"An amazing book, this is a beautiful story of the ties that bind. Two sisters, as different as they come, find the magic in each other's lives. It touched my soul."   —Rosie O'Donnell

I found myself speeding through the monthly accounts, eager to meet the next bus driver . . . But then I'd slow down to savor Simon's keen insights, humor, and evocative storytelling."
—*Newsday*

"Rachel Simon's stirring autobiography about the year she spent riding Pennsylvania city buses with her mentally retarded sister is authentic and impressive, an enriching story of reconciliation and rediscovery. A terrific, heartwarming ride."
—*Rocky Mountain News*

"Wonderfully crafted . . . Anyone who reads this book will come away with a real respect for people with mental retardation, and the families who love and cherish them."
—*St. Louis Post-Dispatch*

"You couldn't get off this bus if you tried. It's about how our journey through life is marked by the kindness of others, and about how lovely the bond between sisters can be."
—*The Arizona Republic*

Rachel Simon is the author of a novel, *The Magic Touch;* a collection of stories, *Little Nightmares, Little Dreams;* and *The Writer's Survival Guide.* She teaches in the Creative Writing Program at Bryn Mawr College. She lives in Delaware.

Visit www.rachelsimon.com

Also by Rachel Simon

Riding the Bus with My Sister

A True Life Journey

Rachel Simon

Ⓟ

A PLUME BOOK

PLUME
Published by the Penguin Group
Penguin Group (USA) Inc., 375 Hudson Street,
New York, New York 10014, U.S.A.
Penguin Books Ltd, 80 Strand,
London WC2R 0RL, England
Penguin Books Australia Ltd, 250 Camberwell Road,
Camberwell, Victoria 3124, Australia
Penguin Books Canada Ltd, 10 Alcorn Avenue,
Toronto, Ontario, Canada M4V 3B2
Penguin Books (N.Z.) Ltd, Cnr Rosedale and Airborne Roads,
Albany, Auckland 1310, New Zealand

Penguin Books Ltd, Registered Offices: 80 Strand, London WC2R 0RL, England

Published by Plume, a member of Penguin Group (USA) Inc. This is an
authorized reprint of a hardcover edition published by Houghton Mifflin
Company. For information address Houghton Mifflin Company, 215 Park
Avenue South, New York, New York 10003.

First Plume Printing, September 2003
20 19 18 17

 REGISTERED TRADEMARK—MARCA REGISTRADA

CIP data is available.

ISBN 0-618-04599-6 (hc.)
ISBN 0-452-28455-4 (pbk.)

Printed in the United States of America

For Cool Beth

AUTHOR'S NOTE

Some of the individuals who participated in this story asked me to change their names. In the interest of honoring those requests in a way that would not tempt readers to sort out the real names from the invented, I chose an egalitarian approach and altered everyone's name, except for my sister Beth's and mine. In addition, I changed details about the location to help preserve Beth's privacy.

CONTENTS

January

The Journey

"Wake *up*," my sister Beth says. "We won't make the first *bus*."

At six A.M. on this winter morning, moonlight still bathes her apartment. She's already dressed: grape-juice-colored T-shirt and pistachio shorts, with a purple Winnie-the-Pooh backpack slung over her shoulder. I struggle awake and into my clothes: black sweater, black leggings. Beth and I, both in our late thirties, were born eleven months apart, but we are different in more than age. She owns a wardrobe of blazingly bright colors and can leap out of bed before dawn. She is also a woman with mental retardation.

I've come here to give Beth her holiday present: I've come to ride the buses.

For six years, she has lived on her own. In her subsidized apartment, a few blocks off the main avenue of a gritty, medium-sized Pennsylvania city, each of her days could easily resemble the next — she has a lot of time, having been laid off from her job busing tables at a fast food restaurant. She has enough money to live on, as a recipient of government assistance for people with disabilities.

But Beth also has something else: ingenuity.

This trait isn't generally ascribed to people who live on the periphery of society's vision. Like indigent seniors, people with untreated mental illness, and the homeless, Beth is someone many people in the mainstream don't think much about, or even see.

Six months after she moved to her fifth-floor apartment, she realized that she was lonely, and had consumed all the episodes of *The Price Is Right* and *All My Children* that she could tolerate. So one day she decided to ride the buses. Not just to ride them the way most of us do, and which her aides had trained her to do a few years before. She wasn't interested in something as ordinary as getting from one location to another. She wanted to ride them her way.

It was, Beth recalls, October 18, 1993, when, for reasons she cannot remember, she first picked her monthly bus pass off her coffee table. Then she pressed the first-floor button in her high-rise elevator, walked through the vestibule to the street, hailed a bus on the corner, climbed the steps toward the driver, settled into a seat, and looped through the city from dawn to dusk, trying out one run after another, bus to bus to bus. Soon she was riding a dozen a day, some for five minutes, others for hours, befriending drivers and passengers as she wound through the narrow streets of the city and its wreath of rolling hills. Within weeks she could navigate anywhere within a ten-mile radius, and, by studying the shifting constellations of characters and the schedules posted weekly in the bus terminal, she could calculate who would be at precisely which intersection at any moment of any day. She staked out friendships all over the city, weaving her own traveling community.

Beth's case manager had not suggested this, nor had Regis and Kathie Lee, nor even Beth's boyfriend. This idea was hers alone.

We hurry down Main Street, the moon setting behind the buildings. My guide, whose fuzzy brown hair is still wet from her morning bath, points out the identifying numbers on bus shelters, the scowls of grouchy drivers. She wears no watch, telling time instead by the buses.

We dart into the downtown McDonald's, already, at six-thirty A.M., filled with early risers: clusters of the elderly playing cards, solitary office workers bent over newspapers. Beth orders coffee, though she doesn't drink coffee, palming out the eighty-four cents before the server asks.

Then we bolt into the dawn, making a beeline for a bus shelter. Head craned down the street, Beth giggles as she once did when I took her to a Donny Osmond concert: thrilled, in her element. She clutches her yellow radio and a tangle of key chains — twenty-nine, by her count — Cookie Monster, smiley faces, peace signs, which hold a total of two keys. She does a drumbeat on her laminated bus pass, stickered 000001. Every month she renews it, arriving first in line at the sales window. That sticker is her private coat of arms, proof that she's queen of these routes.

Our first bus draws up to the curb. The driver, Claude, throws open his door as if welcoming us to his house. Beth clomps aboard, arm thrust forward with the coffee. He takes the steaming plastic cup, then thumbs four quarters into her hand. "Our agreement," he explains to me.

Then she spins toward "her" seat — the premier spot on the front sideways bench, catty-corner from his, so she'll be as close to him as possible. I sit beside her; as a suburbanite who relies on my car and the occasional commuter train, it is my first time on a city transit bus in years. We pull out, past working-class row houses, a Christian lawn ornament store, a farmers' market, an abandoned candy factory, Asian grocers. Short hair, just beginning to gray, fans out from underneath Claude's driver's cap. Beth announces that he's forty-two, with a birthday coming soon. He laughs as she offers the exact date and then explains how he likes to spend his birthdays. "She remembers everything," he says.

He asks if she'll change into her flip-flops should this chilly day become as balmy as the forecast predicts. "If iz over *forty,*" she replies, "you know I *will.*" He tells me they "jam" with her radio when the bus is empty. "*Real* loud," she adds. They recall some trouble with a rider months ago. "She was mean," Beth says indignantly. Claude agrees, and recounts the altercation, in which a passenger vehemently challenged his knowledge of upcoming stops, and which culminated, after the malcontent had finally exited, in Claude's relief that Beth was sharing the ride — he had someone who could sigh along with him.

Moments later, we pass Beth's boyfriend on his bicycle. Also an adult with mental retardation, Jesse has paused at a crosswalk, his maple brown face pointing straight ahead, his blind left eye looking milky in the light, sun glinting off the helmet Beth long ago convinced him to wear. The decade they've been together is more than a fourth of their lives. Claude picks up his intercom mike and calls out, "Hello, Jesse!" Jesse looks over. We twist around in our seats, and his mustached face brightens as we wave.

All day, when we mount Jacob's bus, Estella's, Rodolpho's, one driver after another greets Beth heartily. They tell me she helps out: reminds them where to turn on runs they haven't driven for a while, teaches them the Top Ten songs on the radio, keeps them abreast of schedule and personnel changes, and visits them in the hospital when they're sick. She assists her fellow passengers as well, answering questions about how to reach their destinations, sharing their consternation when the bus halts for double-parked delivery trucks, carrying their third bag of groceries to the curb.

In return, many riders smile hello to her and ask how she's doing; many drivers are hospitable, even affectionate. Jacob asks if she has gotten a new winter coat and if the homeless woman who clashed with her last month has bothered her again. Jack slips her money for soda. Bert squawks out songs, making her laugh at his jaggedy tunes.

Not everyone is nice. Some drivers, I learn, call her "The Pest." When they see Beth at a stop ahead, they cruise right by, gaze glued to the road. Some riders warn them, crying out, "Keep going!" when they spy her waiting on the curb, and, if she climbs on, they bleat in her face, "Shut up! Go home!"

"I don't *care*," she says and shrugs. When we were growing up, I saw a twinge of anguish on her face whenever kids called her poisonous names, and sometimes the hurt took hours to fade. Now I see that, surrounded by friends, she regains her composure quickly.

That's not all that has changed, I discover. Beth, once a willful child who, like many willful children, felt most secure at home, has grown into an extravagantly social and nonconforming adult, one who creates camaraderie out of bus timetables, refuses to trouble herself when people look askance at her — and, in a buoyant refutation of the notion that mental retardation equals sluggishness, zips about jauntily to her own inner beat. My sister (*my sister!* I boast to myself) maneuvers through the world with the confidence of a museum curator walking approvingly through her galleries, and, far from bemoaning her otherness, she exults in it.

That afternoon, as I step to the curb and wave goodbye to her through the bus window, I am pierced by a sudden memory, minted only this morning. She was sailing her short, stout body across the street toward McDonald's, and I was scrambling behind. In the predawn moonlight, as she chattered on about our labyrinthine itinerary, well aware that there are few if any other people in this world devoted to a calling of bell cords and exhaust fumes, she spontaneously threw back her head and trumpeted, "I'm *diffrent!*

I'm *diffrent!*" as if she were hurling a challenge with all her might beyond the limits of the sky.

In the course of my life, cars and trains and jets have whisked me to wherever I wanted to go, and I was going places, I thought; I was racing my way to becoming a Somebody. A Somebody who would live a Big Life. What that meant exactly, I wasn't sure. I just knew that I longed to escape the restrictions of what I saw as a small life: friends and a family and a safe, unobjectionable job that would pay me a passably adequate income. Although this package encompassed just the kind of existence many people I knew were utterly content with, I wanted something more.

Then, in the winter of my thirty-ninth year, I boarded a bus with my sister and discovered that I wanted broader and deeper rewards than those I would find in the Big Life.

At the time, I thought I had my life under control. In addition to having published several books, I was teaching college as well as holding classes for private students, writing free-lance commentary for the *Philadelphia Inquirer,* and hosting events at a bookstore. I adored everything I did, which is more than many of my acquaintances could say.

But, though I wouldn't confess it to myself, I worked all the time. Seven days a week, from the minute I threw off the covers at seven A.M. until I disintegrated back inside them at one A.M., I leapt like a hare through my schedule: Write article → Grade student papers → Interview newspaper subject → Book author for store signing → Teach private class → Take notes for next novel → Eat → Crash.

My life, I told myself, bore little resemblance to the lives of workers in corporate America. After all, I made my own schedule and wore comfy leggings and sweaters at my desk, saving the A-line skirts and blazers and lipstick until I drove out to class or the bookstore. To unwind, I took vigorous walks whenever I pleased, keeping my five-foot build lean and fit. But who was I kidding? I was like most of my peers: hyperbusy, hypercritical, hyperventilating.

As a result, I bricked in all the spaces in my week when I might have seen friends, and so it followed that I lost many of them. I lost my opportunity to indulge in almost all leisure activities as well: no movies or plays, and, though I continued to purchase new novels and routinely carted home any intriguing texts I found on the "Take Me" shelf at school, dust settled on the pages like snow, as I had time to read few books beyond those I needed for my work. But perhaps the greatest forfeit was love. I'd had a few awkward dinner dates in the four years since my longtime live-in romance had come to a mutually tearful and reluctant end, and even those strained opportunities had petered out. Alone in my apartment in the Philadelphia suburbs, dining at my desk most nights, I occasionally browsed the personal ads. But then I'd open my datebook, remember that I had no time to meet for coffee, and turn back to my work.

This had not always been me. Until I found myself single, my evenings had been filled with dinner parties and art openings and reading groups and two-hour phone calls with my girlfriends. That is, when my nights weren't already occupied by relaxed conversations on the sofa with my boyfriend, Sam, where we'd go on about books and politics and the seductive lure of the Big Life, our exchanges interrupted only when he'd get up to flip through his voluminous record collection, then set the needle on recordings by, maybe, Miles Davis, or the English folk musician Nick Drake. I don't know when things stopped working for us; I just know that when he asked me to marry him I could not bring myself to make the commitment. Finally, in a blur of grief and regret, convinced I should let him move on with his life, I left. I took only my necessities — computer, desk, and clothes — and camped out in one cheap rented room after another while I tried to make sense of my life, and of what seemed to be a stony heart. It didn't help that for years I had subsisted on Sam's architect's salary, plus my writing jobs, and now, in one of those unnerving coincidences of fate, they suddenly dried up. Those first few months on my own, I was so lonely and broke that my stomach would seize up during the night and I'd wake on my air mattress, clinging to a pillow, and lie awake until morning. During the day, catching my reflection in my computer screen and seeing only failure, I'd feel my face tighten with terror.

Finally, I accepted a job at a bookstore, and, as luck would have it, started publishing at the *Philadelphia Inquirer*. Then, marveling at the dollar signs sprouting in my check register and discovering that with each newspaper column and wave of bookstore applause I felt myself on my way to the Big Life, I accepted positions teaching as well. I rented an apartment and purchased a bona fide bed, but did not acquire a stereo or TV, as I hadn't missed either enough to replace it. And I worked. I worked until I was so exhausted I fell back asleep easily when I woke during the night. I worked until I forgot I was lonely, until I could not conceive of any other existence.

I hadn't seen Beth in a couple of years. We stayed in touch through letters; once a week I'd scratch out a card, and in return she'd cascade fifteen back. Her letters consisted of two or three multicapitalized sentences sprawling down the page, sprinkled with periods, which she'd then fold into envelopes flamboyantly tattooed with stickers and addressed in fall-off-the-paper print. I relished finding these treats populating my mailbox, whole colonies arriving in a single day. In Magic Marker scrawl, they gossiped about our younger brother (*I aM Glad that. Max got a new rED car. when he Came with his kids. good*) and older sister (*Laura sent Me. a gift Thing for WAlmart*), educated me about the latest Top Ten (*Do you. like In Sinks I want you back. I do*), and revised my knowledge of Jesse's athletic achievements (*Jesse did do that big race. WoW*). Best of all, they climaxed in a spunky declaration that defied the world's cliché of her as an uncomplicated half-wit, signed as they were, "Cool Beth."

But when I phoned her occasionally, the conversations were clumsy and joyless. She never volunteered information about herself, and when I divulged meager scraps about myself, she made no effort to respond. This combination of guardedness and lack of interest annoyed me, as it did the rest of the family, and like them, I didn't know what to say or ask. After "Hello," our dialogue rapidly disintegrated. Finally, resorting to the I'm-the-older-sister-you're-the-little-sister pattern I knew so well, I'd offer blandly, "Did you hear about the Ninja Turtle mug giveaway at that fast food place?" "How was your talk with Mom?" These queries would allow us to trudge ahead for a few minutes, Beth scattering monosyllabic crumbs in my direction, me telling myself, Okay, it's boring, but it's brief. When we got off the phone, my shoulders would be as rigid as if I'd just marched into combat.

Sometimes she'd call collect. "Iz my *birf*day. Can you visit?" Or "Iz nice out. Come over." But she lived hours away, in a city I didn't know my way around; I'd already been long out of the house before she'd moved to the area with our father. Endure both geographic confusion *and* labored communication? "Sorry," I'd say. "I can't."

Besides, she did this . . . *bus thing,* and, like the rest of our family, I found it difficult to accept. Some days its sheer oddness baffled me; other days I was disheartened by her choosing to master bus routes over sticking with something productive like a job. I had long embraced eccentrics in novels and cheered on iconoclasts I encountered in newspaper stories, yet I was too dismayed by Beth's peculiar devotion to the buses to be willing to acquaint myself with her life. In fact, I had rarely even admitted it to friends and colleagues who, once they learned that one of the three siblings I'd mentioned had mental retardation, seldom asked anything besides whether she had Down syndrome (no) and what her "mental age" might be. *Mental age.* It was as if they thought that a person's daily passions — and literacy skills, emotional maturity, fashion preferences, musical tastes, hygiene habits, verbal abilities, social shrewdness, romantic longings, and common sense — could all fit neatly into a single box topped, like a child's birthday cake, with a wax 7, or 13, or 3. When I was unable to supply her "mental age," they'd ask whom she lived with, even if I'd already told them she lived on her own. It would become clear to me then that their understanding of mental retardation had never moved beyond the stereotype of the grinning, angelic child. This exchange was so routine, and had been for so many years, that my dismay had long ago dissipated into acceptance, and with that had come the realization that I would always hover between two worlds, with mental retardation over here, "normal" cognitive functioning over there, and that I would have to convey information from one to the other, never quite belonging to either. My friends seemed relieved to learn that people with mental retardation are individuals. I was relieved to omit just what an individual Beth happened to be.

In letters or on the phone with Beth, I sought to ignore her deepening allegiance to the buses by focusing on practical matters. Has KFC had any openings since they laid you off a few years ago?

Would you like help obtaining a library card? She communicated her resentment with sullen "I don't know"s or a silence as deep as sleep.

So for years I essentially let her become a stranger. Though sometimes at night, when I was at my desk and happened to glance outside and spy the moon saluting from above the treetops, I'd remember how fascinated she'd been by it when we were kids. Sitting at my desk, I'd shake my gaze away from the window, but moonlight would still illuminate my papers. Her stickered letters glared up at me, as the guilt of being a "bad sister" once again reared up inside me.

Then one winter morning when Beth was thirty-eight and I was thirty-nine, and I was too exhausted from my daily triathlon to come up with an idea for the newspaper, I mentioned to an editor that I wanted to visit Beth for the holidays but was, as always, perplexed about how to negotiate the dilemma of her buses. "Say what?" he said, and, embarrassed, I explained. "How interesting," he said. "Take a day to ride with her, and write it up for your next piece."

I did ride with her, and over that day I was touched by the bus drivers' compassion, saddened and sickened by how many people saw Beth simply as a nuisance, and awed by how someone historically exiled to society's Siberia not only survived, but thrived. Indeed, the Beth I remembered from years ago had a heavy, ungainly gait; the Beth I saw now was not only nimble-footed, but her demeanor was exuberant and self-assured. I was aware of my earlier objections to her bus riding, but they began to feel inexcusably feeble.

I wrote the article, and as soon as it appeared it created a stir. Postcards and e-mails arrived from strangers; acquaintances flagged me down in the bookstore to shake my hand. Beth was tickled: people were paying attention to her and her beloved drivers. The piece was picked up by papers all over the country, generating a tide of enthusiasm. I kept calling to tell her, and we started talking more. Her letters, which soon poured into my mailbox in even greater numbers, felt all the more special. I finally knew what to ask, and now she wanted to answer.

Yet I was too busy to dwell upon the pleasure the article's success gave me. Actually, I was too busy to let myself feel much of anything: One day when throwing clothes into a suitcase during the ten minutes I had allotted to pack for a business trip, I glanced outside. A neighboring family was playing together on that mild winter afternoon. There, beside a tree swing, stood the dad — not a Big Person with a Big Life, but an unassuming person with a richly quiet life — as each of his four children lined up for a push. I started to smile as I zipped up my bag, but discovered to my horror that the muscles in my face no longer seemed to work. That night, I lay in my hotel bed in a chill, suddenly unable to keep my loneliness stuffed inside its cage. What if my breathless daily grinds led to only more breathless daily grinds? What if I closed the door forever on human connection — never again shared a relaxed afternoon laughing with a friend, forgetting to look at my watch? Or spent a day, *a whole day,* simply enjoying the company of a man? What if work was *it*?

A few days later, hurrying through my mail, I came upon an envelope from one of the agencies that works with Beth. I opened it to find an invitation to attend something called her annual "Plan of Care" review.

I held up the letter to reread it and slowly comprehended its significance: *Beth had asked that I be included.* In the eleven years since she had left home, this meeting — which I'd been vaguely aware of through the report that gets mailed to each family member, and which seemed to cover matters like finances and health — had been attended only by her aides, not family. But clearly, my ride on the buses had meant a lot more to her than just a few words in a newspaper.

I flipped open my datebook. The January day was not ideal, but if I canceled this and rearranged that, I could manage it. I called to RSVP: "Yes."

On a brisk January afternoon, while last week's snow still dots the streets, the mirrored elevator zooms me toward the eighth floor of the agency's skyscraper. As the numbers light up — 4, 5 — I wonder what to expect. The elevator feels leathery and professional, a part of my world, and with a catch in my throat that falls somewhere between caution and excitement, I know that as soon as I emerge, I'll be in a land of rules and people I don't know — 6, 7 — and will feel as cloddish and bewildered as Alice emerging from the far end of the rabbit hole.

The doors open, and Beth is standing before me in the marble corridor.

At four feet ten, with unzipped regal purple coat, buttercup yellow pants, and an oversized orange marmalade Eeyore T-shirt, she cuts a grand Day-Glo figure in this corporate environment. Although Beth looks like the rest of our family — brown eyes, curved nose, brunette ringlets, squirrelly cheeks — you immediately know when you first see her that she is different in some way, given her unique fashion sense and her loud and spirited manner. "Hi," she says.

I set my briefcase down to give her a hug. I feel as if I tower over her as I lean in close, and my tailored black overcoat, burgundy skirt, and black velvet blazer seem not understated as much as entirely underdressed. We wrap our arms around each other, though I know it will be fast; Beth doesn't care to be touched, she has admitted to me, but hugs me because I like to.

Still, her squeeze, quick though it is, is just long enough for me to uncork a sudden memory: we are three and four years old, admiring a spider web under the house in the shadows of the lattice, and I am tickling her legs in the grass-scented shade. Eventually I grew into my life, smoothing down all the quirks that would make me stand out, while Beth nurtured all the quirks that ultimately produced this imp in my arms. How had we come to evolve as we did, I wonder, as she pulls away from me. We were born into the same family, we relished the same simple moments, and, until a certain sleeting February afternoon when we were teenagers, we shared the same major losses and joys. Yet we turned out so differently. Is it just her mental retardation that made her who she is, or did her experiences after, or even before, that February day somehow spin her personality in this direction? Memories flicker through my mind as I try to trace the thread back to the beginnings of my irrepressible sister.

"Down *here*," she says, wheeling about and hastening along a corridor of office doors, her feet turned out in her customary divining-rod style. "I wore pants today because iz thirty-two, but iz supposed to be forty later so I'm gonna change to *shorts*."

Shorts. Always shorts, and often her trademark violet sandals or blueberry flip-flops, as long as the temperature is above forty. I think it has to do with vanity. Not that she feels she's got Rockette legs, nor does she even have a full-length mirror in her apartment. And, though she draws attention to her sandaled feet by painting each toenail a different fluorescent color, glamour isn't the point either. It just seems imperative to Beth to show that she can brave the cold when the rest of us bundle up.

She patters into a conference room. Around the rectangular table sit three women: redheaded Vera, blond Amber, brunette Olivia. The room is not large, and Vera and Amber, in their casual sweaters and pants, have set up at one end of the table, while Olivia, arrayed in a navy blue pants suit, occupies the other.

"Have a seat," Olivia says to me after I shake their hands. I realize that although Beth has peppered her letters with their names, I know nothing about what each one does for her or, for that matter, anything about the system at all. I settle into a cushioned chair across from Beth.

"Let's start with finances," Olivia says. She is a pretty, tall woman in her early forties, with an alabaster complexion and raven hair that she wears long, her bangs framing a pair of extraordinary eyes. They're turquoise, I see, as she pages through her paperwork. Navajo barrettes, studded with stones the same color as her irises, clip back her hair.

"Okay, finances," Vera says, lifting up a paper. She's somewhat older, petite, pacific, bearing the aura of a no-nonsense grandmother. She speaks slowly, her words shaped by a subtle Spanish accent. "Beth currently receives $527.40 from S.S.I.," she reads from her page.

"What does that stand for?" I ask. "Social Security?"

"Iz my check *evry* month," Beth says.

"It stands for Supplemental Security Income," Amber explains.

Perky and gum-chewing, blond hair swept back from her face, she's the youngest of the three by at least a decade.

Olivia, friendly and easygoing, who seems to be running the meeting, elaborates. "S.S.I.'s a Social Security program that gives monthly benefits to people sixty-five or older, or blind, or who have a disability and can't work, provided they don't own much or have a lot of income."

Vera goes on, detailing how much of the S.S.I. money goes to Beth's subsidized apartment, groceries, phone, cable, burial fund, spending money, and bus pass — "the most important thing."

"It sure *iz*," Beth says. "You *know* it."

I suddenly remember that Vera visits Beth in her apartment a few times a week; she must be the person whom the drivers call Beth's aide. Amber seems to work with her. At last, the cards are shuffling into order. I find myself nodding, suddenly understanding — and almost miss Olivia saying "On to health."

Amber pulls out a report written by Mary, who, I'm told, is Beth's medical caseworker. "Your weight is 166 right now," she says as Beth shrugs, "and your cholesterol is still too high."

Vera says, "It's those Ring-Dings and chocolate pudding, and the way you eat on the bus instead of going home for meals."

"I eat what I *like*," Beth says. "I eat hot dogs too, and spaghetti and meatballs, and cream cheese on bagels, and macaroni and cheese."

Vera says, "Those foods are not going to help your cholesterol. You could develop heart problems."

"Thaz not gonna *happen*."

Amber simply continues. "It's been a few years since you've seen a dentist."

"I brush my *teeth*."

"For a thorough cleaning, honey," Olivia says.

"They can look in my mouth, but I'm not letting them put their fingers in. I'm not doing *that*." I learn that when dentists have tried *that*, her reflexes have immediately assumed command, compelling her to shove them, quite forcefully, away.

They drift off into a discussion of where to find someone who'll take her medical assistance card, and who also has experience with patients with special needs. My attention strays, and I glance at Beth. She's not engaged either, so we make eyes at each other, as if once again we're little kids at a dinner party of adults who are up to important and mysterious business. It's easy to fall into this secret silliness with Beth.

"Your uterine fibroid seems to have stabilized," Amber goes on, as we return to the discussion. "But the eyes really worry me. She has a rare condition. Her corneas are becoming scratched and opaque, and it's affecting her vision."

"Is that why your eyes have looked foggy for the past several years?" I say.

"I don't know."

"Does it affect your vision?" I ask.

"I don't *know.*"

"Yes," Vera says. "I help her with eyedrops a few times a week. And she's got a follow-up appointment with the doctor in a few months."

I peer at Beth with concern. Again, she shrugs.

Then they review what Beth is not: a drug or alcohol user, a smoker, a person with high blood pressure. I peek across the table at the paperwork. Olivia is updating a typed sheet that lists "Diagnosis: Mild Mental Retardation." I also make out, on a different set of papers, that Olivia is Beth's "case manager," Vera her "program assistant," and Amber her "team coordinator." Whatever all that means. I have never thought about any diagnosis besides the blanket term of "mental retardation," and God knows I haven't a clue about what any of these titles designate. It all seems quite complicated, but I feel too self-conscious about my ignorance to ask them to clarify anything for me.

"Safety," Olivia says.

"Sometimes you walk in the street," Vera says.

"When there's *snow.*"

"Can you walk on the sidewalk?"

"I'll *try.*"

"You need to do better than try," Vera says.

"You could get hurt," Olivia says.

I glance around, and detect what my own little-kid mode had prevented me from noticing: their tense brows and exasperated slumps. Beth notices too, but rather than give in to what they want, she says, "I know how to use 911. I know what to do if there's a *fire*. I don't go out in the dark 'cept for the early bus. And if anyone gives me trouble, Jesse'll look out for me."

"We just want to make sure you're safe," Olivia says.

With quiet defiance, she says, "I'm *safe*."

"Okay," Olivia says, writing, as I hear a sigh coming from one of the others. "Now, what are your important relationships?"

Beth gives everyone at the table an as-if-you-don't-know grin. "Jesse. The *drivers:* Jack, Bailey, Rick, Timmy. And my little brother, Max, brings his two kids to visit sometimes, they live a few *hours* from here, and I talk with my mother on the phone sometimes, she lives in North Carolina. Dad lives across town, and Rachel near Philadelphia, and our older sister, Laura, lives in Colorado. I write them letters — *some*times."

She sits back, giving me a different sisterly look, one that says, *Of course we both know why it's like that.* I glance at Olivia and Amber and Vera, and I can see in their eyes that they know it too: the family rarely visits Beth because there's too much friction. I think about the issues we discuss when we talk about Beth. Some family members say they're tired of speaking with a person so disinclined to respond that she might as well be mute. Others have waged a campaign for her to shrink to a healthier size, only to retreat from the futility of it all. Then there are the buses. Our mother has actually met with Beth's support people over the years, begging them to make Beth get a job, a volunteer position, just something to encourage her to be a fuller member of society. They replied that they'd do whatever Beth wanted, and that wasn't what she wanted. Since then, the family has spoken of "them" with distrust, or sometimes disdain. We're suspicious of their guiding principles, not that we know what those principles are. We haven't asked, and they haven't thought to offer.

But they are sitting before me now, one, two, three individuals, not a "them" at all, and I see that they *are* only doing what Beth wants. Besides, I know how contrary she can be when not given her own way. If she doesn't want what you're proposing, no matter how kind or encouraging you might be, you're bound to hear this response: "Stop bossing me around."

"What are your dreams for the future, honey?" Olivia asks.

"To go to Disney World with Jesse. To live with my niece and nephew for one day."

"What about the coming year? Do you want to take any classes?"

"No."

"Do you want to join any organiz —"

"No."

"Do you want —"

"No."

"— a job?"

"*No.*"

We get up to leave and, as we shake hands, Olivia tells me to expect her written report on this Plan of Care meeting in a few weeks. But now that I understand what it is, I also know what its conclusion will be: "Beth does not wish to change anything."

Though that's not quite true. There is one thing she wants to change.

I discover this after the meeting. I'm all set to take her to lunch, some cheery place where our worlds can stay merged from the menu to the check before we exit into our separate lives. But the moment we finish up with Olivia and the others, shuttle down the elevator to the lobby, and open the doors into the sunlight, Beth launches herself full speed up the street. Her purple jacket billows behind her, and her tiny feet fly like wings.

"Where are we going?" I call out, stumbling behind in my pumps and overcoat, clasping my briefcase to my chest.

"Jacob, or Bert, or Henry — whoever we can get to first! Come on!"

Wait a minute, I think, jumping over ice patches. I volunteered to ride along for one article. I wasn't enlisting for life.

At a corner she slows to a stop and sights a bus bearing toward us from the distance. "Look! I knew we'd make it!"

"So this is what it is?" I say, catching up to her. "Whenever I see you, I ride the buses?"

"Iz *fun*."

I check my watch. A student is expecting me after lunch, some-one whose novel-in-progress I care about a great deal. Then I peer back at the skyscraper we left minutes ago, where I met with people who care equally deeply about Beth. A coldness rolls through me; it occurs to me that I couldn't assemble a crew who would know so much about me, and, should I be asked about my important rela-tionships, I could no longer supply such a long list.

"You could *try* it," Beth says. "Just for a *while*."

The bus is one corner away. I know my student is eagerly waiting to show me his next chapter.

"I don't think I . . ." But Beth is giggling, perhaps in anticipation of the driver at the helm, perhaps in amusement at me; and my ha-bitual refusal trails off into silence. Well, I consider, buoyed by her laughter, greathearted and wily at the same time, it *is* beneficial for her to see family under her own flag. I *could* stop feeling like a bad sister — stop fleeing from intimacy with this person I have known all my life — if only for one afternoon.

"Um, how much of a while?" I ask. "Like till three or four o'clock?"

"No-oh," she says, drawing out the word as if coaxing me to guess a secret. Then, as the bus swings toward the curb, she ex-presses her wish. "They see me *evry* year," she says. "So do it like me."

"What do you mean?"

"A year," she says.

"What?" I can't have heard that right.

She grins. "Do it for a year."

I look nervously at her. "*A year?*" That's two semesters of student papers up in smoke! Four seasons of newspaper pieces — twelve whole months of articles and authors and conferences and my comfortable bed and mornings that begin *after,* not *before,* the birds, and salads at a *table* instead of Ho Ho's on a bus. *A year.* "You're kidding," I say.

"You could *try*," she says. "You don't have to ride *evry* day."

I see the thrill of the dare on her face. All right, I think, let's say I didn't do it with the full dedication that Beth has . . .

She tilts her head back, as if waiting for me to chicken out. I hold her look, calculating wildly about when I could shift my meetings.

The bus berths at the curb, and the door opens before us. "So?" Beth says, wearing a teasing face that's melting into hope.

I stare at her.

"Well?" she says.

And I think, *You need to do this, even if you don't know where it will take you.*

I draw in a mighty breath. "O . . . kaaay," I say to Beth.

"Really?" she says.

"Yes," I say, more emphatically and, as I say it, I know I will do it.

"And how much will you come?"

"Uh," I say, stalling. "What about every two weeks?"

"What about *more*?"

I pause, and exhale. "I'll try my best," I say. "Whenever I can, I will."

"Oh, good!"

With trembling hands, I fish in my coat pocket for a token. A golden token that cost $1.10: the price of admission for this odyssey. Beth is bounding up the stairs toward the fare box, radio in her hand. I look down at my briefcase, then up at Beth standing at the top of the steps, ushering me into her world. *A year*, I think. *For her. Just one year.* I rest my hand on the railing. Then, not knowing where this bus is going, I hop aboard her life.

The Time of Snows and Sorrow

This is a story we tell in my family.

"I'm worried about the new one," Mommy says to our neighbor Mrs. Stein. "I think something's wrong with her."

Mommy is holding baby Beth in our New Jersey yard, leaning over the picket fence between the two houses. Roses bloom everywhere. Laura and I run around on the grass.

"Oh, now, don't worry," Mrs. Stein says. "She's only two months old."

"But her birth . . . it wasn't like the others. They gave me a drug so I wasn't conscious during the delivery. Later they told me they'd had to use forceps, and they squeezed her head."

Mrs. Stein moves closer. Her two girls wave to Laura and me through the picket fence.

"Maybe your hands are too full," Mrs. Stein says. "Laura's only two and a half, and Rachel's just over one year. With three under age three, I know I'd be meshuggah."

Mommy sighs and looks down at Beth. She just lies there like a doll, not moving at all. "I think that's why I didn't notice anything at first," she says. "But then, when she was maybe five weeks old, something struck me as not right . . ."

Mrs. Stein's girls come over, they stand as high as her knees. We can't reach them, so Laura and I start spinning round and round and then they giggle and do the same.

"Ach, what can anyone really see at five weeks?" Mrs. Stein says.

"She just wasn't reacting like the other two had. She'd lie in her crib, staring for hours. You could clap your hands above her head, and she wouldn't look. You could come near, and her eyes wouldn't focus on you. Her expression was always . . . empty."

"She'll catch up."

"She's still like this. Except when she arches her back and holds stiff, but she barely moves her legs or arms. And she doesn't cry."

"Even when she's hungry?"

"No. I'm afraid that she's . . . I don't know."

Laura and I spin into a heap. The girls over the fence do, too. Mrs. Stein is looking into Mommy's arms at Beth.

"She's just a little baby," she says. "Don't worry about it."

Mommy's eyes are fixed on Beth. Her face is tight and scared.

Every day, Mommy stands beside Beth's crib. Sometimes Mommy holds her up to sit, but then Beth's head just droops to the side. She can grasp a little, but she won't reach.

Grandma comes over some mornings, and Mommy sits with her in the dining room, drinking coffee, whispering. At night, Daddy comes back from the school where he teaches and stands at Beth's doorway, staring with Mommy. "Tell the pediatrician," he says.

Laura and I are waiting with Grandma in the doctor's office, and Mommy comes out with Beth. She's got that sad look. "He did the exam," she tells Grandma, putting us in our strollers. "But he says nothing's wrong."

"He says I'm just a worrying kind of mother," she says the next month.

"He says I should just relax," she says a month after that.

Finally, when Beth is six months old and Mommy goes to the doctor with Beth again, he picks her up in his arms and throws her up in the air. She does a somersault up by the ceiling, right in front of Mommy's eyes, and he catches her as she comes tumbling back down.

Beth's expression doesn't change at all.

"You're right," the doctor says. "There's something wrong."

"I'm finding another doctor," Mommy says to Grandma when she comes back to the waiting room. Then she whispers, "We're thinking she may be retarded." Mommy fits my boots onto my feet. "But, oh God, I hope we're wrong."

Right after the new year, on a windy, flurrying morning when Beth is seven months old and still not sitting up, she goes to stay for many *weeks in a children's hospital in Philadelphia. A special doctor there will try to find out if Beth is what our parents worry she is, and why, and what to do about it. Mommy and Daddy are both from northern New Jersey and have never been to Philadelphia, but they've been told this doctor is the best. They'd drive to Mars for the best.*

The doctor studies everything medicine knows about in 1961 — the papers I later see use words like red cell fragility, platelet count, electrolytes, spinal fluid, amino acids in the urine, skull x-rays, EEG. *He biopsies some tissue on her leg to search for signs of diseases common to Ashkenazi Jews, because that's what we are. The biopsy leaves behind marks on Beth's thigh, white lines like a train track to nowhere.*

Every weekend, Grandma takes care of Laura and me while Mommy and Daddy drive the three hours to the hospital. Snow pelts the roads. The icy streets are narrow, and sometimes the car skids. Week after week, they enter the hospital and walk to Beth's room, seeing things they've never seen: babies with oxygen tubes, babies with IVs, the hollow faces of bald children, weeping parents. Then they reach Beth's room, and the doctor turns to them, and announces that there are still tests to be done, but that Beth has shown no improvement.

They drive home in the snow, demoralized.

Then, after four weeks, the doctor calls and requests a special visit. This is the one, they know. The one where they'll finally learn it all.

They get to the hospital. Someone tells them the doctor will meet them soon, and they stand at the end of a long corridor, trying to breathe through the moments. They stare down the hall, waiting for a glimpse of his approaching form.

Finally he rounds the far corner and comes toward them, walking slowly. His face darkens as he draws near.

Then he is in front of them. They stand in silence. At last he puts his hand on Daddy's shoulder, and takes a deep breath. "We know she's retarded," the doctor says, "but we don't know what caused it. I'm sorry. There is nothing left that we can do."

Mommy collapses into herself. Daddy stumbles back. Their daughter is mentally retarded, and they don't know why. All they know is what they've learned in the last month: that she will not develop normally; that she will have limited intellectual, emotional, and maybe even physical capabilities; that, given her current progress, she might be bedridden for life and communicate in grunts and groans.

They bundle her up and take her home, wipers clearing the snow from the windshield. Laura and I run to hug them as soon as they come in, and then they teach us the two biggest words I'll ever know, two grown-up words about our sister.

February

Hitting the Road

5:15 A.M. "Uhhh," I groan, throwing the covers over my eyes as Beth, in green pajamas, spins on her halogen lamp. "Do you have to get up so early?"

With no alarm clock except the one inside her, Beth has just burst awake and out of her bedroom, heedless of the stars still visible in the sky, and of me, still half-asleep in her living room. Her linoleum floor is my bedroom, and since her teal velvet love seat doesn't accommodate a full-length body, three sofa cushions from my apartment have become my bed. Though with the winter wind tom-tomming at the windows, and the gaps between the cushions opening up every time I turn, I can't say I had a cozy sleep.

"*Thiz* when evrything be*gins,*" she says. In my sleepy state, the irregular cadence of her voice reminds me of the higgledy-piggledy way she uses capital letters in her writing.

I hear the weather channel come on, and then her dialing the phone. "Who're you calling?"

"'Livia."

I peek out from the covers. "Olivia's not in her office now, is she?"

"No. Iz her machine." There is a pause, and then she says into the receiver, "Iz a high of twenty-five today, so you better dress *warm.*" She hangs up.

"You called to give her the weather report?"

"*Evry* morning," she says.

"But by the time she comes to work and hears it, she'll already be dressed."

"Iz okay," she says. "'Livia likes it. Iz good for her to know. I don't do it on weekends. Iz okay." Then she shuffles into her bedroom for a bath, leaving the light blazing.

I straggle off my sofa cushions. I may not have slept here before — in fact, besides her boyfriend, Jesse, I don't think she's ever had an overnight guest — but the scents of Crayola crayons and Hershey's syrup, the Pebbles and Bamm Bamm throw pillows, the kitten calendar from the dollar store, give me a sense of déjà vu, since, as teenagers, right after the worst times, Beth and I shared a bedroom. Beth used to laugh at my nighttime compulsions, which helped me drift off back then: my stuffed rabbit, the blankets placed just so. But has anything changed? Last night, when my meticulously arranged bedding slid off my cushions and I fumbled about for them, I heard her old "aaah-hah!" with its touch of wicked glee. I'd grabbed at the quilt and laughed back weakly.

Now, I pull on black leggings and a black shirt. The living room contains only her small dining table, the love seat, the television set, a coffee table, posters of 101 Dalmatians and Casper the Friendly Ghost, and a tidy formation of toy cars for Max's kids. The dining table is not for meals, but for holding Beth's backpack, key chains, radio, and cassette tapes, which today include K-Ci & JoJo, Right Said Fred, Gloria Estefan, and her old favorites, the Osmond Brothers.

Occasionally, in the evenings, the room also houses Jesse's bicycle, when he pedals to her apartment building to see her in the few hours between her last bus and her nine o'clock bedtime, at which point he pedals home to watch martial arts movies on late-night television. Or sometimes he comes over at sunrise on Sundays, the one day when the buses don't run. By mutual agreement, however, those visits are brief, too, with Jesse leaving by midmorning. This way, they can each spend Sundays as befits them: he goes off to tool around on his twelve-speed bicycle and she, whose only athletic interest seems to be the three-block dash for the buses, settles down for a marathon of pretzels and television. Beth and Jesse seem to prefer to keep their relationship private, so I already know that I probably won't see Jesse much. But, based on past visits, if we're in her apartment when they're on one of their nightly phone calls, Beth will probably hand me the phone, saying, "Jesse wants to speak to you." Then, as *Full House* blares away on her TV, he'll talk to me about bikes, and life, for an hour.

I turn to her fifth-floor window. Her eight-story building, occupied mostly by senior citizens, is one of the only high-rises in the city, so I can make out blocks and blocks of small row houses sweeping away to the north. Though I can't see that far, I know they extend to the bus terminal two miles off, then thin out as they spill into country. To the east, a wooded mountain interrupts the view of the sky, an evergreen wall at the edge of the city.

Beth moved here after living in group homes for five years; before that she'd always lived with the family. I've long wondered how she felt, as she took in this view in the beginning, alone with the bray of traffic. When I asked, she would say, "Fine." A few years later I wondered about it all the more, when I left Sam and was alone for the first time, too. In the gloom of those days, I remember telling myself, Well, if Beth can do this, so can I, and maybe someday I'll feel fine, too.

I'm two rooms away from her now, but I know that, while I load my deep coat pockets, outfitting myself for our journey — tissues, Chap Stick, pens, book, tokens, toothbrush, herbal tea bags, hand lotion, cell phone, apple, and journal — Beth is dressing with nothing but style in mind: mulberry-colored sweatpants, lilac socks, lemon-lime Tweety Bird T-shirt, and, though we both have ample chests, no bra, because bras "dig in," and she can't seem to command her fingers to hook them. Besides, like pants in "warm" weather, bras are something that only other, more mundane, humans wear.

Out in the living room, she pops open a diet Pepsi (*diet,* she'll stress, and only in cans). "Boy, you're a *slow*poke," she says, as I sit down to put on my sneakers.

"Mmph. I'm not used to this hour. It's still dark out, you know."

"I do this *ev*ry day. You're missing too much. Thiz what I *do*." On the love seat, she devours a bagel and cream cheese before I've finished tying my laces.

Downstairs, she sashays into a bitter gust, hatless, gloveless, jacket unzipped. "Brrrr!" she says. "Iz *cold* out *here*."

I skitter after her, buttoned up against the cold. She calls back over her shoulder, "Hurry! Come on!" A cradle-shaped moon still rests above the buildings, and only a couple of the row houses have lights on. But the hourglass of our day has already started running, and Beth is not going to be late.

The Professor

6:00 A.M. We shiver on a stoop at Tenth and Main, peering up the steeply rising street for the first driver of our day's wanderings. Beth looks carefully into the windshield of each passing bus. "Thaz K.T. driving," she says. "Sharon." "Thaz Eric." Some she waves to, some — the ones with whom she feels no solidarity — she pretends not to see. She tells me about them all, as she shifts her weight back and forth, playing her radio, cupping hands in her sleeves. She makes clear that each bus is distinct, noting their four-digit identification numbers, as unique as fingerprints. "Hope you're staying *warm*," she says to a newspaper delivery girl, the only other pedestrian in sight.

Then our bus sweeps around the corner. With glee Beth looks through the window to Tim, who is so cheerfully outgoing that Beth has nicknamed him "Happy Timmy," though some of his colleagues call him the "Professor." Right away, I see the reason for both names, as I scale the steps to meet a man who reminds me of the kind of amiable bookworm who might amble down the corridors of my college: lanky, long-faced, intelligent-looking, and forty-ish, with parchment-colored hair, mirthful brown eyes, and a trim goatee. I half expect him to be wearing the rumpled khakis and tweed jacket my jocular calculus professor wore twenty years ago, but there the resemblance stops, as he's clad in the uniform of this company, a bland blue tone somewhere between Union and Confederate. Though above the collar, he sports a wisecracker's grin.

"Good morning!" Tim says heartily, extending his hand for — not my token, as I erroneously assume, but a greeting. "Welcome to the world's most edifying one-room schoolhouse," he adds, pumping my hand. Only then does he nod toward the fare box.

As I slip the token in its slot, I give Beth a look: *This is a bus driver?* Smiling, she settles into what I already think of not just as her seat, but her throne, which, I realize, is in the most secure — indeed, the only — nook on the bus, tucked against the panel that separates the seats from the entry steps. Thus, in addition to being, quite literally, the driver's right-hand man ("but I'm *not* a man," she corrects me when I tease her later), she can take in the entire length of the bus at a single glance. Perhaps even better, she can peek over the handrail atop the partition, ensuring that she knows who's boarding before anyone but the driver can see.

As before, I sit immediately to her left. I could, though, choose from Tim's entire lecture hall, because, as Beth says, "I pick runs that aren't *crowded,* and when the seats get too full, I'm *outta* here."

"If I might add an addendum to that," Tim notes, pulling the lever that closes the door. "It's because she likes to be the center of attention."

"No I *don't,*" says Beth with a giggle that belies her words. "I just like to *talk.*"

"She fills me in on what every driver's up to, their vacations, their ups and downs," he says to me. "She's the town crier." Then he steers the bus back onto the street, heading up an eastern cut in the mountain, directly toward the sun pushing into the morning sky.

As he's driving, I follow Beth's gaze, which never wavers from him, and notice that beside his seat, he keeps a quart-sized plastic mug of coffee, a *New York Times,* and a glossy photography magazine.

"Ah, look at that sunrise!" Tim says at the first stoplight, lifting his arms toward the windshield. "Four billion sunrises, over the dinosaurs, the pharaohs, and now ours today. And no one's ever the same. Isn't it just the most remarkable thing? Each day is fresh and unique, yet each is also a link to every dawn all the way back to the Precambrian."

"Whuz that?" Beth asks.

"A long, long time ago," he says. "Before there were even people."

"You always use big *words,*" Beth says with a touch of disapproval. "I wouldn't want to be *around* before there were *people.*" She pauses. "*Some* people."

Tim's smile now develops a knowing curl. He turns the bus toward a neighborhood of brick houses, and at the first stop sign, he glances at me and explains: a senior citizen recently flew into a rage because Beth was holding on to her seat — "Which the lady saw as the optimum place for her to sit as well," he clarifies. "I told the woman very nicely that all six of these sideways seats up here are for the elderly and handicapped; she could take any of them. She eventually did, but she sure made her feelings known. Whew! That was some day, wasn't it, Beth?"

"Oh *man*, she went *on*," Beth mutters, and then declares, "It doesn't pay to be nice."

"Certainly it does," he says. "That's why people admire Abraham Lincoln so much, and Eleanor Roosevelt. That's why the Gettysburg Address says, 'Four score and seven years ago our fathers brought forth on this continent, a new kind of bus,'" — I laugh — "'conceived in liberty, and dedicated to the proposition that the nicer you are, the more they'll leave you alone.' Or, as Mahatma Gandhi said — you ever heard of Mahatma Gandhi?"

"No," Beth says, rolling her eyes.

"He was from India. Remember, we talked about where that is? And he once said, You can kill them with kindness."

"He did not," I say.

"Then he should have," Tim says.

Smiling, I whisper to Beth, "What a great start to the day. He's so personable."

She looks at me curiously, and I remember that, with her limited range of vocabulary and difficulty with abstract thought, our communication usually flows more smoothly if I use simple words and rephrase complex concepts so she can follow me more readily. But I wonder if, like Tim, I should just speak as I usually do, twenty-dollar words and all, and let Beth ask questions, and therefore learn.

"Whuz that mean?" she asks.

"Personable? It means he's nice, that he has a pleasing personality."

"Yeah," she says with a quick nod. "He's *cool*."

Ah, yes. Cool. As my speech might sometimes seem unintelligible to Beth, so can hers seem to me, because Beth has her own lingo. And in Beth-speak, as I have gathered from her letters, "cool" does not concern hip attire or trendy indifference. Instead, it is the term of highest approval, bestowed only upon those people Beth deems worthy of her attention and trust, and crucial if one is to be promoted into her personal Top Ten (though, in truth, hip-hop shades or chiseled Brad Pitt features — neither of which the Professor possesses — are apt to increase the likelihood of admission). "Yes," I say. "I guess I do mean he's cool."

As Tim accelerates away from the crosswalk, Beth tells me that he's one of the drivers who truly loves his job, a quality without which, I realize, one cannot ever be deemed cool in her lexicon. Furthermore, she tells me, he smiles all the time, in glaring sun or fog, when the heater has broken, whether the riders have become deafening, or even if, as she sometimes observes from a bus shelter, he's gliding down the street alone. I'm impressed, especially after she mentions that he's been driving the buses for ten years. "What did you do before this?" I ask.

"I took an evolutionary route," Tim replies, slowing to a stop at the edge of this suburban neighborhood.

"Seven minutes," Beth says, reaching for her backpack. At first I'm confused, thinking she's referring to Tim's past, then realize that she's simply engaging in the kind of free-flowing talk that can characterize conversation on a bus. This time, she sees the question in *my* face, and clarifies, "Thaz how long he has to wait now."

"It's a layover," he adds. "They're put right into the schedule: idle time where you just sit before departure. Good opportunity to stretch my legs and get some real discussion in."

"Thaz what I *mean*," she says, as she pulls out a pad of paper and a set of Magic Markers and begins to draw.

Tim reaches his arms for the ceiling, flexing his hands. Then he steps into the aisle, holding his mug, facing us. "So, to answer your question. I used to be what you might call searching, except I'm not sure how much I ever let myself see." He takes a sip of coffee. "Funny, when you consider that I've always enjoyed photography. In any event, I came from a college-educated family and dreamed of being an archaeologist, but I got so lost in my own head that I couldn't buckle down to a career or even school. I was working in a factory, which was actually nice because I saw I really liked being around the other people, but I knew there was more out there for me. Finally I realized that I needed to look at life with a different eye. It took a lot of effort, but eventually I went back to college at night.

"I loved learning. Paleontology, history . . . Looking back in time was very exciting to me. But looking forward is more challenging — nothing unfolds as you anticipate, and it's the small things, not the huge geologic shifts, that make or break you. There I was in college, and I went on my first dig, thrilled to know I would at last be excavating artifacts. But when I squatted down at the site, I saw that the earth was packed down hard, the work was backbreaking, and the sun was baking me head to toe. I said to myself, This is *not* my destiny. I came home and switched my major to photography."

He pauses to finish off his morning coffee. "And life," he continues, "just kept happening; I began dating one of the teachers I met at college, and we ended up getting married. Then I heard that the bus company was hiring people. We wanted children, so I needed more income. That meant leaving college, but now we're looking forward to having our third kid.

"It's a rewarding life. Not the driving of the bus so much, though that pays the rent. But there's much more to this than taking people for a ride. It's like William Blake said, how you can see the world in a grain of sand, in the smallest moments of life. I couldn't see that when I was younger.

"This ties into my photography, too. I take pictures of all the things people don't normally look at." With his empty mug, he gestures at a jade plant inside a front window. "Like that little green guy over there. I pass him every day and watch him get bigger, and it makes me think about the way everything wants to grow, even if it's in a tiny pot."

I look out the window. Above the single-sprinkler lawns, now fallow with frost, rises a neighborhood of rectangular, two-story houses, their brick exteriors as red as apple skins. In the yard beside the house with the jade plant, a branch tilts upward from a puddle of slush: the remnants of a snowman. In another yard stands a stocky man in a cap, clipping a flag to his own private flagpole.

Then he hoists it up, arm over arm. Tim lifts his hand in a wave as the man cinches his rope to the pole; the man raises his gloved hand back.

"You could say I left college behind," Tim says, getting back into his seat. "But I think all I really did was find another major: the details — the ones that are so easy to overlook."

I glance at Beth. She is shoving her markers back in her bag, with her finished work of art still on her lap. It is a variation on the many drawings she has sent me over the years: an intricate, mandala-like face, with a crown of many hues, a fan of dazzling hair, and what appear to be earrings and a necklace made up of small, smiling faces. Go-light green, merge-sign yellow, caution-cone orange, railroad-crossing red — each detail, I note for the first time, resplendent in its own color.

The bus resumes its loop. Now, with the morning rush hour under way and with us headed back into the city, commuter after commuter gets on, each of whom Tim welcomes not as a mere fare, but as an individual who deserves a "Good morning, Louise" or a "Ricardo, how are you today?" Slowly we fill to capacity, though Beth, despite her stated preference for emptier buses, seems satisfied to remain on this line a while longer. So I settle in, too, and, keeping Tim's "lesson" in mind, I find myself taking in the individual faces around me: the jowls and curlers and nose rings, the bifocaled and puffy eyes, hair every color from snow to flamingo to ebony, all of it enveloped by a bouquet of perfume and after-shave. I become more attentive to the symphony of sounds, from the *rrrr* of the bus's transmission to the *Ay, Dios mío!* of heart-to-hearts to the frequency with which *ain't* and double negatives like *he's not doing nothing* pepper the meandering chitchat. I note the advertisements above the seats, for denture services, gas payment plans, funeral homes, Shriners hospitals. Beth points out passing buses, able to detect, from subtleties I don't yet see, the different varieties: "Conventional, like the one we're on," Tim elaborates when she can't find the words to articulate just what she means, "and then there are the new, low-rise variety, and then the ones wrapped in an advertisement like a birthday gift, called, you guessed it, 'wraps.'"

But as Beth begins to fill Tim in on the medical status of a driver who hurt his back, I find myself growing a bit skeptical that Tim is as content as he seems. He bailed out of college for this: a dozen daily circuits in this grungy, lumbering vessel? How could there possibly be enough here to sustain him?

Somewhere not far from downtown, though, as we're drawing up to a curb, an elderly woman on the front-facing seat to my left lets out a sigh. I turn. She's short, with white curls that she holds in place with a polka-dot hair band. I already know her name is Norma, because she'd greeted Tim and Beth by name upon her arrival, as they had greeted her by name, too. "Know what today is, Tim?" she asks.

"Wednesday," Beth answers authoritatively.

"It ain't only that," Norma corrects. "It's my anniversary."

"For your *wedding*?"

Tim, discharging passengers, says, "Isn't it the anniversary of when you met your first husband? You mentioned it last year, didn't you? That would make it sixty-one years now, I think."

"Yeah, long ago, may he rest in peace. God, that war . . . But when I think about it, it was a day like this: cold and sunny."

Then, as Tim tacks back onto the road, Beth lets Norma take the floor. "It was in one of them great dance halls," she says. "I'll tell you, those were some times. We'd ride the trolley down from where we lived — only seven cents, that's what it cost then —"

"Right, I remember," says a white-bearded man a row behind her, nodding. "Had a newspaper they sold on board."

"The streets, they was all lined with shops. Imagine it. My daddy used to say you could start naked at one end of Main Street and by the time you got to the far end you'd be dressed like a king. He worked in a knitting factory, and on weekends he'd give us money for the pictures. Well, the *theaters,* all gone now . . . I remember one with a domed roof that looked like the sky —"

"The Palace," adds a woman who wears a kerchief over her gray curls. "I had my first date at the Taj Mahal."

"The Taj was something," the bearded man says. "Not like them megaplexes now."

"And at the end of the trolley line," continues Norma, "was a grand park with a lake so wide I bet not even your finest athlete could swim it. There was a Ferris wheel, a carousel. Not that they ran at this time of year, and, anyway, the dance hall was all we cared about. The Silver Pavilion." Her listeners murmur in agreement. "You'd wear your smartest skirt and blouse, probably the same one you wore to church — we didn't have the means for lots of clothes — and you'd walk in the doors. It was so enormous, you could fit the whole town inside. But only young people came. There'd be a stage at the far end with a big band playing the hits: Tommy Dorsey, Guy Lombardo, all the orchestras you still hear about now.

"And that day I went with my sister. I was shy, so she brought me with her date. When we got inside the Pavilion, he saw his cousin. His hair was black, he was as handsome as Errol Flynn, and the very next song he asked me to dance."

As Tim drives, she goes on. Not everyone is listening — Beth has already floated off course, entranced by Tim's back — and most other riders are sorting through handbags or gazing out the windows. But for the few around this woman who grew up when she did, she is playing a newsreel of their youth. For a moment I too find it easy to see back sixty years, and I envision this woman, young and slender, and a boy taking her into his arms. Though the city might have declined since then, and though the war broke her heart, and, though, as Beth tells me, Norma later went through two more husbands, both of them louts, she chooses this moment to remember now: when the band struck up "In the Mood" and her hand first touched his.

Then I sense eyes on me, and look across the aisle. An attractive man about my age, wearing a chestnut-colored bomber jacket, nods at me. "Looks like you like to dance," he says.

I am startled. Strangers mix with strangers all the time on these buses, but this stranger's eyes are flirtatious, though I tell myself I must be imagining it. "Well, I . . . I haven't really . . . danced for . . . for quite some time . . ."

"It comes back fast," he says with assurance. "You just get out there and go for it."

"I guess so."

"You ever get out to Club 86? The Lion's Den?"

"Uh, no."

"So you're new to the area?"

"I'm . . . just visiting . . ."

He glances out the window, then back at me. "So where are you going?"

You'll never reach the Big Life by dancing, a dark voice deep inside me says. *And, besides, this journey's not about you. He wants to know where you're going? You know what to tell him: Nowhere.*

I square my shoulders and say, "Actually, I'm going wherever she's going," and gesture to Beth. "She's my sister." He laughs politely. Soon afterward he gets off, nodding a quick goodbye.

Norma is now talking about her wedding to the boy, but I can no longer bring myself to listen.

Later, virtually all the passengers except Beth and me pour off at a glossy, platinum-colored mall. I know, because Tim thanks Norma as she exits, that I missed hearing all about the reception and how everyone loved her mother's wet-bottom shoofly pie. I know other exchanges escaped my attention as well, when a woman in a nurse's uniform brings up the rear, and Tim says to her, "It might seem hard now, Annie, but you have to have bad days to know how to appreciate the good ones."

Finally, when we're once again a threesome, waiting at the curb for new riders to emerge from the mall, Tim angles toward us in his seat and says, as if in response to my earlier inner criticism of him, "See, it's not the driving. I spend my day meeting people who lived important parts of their lives before I was born. Shakespeare says all the world's a stage and everybody's an actor, and that's very true in the microcosm of the world that's a bus. And a lot of the riders on this run are playing, like Robert Frost says, in the winter of their lives, and they're like an open history book. Actually, it's better, because you don't get feelings in a history book. Every day right here in this seat, I have history riding with me.

"And that's what I like about it. There's so much richness on a bus — really, so much richness everywhere — if you just develop the ability to look at life with a different eye, and appreciate the opportunities offered to you. It's like what Marcel Proust said — he's a famous writer, Beth." Beth had lost interest in the conversation, but now she turns back to us. "He said that we need to look at every second, past and present, to truly see the whole oatmeal cookie of life, as it manifests itself all around us."

"No way did he say *that*," I say.

"Maybe not," Tim says. "But he might have if he'd driven a bus. Right, Beth? Don't drivers have all the answers?"

"No," she says, waving her hand at his question, and I laugh. "Only about *some* things. Not *all* things. Nobody does."

Still wearing his smile, he throws up his arms in surrender, then turns back to the wheel. "So much for my MacArthur genius award," he says.

Beth has already mailed her thank-you note to me before I've merged my car onto the highway home. It arrives at my apartment the next day:

> *to sis.*
>
> *thanKs. So very very much. For. hanging out with me. and TakinG Me. out and take carE. of me. too you are s☺ great. who I DO Love a whole whole lot. And forever too.*
>
> > *Love*
> > *Cool Beth*

A second letter arrives as well.

> *to Rachel. Hi.*
>
> *Happy TiMMy said. he saw Jesse riding his bike beHinD us. Jesse says. he Wanted to do a surprise. On his New bike. that. was Great. to hear. Happy Timmy said its just like What he said. now.*
>
> > *Love*
> > *Your Coolest sister of all*

I stick the second letter to my refrigerator with a magnet, and, at first, every time I glance at it over the next few weeks, I imagine Jesse sitting on his bicycle at an intersection, catching a glimpse of us through the bus window, then swerving away from his route and pedaling along swiftly behind us, unseen by anyone except Tim. But after a little while, when I look at this letter, I think instead of Tim, who keeps as aware of what's behind as of what lies ahead. I wonder how he developed a different eye, and in what kind of schoolhouse he learned.

Fighting

"Get ready for some Halloween pictures," Daddy says, grabbing his Polaroid, which means it's time to pull on our costumes. Laura is six, I am five, Beth is four, Max two. Mommy has spent weeks sewing our outfits, in between her classes at library school. Now Laura jumps into her princess dress, I get into my clown suit. Max is too little for a costume this year, so he and his Captain Kangaroo juice cup watch everything from my bed. Then there's Beth. Mommy still has to help her with sleeves and collars, so she takes the witch's costume she made for Beth, a pretty black dress with a hood for the hat, and starts to put it over Beth's head.

But Beth will not wear dresses. How can she know it's not just a big shirt, we wonder, as Beth starts shrieking and Mommy begins wrestling the cloth down to Beth's shoulders, saying "Stay still!" as Beth flings her arms around like she's a genie that won't go back in her bottle.

We watch in amazement. Beth sure can put up a fight. Even though she still wears diapers, and never crawled but just pulled herself along on her front arms till finally she stood up. Even though she talks funny — "Be quiet" is "Dee-DIE-ak" — her voice like a song and a quack at the same time. That doesn't stop her from kicking and howling as Mommy hauls the collar over her head. She doesn't want dresses in any color or for any holiday, and when Beth doesn't want something she doesn't give in. Not till — like now — the zipper is tugged all the way to the top.

Mommy stands breathless, letting Beth go. "You look so cute," Laura and I say, but Beth doesn't glance at the mirror. The best she'll do now is go along. Not smiling the way we do when Daddy sits the three of us on the lawn and snaps our pictures. But at least that fight is done for today.

*   *   *

She's fun to play with. She'll do the things that Laura's too big to do, and Max too little. After all, we're only eleven months apart, which means one month every year we're twins.

She'll suck on wet washcloths with me after a bath. She'll ride her big sturdy tricycle, which our parents had specially built for her, alongside me and my Schwinn. She'll go "Oooh" when I show her my booklet of spelling tests because my teacher puts stickers on each page where you get 100 and I'm going to save that book forever because there's a sticker on every page. And sometimes in the afternoons, she'll crawl with me into that quiet place under the house where Daddy piles the cut grass, and it smells all fresh and green. We'll lie on the soft blades, and look up into the sunlight coming through the lattice between us and the outside, and one of us will surely spot it: the beautiful strands of the huge spider web in the corner, shining like diamonds in the sunbeams. As we watch it sparkle, and point to how each thread runs magically right into each other thread, she'll hold her arm out for me to tickle. I'll skim my fingers along her skin, and she'll say, "Oh, dee-lee-shus." Then we'll reach beside us and toss the grass cuttings into the air. They sprinkle down, from light to shadow to light, our own private fireworks in the shade.

This is the second most scary time I remember.

Before Mommy goes to librarian school, she does paint-by-number landscapes with trees and streams. She props her canvases on an easel near the living room fireplace and paints when all four of us kids are just a few feet away in the sun parlor, singing to Meet The Beatles! *This makes it easy for us when the needle gets to the end of the record, because we can just run up to her, and Laura can ask, "Will you turn it over, please?" Mommy sighs every time, and puts the brush down in that slow way she does when she's sad, and she's sad a lot. She's sad in the way Laura wears glasses and Max has freckles and Beth is retarded. There's no reason, it's just the way it is. She goes to the hi-fi, slow and not smiling, and flips the record to the other side.*

One night when Daddy's working late, Mommy leaves a partway finished painting in the living room when she goes to make dinner. Laura and I are at Linda's house down the street, playing Colorforms and cootie catchers, but Beth and Max stay home. When we come in from Linda's, there's Mrs. Stein, looking serious. She says Beth went to the easel when Mommy wasn't looking and drank up the tubs of oil paint like they were punch at a picnic, and now they're at the hospital. Laura and Max and I sit waiting in the living room, staring at the half-empty landscape. We don't sing now. We don't even talk.

Then we get the call: "She's all right." The easel disappears, and Beth comes home, and Mommy starts her library studies, and her eyes grow even sadder.

This is the first most scary time I remember.

One morning, Mommy is in the kitchen, holding baby Beth in her arms. There's no Max yet, and Laura and I are playing dress-up through the archway in the dining room. When the phone rings, we know it must be ten-thirty, because every day Daddy calls us on his ten-thirty break from his classes, and Mommy really looks forward to it. She's lonely, and wears a drawn face, and asks Grandma over coffee how other people ever feel okay with themselves. Once she got so low she took us out for ice cream and had to call Daddy to find out if she should buy vanilla or chocolate. Daddy says she should take up a hobby like folk guitar or painting, or go back to school to get a job, they could use the money, and then she wouldn't feel so lost. You can tell she feels lost because she naps so long every afternoon that I get bored lying beside her, and if she ever laughs it's only a tiny "ha" next to Daddy's great big "Ha-Ha-Ha!" And sometimes after the laundry and shopping and dishes, she sits us on her lap and in that gorgeous Judy Garland voice she sings songs that make you want to cry, like "Cockles and Mussels" and "Puff the Magic Dragon" and "Kisses Sweeter Than Wine," and then says softly, "You know, I could have had a career as a singer." Daddy doesn't sing like that. He wakes us every morning by putting on bouncy records like "Hi-Diddle-Dee-Dee" from Pinocchio and "Hello, Dolly" by Louis Armstrong and "Where's My Pajamas" by Pete Seeger, and then comes upstairs clapping his hands and singing and he throws back our covers and pulls us to our feet and gets us dancing so we start the day all giggly. Mommy says, "I wish you wouldn't get them so worked up," and goes off to scramble the eggs.

Now, Mommy's talking to Daddy on the phone. Laura and I are hooking slips over our heads for long, princess hair, and suddenly Laura grabs me and points: there, in Mommy's arms, Beth's neck is going back, and her eyes are rolling up into her head. She isn't gurgling. She isn't breathing.

"Oh, God!" Mommy blurts out to Daddy. "What'll I do? Oh, God! What?"

Daddy tells her something so loud, we can hear him say, "Now. NOW!" over the phone.

She hangs up, looking with this sick face at Beth, and then she's dialing the phone with her finger so shaky she messes up and has to start again. Then she's talking high into the phone, and when she says, "Help me, Mort!" Laura whispers, "That's Linda's dad. He's a doctor."

We hold each other as Mommy says, "Okay, I'll try, I'll try," and throws down the phone and races with Beth to the sink, limp as a towel in her arms. She rips through the clean dishes, seizes a spoon, and sticks the handle in Beth's mouth, pushing on Beth's tongue. But Beth just lies there. "I can't do it, I can't!" Mommy's saying, her mouth all crumbly, eyebrows sucking together. She tries again, moving the spoon around like she's trying to dig something off the bottom of a pan. "Oh, God!" she wails, and then she drops her arm. It's like she's giving up. "Oh, no." The spoon clinks onto the floor.

That's when Laura steps into the kitchen. I follow, and with the slips still on our heads we walk up to Mommy. She's facing out the sink window, holding Beth against her chest, her body shaking.

"What's the matter, Mommy?" Laura asks.

Mommy turns. Her eyes are red, and she looks down at us. And we stand there, just like that, staring up at her, until the scare in her face suddenly turns into something else.

She spins around and scoops up a new spoon and then it's into Beth's mouth and she's got it shoving against the tongue like a stick pushing a stuck rock. "Uh!" she says, and then we hear a gasp from Beth. Mommy keeps pushing, and then Beth breathes.

Later that morning, Mommy calls Daddy, and cries when she tells him the story. "I did it because they were there with me," she says. "I just couldn't let them see me not knowing what to do. They saved their sister's life today."

March

The Pilgrim

8:10 A.M. "You know how you can tell the selfish from the unselfish people?" Jacob says to us. "On this bus, it ain't hard to do." An ivory-skinned man of average height and average girth, he grins hugely. His single distinct feature, especially striking for a man in his fifth decade whose Pennsylvania Dutch ancestors all went bald, is a tumble of dark hair. He has paused his bus at a stop sign at the bottom of a steep road. "When we had the older buses years ago," he says, as we peer up the almost vertical block to where this street will T-intersect at the forested mountain, "they lacked the power to climb this hill, so we would get to about halfway and then be stranded. I would then ask people, 'Is anyone willing to get out and walk the rest of the way up the hill and meet me around the turn?' You could tell the unselfish people because" — and he quiets for the ascent, then leans in for a hard left, arm crossed over arm, banking us onto a long ridge and over to the first shelter — "they would be the ones to volunteer to brave the demanding hike in sometimes harsh rain and snow. And then they'd get back on the bus with a good feeling."

It is about ten days after my first round of rides, and I have returned to spend another couple of days on the buses, a schedule I will try to stick with through the year. I came to this conclusion last night, as I cut my Toyota's engine in the bus company's visitor parking area. Beth, worried that the city's two-hour parking signs would keep me from being able to join her for whole days, had asked some dispatchers what to do, and they suggested that I leave my car here. She's making it so easy, I thought, as she hailed me to a shelter to catch the last bus home; I'll be able to handle this.

The seasons are already cycling, I see. The sun slants higher in the east, melting frost from parked windshields, and opening crocuses in window boxes. Jacob stops and starts the bus, block by block, so rhythmically that I almost don't notice when we're stationary and when mobile. In fact, we pause and go so predictably that Jacob — and all the drivers, I eventually see — time their talking for when the bus is not in motion, and do so with such skill that the exchanges appear to flow smoothly.

As we continue our pulsing course along the ridge, Beth tells Jacob about a driver she'd never ride with. "That Gus, he keeps saying I shouldn't go into the drivers' room. He's a *jerk*."

"He might just be in a bad mood," Jacob tells her.

"He's ob*nox*ious."

"You can try to understand him," he advises. "When you listen to somebody's story, and you see the troubles they have, you get a better sense of why they act a certain way. It might not excuse lousy behavior, and not everyone who has a difficult life acts badly. But going deeper, and really listening to someone, can help you see that they don't mean nothing against *you*, they're just hurting."

"I don't *care*."

"Remember that driver who died?"

"Yeah."

"He was a difficult driver," Jacob explains to me. "Gave Beth a hard time. Didn't like her talking and talking in the front seat. I kept digging at her to send him a card when he got sick. She finally did. It made him feel so good."

"But he wasn't nice to people. He was nasty," Beth says.

Jacob asks, "How do you feel about making him feel good?"

"I don't *kno-oh*."

"Ah, yes you do. You're blushing."

"No I'm *not*."

"You're really a good person."

"I'm tough," she says.

"You're tough and good, too."

"Thaz *right*."

"You like people too much not to be good."

"*Some* people."

"Don't I always hear you say," he teases her, "that you love all mankind?"

"*What?* I don't say that. I never say that. You're making that up. I love people that are nice to me. I don't love *evryone*."

"I'll be patient," he says. "I'll wait a year. I'll wait ten years. Because everyone's got it in them to treat others as they wish to be treated themselves, and I know you do, too."

"No I *don't*," she says.

"Ah, you're blushing again," Jacob says.

"You just passed into Zone 1," a woman bursts out, accusingly. "And *she* doesn't have a Zone 1 pass."

I turn. A squat, seventyish woman diagonally across from us who'd been watching this exchange is now pointing at Beth, who has not even glanced over.

"All she has is an inner-city pass. You should put her off. Unless she pays you the extra, and she never does."

I look to Jacob; the mood in the bus has suddenly plummeted. He drives on, saying nothing.

"Can't you hear me? You're letting her get away with this! She's just cheating the system. She should be out on that road, right now."

I feel tense in every muscle, and glance at Beth. She acknowledges me with a slight tilt in my direction, and a rolling of her eyes. The woman, lips puckered, rattles on and on. What business is this of hers?

Finally, after maybe a mile of her demands, Jacob reaches a stop. I pull on my gloves, expecting Jacob to turn to us and tell us, sorry, we have to leave now. "Hey, Beth," he says, and I am puzzled to note the same pleasant tone as he had before. "Lift up your pass, Beth."

Beth turns to the woman, and hoists her pass as if raising her fist in a *Yes!* "Zone 1," it says quite clearly. Then Beth lowers it to her lap, wearing the aaah-hah grin that I know so well.

The woman clamps her lips shut, and stares out the window, fuming in defeat.

"Nothing bothers Beth," Jacob says, after the woman departs, hissing at Beth on her way to the door. She might as well have been invisible; Beth shows no response. As the door closes, Beth steps forward to hand Jacob a box of raisins, a treat she offers the drivers once a week.

"Some of the old people, they don't like me," she tells me, as she sits back down.

"Why? You have a pass; your riding has nothing to do with her."

"Thaz just what they're like," she says with a sigh. "*Some* of them."

"And know how much she'd have to pay if she hadn't had the Zone 1?" Jacob adds. "A big twenty cents."

"Iz just to be mean," Beth says. "But I don't *care.*"

"I'll tell you," Jacob says, "you could get the Marine Corps in here, and they wouldn't take Beth down. *Oh well* is her attitude. Whatever happens happens, she's going to get through it, and good things are going to happen after that. That's all there is to it."

He thanks her for the raisins as a family gets on, and the two little girls, in matching yellow coats, give Jacob high-fives. They and their mother take the seats across from us, and Beth is instantly captivated by them. With her seated posture resembling a macaroni noodle, she's at kid level. As they begin playing clapping games, singing, *A sailor went to sea, sea, sea, to see what he could see, see, see,* Beth acts as she often does with children: chuckling along, answering questions. Their mother acknowledges her with a cordial smile.

I've seen this before. The mother views Beth as another of the impromptu aunties whom they might encounter in public places, like waitresses who say *Hon.* Her kids, though, probably sense that this heavyset auntie doesn't seem like the usual authority figures who constitute the adult world, and welcome her as an ally. Some people — those who don't know better — might think that Beth gets along so well with children because she is simply a large child. But kids see that, unlike other grown-ups they know, she treats them as she wants to be treated: with no restrictions, no judgments, no authority.

I envy her connection with kids. When I felt myself backing away from Sam, it drained away any thoughts of having children. Now, sharing my bed with books, I have no room in my life for a man, much less a future family.

"She knows the good ones out there," Jacob says, nodding toward Beth as the kids grow louder and more giggly, and she seems increasingly spellbound. "She can pick out who to trust better than I can.

"But she and I have little debates," he goes on. "She feels, An eye for an eye. I argue, Do unto others as you would have them do unto you. That's the biggest debate in life for all of us. I see her struggle with this, and it's a tough one for everybody. Like I just wrestled with myself back there about how to handle that lady. An eye for an eye would have meant getting angry, shooting my mouth off, or, like Beth puts it, 'telling it like it is.' It's a lot easier to do that. You get that immediate rush of power, that excitement, and some of the other drivers, that's how they advise her. But do unto others — living by the Golden Rule — that means you stay calm and don't get revengeful. Then truth will come out. It's harder, and it ain't instantly satisfying. But it's the right choice.

"She asks what I think, and I tell her. Of course, then she tells me back. Some drivers get impatient, especially if it looks like her mind's made up, which it probably is" — he laughs — "but I don't get bothered. It's good for me that she tests my patience. If I see myself growing irritated by Beth, I know *I* have a problem. I know Jesus wouldn't act like that. It's how unselfish can *I* be, because when I'm not, that's my problem."

I feel a twinge of those old bad-sister feelings, wondering if I have it in me to be as openhearted as Jacob. I glance at Beth to see her response. Her eyes are not on us, but on the children's hands, though her canny smile reveals she's been following every word. Then a commotion startles me back to the goings-on across the aisle. The girls' game has leapt to new heights, their voices bellowing, their whole bodies engaged:

> *A sailor went to sea, chop, knee, ankle, toe*
> *To see what he could see, chop, knee, ankle, toe.*
> *But all that he could see, chop, knee, ankle, toe*
> *Was the bottom of the deep blue sea, chop, knee, ankle, toe.*

"Thaz good!" Beth says, as the girls zip flawlessly — hands, wrists, ankles, feet — through their routine. "Do it again! Louder!" She laughs, as complete a practitioner of the Golden Rule, at least when it comes to kids, as anyone could hope to be.

Last night, Beth sat me beside her on her love seat and, as she often does, laid one of her scrapbooks across our laps. As we were paging through, admiring her cherished collection of every letter she's ever received, she looked away. "Sundays are the hardest days." She sighed. "The buses don't run and the mail don't come. Iz too *quiet* on Sundays for me."

The brakes squeak; we are coming up to a railroad crossing just as the gates drop down. Jacob stops the bus, windshield facing the flashing red lights, and the first car of what turns out to be a freight train rumbles past us. I don't know that we will be at a standstill for something like fifteen minutes, though Beth and several passengers groan, the children's mother reaches into her bag for picture books, and, after a few moments, a fortyish man with a Rod Stewart haircut mutters, "Jeez, we'll all be dead and buried before that thing's done."

"*Jacob* died," Beth says, turning to me.

"What?" I say.

"He says it was *good* for him."

I give Jacob a look. He'd turned around at Beth's comment. "She's right, you know. I guess that's *my* story."

"Iz a *long* story," Beth says.

"Believe me," the Rod Stewart look-alike says to me, "you got time to hear anything. You got time to hear the whole damn *War and Peace.*"

"You can *tell* her," Beth says, waving her arm at Jacob. "I'm gonna *sleep.*"

Jacob looks questioningly at me. I nod. "Sure. Go ahead."

"Well," Jacob says, pivoting in his seat to face us fully, "you could say my life before I died was a total drop to the bottom. I was a rebel in Catholic school. Then I went through hippie times and married young. My first wife, she'd be gone days at a time, and then come back and describe in detail to me who she'd been with.

"I got deep into alcohol. I was a bus driver then, too, and I was almost fired from my job. My marriage fell apart. I couldn't have cared less if I lived or died.

"Then I started feeling very sick. I was about thirty. They diagnosed it as hepatitis B. I could barely drive the bus. And one day" — he sighs — "I got so sick that I just came home and lay on the sofa and couldn't get up. A day passed, then a week. My wife and I had split, and my girlfriend called the hospital. They took me in, and I went into a coma. It ain't a bad way to die, believe me, you just slowly fade out.

"I was in the coma for three weeks, and then for some reason they put me as number one on the transplant list for livers. They figured I had about seventy-two hours left. This is twelve years ago, when there weren't many donations, and it didn't look like it would happen. But somebody, and I still don't know the age or sex or race, said they wanted to be a donor before they died. It was a miracle for me. They helicoptered the liver here just in time, and they wheeled me in for surgery. It took a long time, and my girlfriend was really scared. They tell me my heart stopped while I was under. For a minute there, I died.

"But here's where it all changed," he goes on. "I woke up in the hospital after the operation, and even though I could see and hear, I didn't know a single thing. My mother. The day. I didn't know the button on a shirt. I was totally erased."

I'm thinking, *Your mind was erased?* Yet he's smiling serenely, and his eyes seem to take me in and at the same time to look at a place I cannot see. "Then," he says, "as my mind got functioning, everything was just beautiful. There was no right or wrong feeling, no social pressure. I believe that's what heaven's going to be like.

"For six months after, I remained in that state. It was total purity. I'd admire everything I saw, like a baby. You don't worry about what you have to do or what you once did, you just look out there and admire God's creation.

"Everything I asked for came to me in that state. If I had a thought about something and then couldn't remember it, I'd pick up a newspaper the next day and there it'd be. It went through my head one day that I wanted to see a turtle, and the next day I was driving the bus and a turtle was crossing the road. I got out of the bus and picked it up and brought it home.

"I said to my girlfriend, We're going to have a little girl. That's what happened. We had our little girl within the year.

"For a while, I struggled with going back to college or driving a bus. This is my second chance; am I chosen for something? Should I be the achiever I was supposed to be? But it didn't click. Driving a bus is where I belong.

"But when I went back to work, things inside me started to slide back to the way they used to be. I didn't want that, not after I'd tasted the pureness of existence. It made me wonder what we're here for. So I started reading the Bible. I took a notebook on the bus every day, and wrote down everything I thought about — love, suffering, death — and the Scriptures made sense for the first time in my life.

"The first part was all about getting close to God. The next step was understanding Jesus.

"I said, 'Okay, now I'm being good, I'm close to God.' Wrong. Because once you look at Jesus, it tears you apart piece by piece. All your pride, your anger, your selfishness. That's where I'm at now, working on every part of myself.

"And it's all because of my organ donor. Organ donors jump over all barriers of human selfishness. Let me ask you, Would you walk by someone dying without trying to help them?"

"Of course not," I say.

"Organ donation is the greatest thing you can do for another person. You don't need courage, muscles, or money. Just a commitment to do unto others. And then you can help someone who's died rise again."

"Caboose!" the girls cry out. Beside me, Beth starts; I realize that she had indeed fallen asleep. As she yawns, Jacob says, "Good morning" with a laugh, and turns back to his business. The gate lifts up and his bus carries us over the tracks.

I let Jacob's story ring in my ears as we trace along the ridge that separates the peak of the mountain from the valley. To our left sprawls a grid of streets, as bare of vegetation as a desert, and densely lined with row houses. To our right stretch three blocks, as tree-filled as vineyards, dotted with grand stone houses and Colonials. Maybe it's his words, maybe our vantage point on the mountainside, but for the first time in my journey, I see where one neighborhood, and class, borders another, and how, except for this ridge, they could easily blend into each other.

"So here's how I feel," Jacob says at the next stop, "and I say this to Beth all the time, right, Beth?"

"Huh?" says Beth, who is watching the kids across from us get off the bus, and as she waves goodbye to them, she says, "*What* do you say?"

"If you think of yourself only," Jacob offers, "you get nowhere. Yeah, we all could be an eye for an eye. But I prefer the Golden Rule, at least for me. Because money ain't going to satisfy me, and women ain't going to satisfy me. The only thing that's going to satisfy me is to do good in this life."

With that, he pulls away from the curb.

"What do you think of this?" I say to Beth.

"I don't *kno-oh*," she says. "Iz time to find a baffroom."

I laugh at her timing. "That's all?"

"Ah, you know it's right, Beth," Jacob says, already at the next stop.

"Well, thaz what you always *say*," she says. "*Evry day*."

"My battle's not won yet, huh?"

"Thaz *right*."

"Oh well," he says, as she tumbles down the steps. "Cool Beth keeps on rolling and Jacob keeps on driving. We're just rolling, rolling, rolling down the river. But hey, I'm not giving up yet. Have a good day today and a better one tomorrow. God bless you both."

I jump onto the curb, wondering if, on the older buses, I would have been one of the passengers who got off when he made that turn on the hill. And if I passed someone hurt on the road, would I really stop to help?

I run after Beth up the street.

Streetwise

"What about the bathrooms in city hall?" I ask, as we're flying down Main Street.

"I tried it once," Beth says, "and there was a lady in there who was *na*ked. I think she was a drug addict. She jumped out of the toilet and started *scream*ing at me, 'Get out of here! Get out!' Boy, did I *run*." She shudders. "I'm not going back *there*."

Bathrooms are the greatest recurring difficulty in Beth's day. First there's the question of *when,* which is usually during the five galloping minutes between goodbye on one bus and hello on the next — the kind of breathless five-minute break on which we find ourselves now. Then there's *where,* which means knowing every public restroom in town, information she seems to have amassed through six years of foraging from establishment to establishment, and soliciting pointers from passengers and drivers, and then keeping her list updated, since not all public restrooms remain accessible to her.

We charge past a popular fast food franchise. "What about here?" I ask between breaths.

"They let me for a *while,* but one day the manager came up to me and she said, 'You can't come in here anymore.'"

"But you told me that you sometimes buy the drivers coffee here. Did you tell her you buy things, so you should be able to use the bathroom?"

"I told her, but she said I still couldn't come in. If they don't want me there, I don't want to go there."

I try to wash the outrage from my face, as well as my surprise at her reaction. I think of the bookstore customers who'd call the president of the company if we dared say such a thing to them. I think of the libraries that homeless people have sued successfully so they could pass their days at a reading table. But lawyers, and the right to demand rights, are part of a world that Beth's aware of but doesn't seem to want to inhabit.

"Where are we going?" I ask, my overstuffed coat pockets bouncing against my legs.

"You'll see," she says, with a sly smile.

She barrels on, in her flamboyant Big Bird yellow, her curly hair as wild as Little Richard's after an elbow-flapping performance. Today, her eyes are also bejeweled with the hippest one-dollar sunglasses available, her head crowned by a lavender baseball cap worn backward.

I scamper behind, dodging smatterings of pedestrians in hooded sweatshirts and blue jeans or pullover sweaters and gingham housedresses. The sidewalks are bordered by the kind of humble dwellings and mom-and-pop stores that can be found in countless other northeastern industrial cities past their glory days. At some point early in this city's decline, young people dreamed of emigrating to more sophisticated cities, but the passenger train toward the coast was discontinued decades ago, perhaps also diminishing that lure; many people born here are still, as they always were, buried in these hills. In addition, for reasons that seem more associated with family ties than career opportunities, populations drift in, not out. Not in a census-shattering way, though — if all the doors in this Zip Code opened at once and every inhabitant spilled onto the streets, they would fill only a good-sized football stadium to capacity. But the palette of complexions has changed; the almost homogeneous white of the past now accounts for only slightly over half of the population, the rest being shared by every pigment from biscuit golden to well-steeped tea.

It seems that most people who are of Hispanic ancestry moved here within the last ten or twenty years, settled in the downtown area, and still retain the inflections and traditions of their native Puerto Rico, Mexico, or the Bronx. A few African-American residents have roots extending back many generations, though again, whether old-timer or newcomer, most seem to live closer to the city center, as do Asian immigrants. Only white people, who mostly have Italian, Polish, or German surnames, increase in number the farther one gets from the core of the city.

But another influence, which is perhaps as important as race for some people, if not even more so, runs from the most urban corner to the most rural pasture: Pennsylvania Dutch, or Pennsylvania German. Their ancestors came to this area from Germany over two centuries ago, though few people from middle age on down here would now identify themselves as Pennsylvania Dutch. But the legacy of their culture remains evident in the homemade pretzel shop we're now passing, as well as hex signs on barns, chewy funnel cakes at state fairs, and dishes like dried snitz pie at diners. This history also seems to explain the occasional broken grammar and Germanic phrasing I've heard on the bus, which, I will later learn, are what remains of the original dialect.

But I do not grasp all this at once. There are still the bus lines to figure out, and the layout of the city, and the protocol — on both the bus and the ground — and the social service system, and, most important of all, my sister. Besides, at the moment, I am racing down Main Street, just trying to keep up with my tour director.

"See them?" Beth says. She points to men in red jumpsuits, pushing brooms on the sidewalks and emptying trash. "They're from jail," she whispers, and I observe a supervisor hovering nearby. "They work on the *street*. I don't talk to them."

"Thaz the store that makes chocolate chip mint shakes." She is indicating a family restaurant. "But the stairs to the baffroom are *scary*. They're hard to go down — they're so deep!"

"You mean they're steep?"

"Yeah. Thaz what I *mean*. I can't go on them. A long time ago I tried, and they had to help me get *up*. I won't do that again. And see there?" She directs me toward a broken sidewalk. "Once I didn't see it and I *tripped*. I got all scraped up. But it's over with now, I'm all right now, I don't fall anymore."

In this way I am introduced to Beth's city, as we hurtle past its ragtag assortment of the unpretentious: used furniture showrooms, beauty salons, pizzerias, apparel establishments, swivel-stooled lunch counters, wig stores, Spanish grocers, churches, Veterans of Foreign Wars clubs, a factory, a newspaper building, funeral parlors.

"Does it ever get more crowded than this?" I ask, panting, noting that there are only a scattering of people out and about. "Is it safe?" My gaze is drawn to some police officers.

"Iz getting *worse*. Thaz what the drivers say."

At last, at the far end of Main Street, Beth scoots up to a renovated Victorian firehouse, which has been converted into a restaurant and offices, zips around the side, and swings open an unmarked glass door. "Down *here*," she says, shooting through an obscure corridor of small businesses and janitorial closets.

"How did you ever find this?" I ask, trying to see as we pass out of the sunlight.

"There were people in some office upstairs who helped Jesse out for a while, with money and stuff, and I'd just walk around when I went there with him, and I just found the baffrooms. But sometimes the doors're locked, so then I can't go. They don't always want us in here."

"Us?" I ask. "Who do you mean?"

She frowns, and opens a bathroom door. "Anybody who's not *them*," she says.

We're on our way back up the street, only now we're walking. There's no need to rush; in the bathroom I removed a sweater beneath my coat, lingering for more than the three minutes Beth had allotted before our next bus. It was pulling away just as we stepped out of the firehouse.

Annoyed, Beth storms on ahead of me. "You take too long," she says. "I'm fast, why'd you take so much time, iz too slow, now iz all messed up, now we have to *wait*."

"Sorry," I say. "But I was getting warm."

"You need to be fast to keep up with me, I'm not slow, I don't stop, I do what I want, I just keep going, and I can't keep going if you're so slow so you better get *quick*, you better, if you wanna ride with me, thaz how I *do* it, and thaz how you have to —"

"All right!" I snap.

Silence. Both of us steam. We're at an intersection, stuck waiting for the red to change. Ah — a distraction: I see a familiar form crossing up ahead, a woman with Native American jewelry and bouncing dark hair.

"Isn't that Olivia?"

"Who? Where?"

"Right there." I point. I turn and notice that Beth is staring at her, but cannot gauge who it is. I grasp now that Beth's vision, damaged by the cornea problem I learned about in her Plan of Care meeting, is deteriorating. "Oh!" Beth says at last. "Hey! 'Livia!"

Olivia whirls around and smiles. She's got a winsome, girl-next-door face, and since she has the walk sign, she U-turns back to us.

"You're visiting?" Olivia asks me as she reaches the sidewalk.

I say, "I'm touring the buses, and Beth is my guide."

"Well, you'll learn fast," Olivia says. "Beth is really quick."

"I sure am," Beth says. "I'm quick and she's *slow*. She was in the baffroom so long we missed Rodolpho and now we have to *wait* and I hate to wait and if she didn't take so long —"

"You don't have to blab it to the world, Beth," I say, realizing that for the rest of the day, she will.

Olivia says to Beth, "Does that mean you've got a minute for me?"

Our light has just turned, and Beth has a *let's go* look on her face.

"I just need to cover a few questions, honey," Olivia adds. "I'll only be a second."

Beth stifles the look, and Olivia explains to me that as Beth's case manager, she has to check each month to see if everything's going well, and because Beth is out all day and has no answering machine on her phone, they usually have this exchange when she bumps into Beth on the street. "Are you getting the services you desire?" Olivia asks speedily. "Are you getting the help you need?"

Off to the side of this exchange, I quickly put more of the system together: Olivia must work at the agency that monitors the services Beth receives, including those of the *other* agency, the one that employs Vera and Amber. That's why she was running the Plan of Care meeting, which was held where *she* works, and why she needs to know if Beth is satisfied with how she's being served. Once again, I'm a bit uncomfortable as I realize all I haven't known.

"Yeah, *ev*rything's all *right*."

Olivia nods, listening hard. Then, "And how are your eyes doing?"

"I'm *fine*."

"When's the doctor appointment?" I ask.

"I just *had* one," Beth says. "He wants to have me come in again this summer."

"To see if it's getting any worse," Olivia adds.

"We done?" Beth says.

"All done. I'll see you in a month," Olivia says, but as she steps off the curb she turns to me. "I really like Beth. She's so cool." At this observation, Beth grins. Then Olivia hurries across the street.

We're sallying up the slope of Main Street, toward the *you'll see* of our next stop, when I realize, though Beth doesn't say it, that as far as she's concerned I am *not* cool. Having apparently forgotten her annoyance with me, she is chattering about the different stores along the way when we see a scraggly, bowlegged man walking toward us. His pants cuffs are unraveling, and his beard is a waiting nest for birds. I avert my eyes, figuring, as always, that it's better to ignore homeless people than to get a request for a handout.

As we pass him, Beth says, "Hi, John." He looks directly at her and nods back.

A moment beyond, I ask, "You know him?"

"Yeah. He lives on the *street*. He's nice."

I turn around and watch him walk away.

After a few more blocks, I realize that she knows all the misfits. Every time I notice one — the mustached guy with the loping belly and duffel bag, the frog-faced woman whose scarlet shoes match her hair, anyone who seems homeless or "different" — I, preset to tune them out, turn away. Immediately, as if reading my dismissiveness in the swing of my head, Beth will say, "He lives in a shelter. He uses Tide in the Laundromat." Or "She works at the drugstore. We talk about Whitney Houston." I walk on, my footing less sure than only minutes earlier.

But Beth's goodwill toward other outsiders doesn't extend to everyone.

A sallow man wearing a toupee, who's driving a rusty station wagon, screeches over to the curb. "Hey, Beth," he calls out, but she just treks forward, saying nothing.

I say, "He's calling you."

"I *know*," she says, without breaking stride.

"Beth," he says. "I got something for you." He thrusts an arm out of the passenger window. Dangling from his fingers is a photo album with Tweety Bird on the cover.

She swerves over, snatches it from his hands, and resumes her march.

"Aren't you going to thank him?" I say.

"I'm gonna throw it a*way*."

"Why?"

"Because he likes to give me things. I don't like that. He shouldn't do that. Iz *creepy*."

"How do you know who's safe?" I ask.

"He's not," she says, pointing to a man in a wheelchair sitting in front of a fast food restaurant.

"How do you know?"

"He asks people for *money*. The drivers and Vera told me he's bad news."

"That's how you know? You listen to what people say?"

"Yeah, but I also see if they're nice. I give them two chances. If they're nasty twice, then they're not my friends."

"For good?"

"Unless they change. *Really* change. Like, you can't fake being nice. If you have to fake being nice, thaz not who you really *are*." She sees a trash can, and, without elaborating on who this man is or how he knows her, she flings in the offering.

She's got her own streetwise code of behavior, I see, as she finally stops at a corner. It's a code born of circumstances she has not shared with me, and that have taught her a level of discernment I do not possess. Indeed, throughout this break from the bus, I've felt far more naive than the street urchin chugging along in front of me.

"So is this where we're waiting for Rodolpho?" I say.

"Yeah." She sets her radio on a bus bench.

It's Fifth and Main. I realize that, even though it is a fairly nondescript intersection, with a bank, luncheonette, bankrupt department store, and McDonald's on the four corners, it is where the two most important downtown streets cross. Not surprisingly, many buses stop here; each corner has one or more shelters.

"A *while* ago," she then says, "I was waiting for a bus here, and a homeless girl on that corner" — she points across the street — "started giving me crap. She called me names, and I tried to ignore her, but then she came over here and jumped on my *feet*. I'd heard that her boyfriend sometimes hit her, so I said, 'Why go after *me*? Did your boyfriend hit you again? Why not go after *him*?' Then she put her hands around my neck, and said, 'I'm gonna kill you.'"

"Beth, this sounds awful." But I notice that she doesn't sound troubled. Actually, her voice is gleeful, and each sentence is taking her higher.

"I pushed her hands and broke away and ran to Jesse's. I told him what happened, and he rushed back there on his bicycle, and I ran back, too. When we got there, we saw that she'd brought *her* boyfriend, too. He whacked Jesse, and Jesse let him have it! Then the cops broke it up," Beth crescendos in triumph, "and the boyfriend went to jail!"

I pause, aghast at how rapidly this incident went from ugly to life-threatening, and I'm terrified for Beth's safety. "Maybe you could have just walked away. Jesse and you could both have gotten hurt."

"And now the guy's out of jail." She giggles. "And I hear he has a *knife*!"

"Beth, please watch what you do out here," I say. "This isn't something to laugh about. This could be dangerous."

"Iz okay. Jesse will take care of me."

"And who will take care of Jesse?"

"Nothing's gonna *happen*."

"But it could, Beth."

"It won't."

"What if it does?"

"It *won't*."

Now I grow irritated. I glare at her, remembering how I used to get fed up with her stubbornness, and how much that made me disappointed in myself — and in a flash, anger spews through me, at her bullheadedness, at my inability to get through to her, at my years of excuses for not being a good sister. And there it is again, that deep voice grumbling on inside me: *How can she be so blithe about the possibility of trouble? You can't let her do that. She may be putting herself in real jeopardy!*

I take a deep breath. Despite her familiarity with this city, I'm not sure she fully understands, or accepts, how perilous the world can be. Yet if I get too "bossy," I know she'll dig in her heels all the harder. I also know it would be a great loss if I let some inner voice of criticism come between us. I'm enamored of her feistiness and her keen-witted street savvy. I feel privileged to be her sidekick. I want this year to go on.

So maybe I should back off. Even if I don't think it's safe here. I think of her words: "Iz getting *worse*. Thaz what the drivers say." Oh, how I wish someone would tell me what to do.

"I'm sorry, Beth," I say. "I don't mean to be bossy. I really don't."

"Iz all *right*," she says.

"I just don't want anything bad to happen to you or Jesse."

"I *know*."

"And I don't want us to grow apart again."

"Iz okay. I like having you here."

"Do you really?" I ask.

"There's Rodolpho!"

"Do you really like having me here?" I ask again.

"You worry too much," she says, turning toward the approaching bus. "*I* don't worry. You should try being more like *me*."

"Oh, Beth, what am I going to do with you?" I sigh, not caring that I may be uncool forever.

Into Out There

"My turn," Laura says from the back seat. "Alaska."

"Oh, not an A word," I say from the front. "All the A place names end in A, which means you start the next with A, and it goes on forever."

"If she wants an A word," Mommy says next to me, her eyes on the dark road, "she can do that."

"It's a free country," Max calls out from the far back of our Dodge station wagon.

"Yeah," Beth says, next to Laura.

"Ruff," our puppy, Ringo, barks. He rides shotgun in front with me.

"How about Name That Tune?" I say. "I'm tired of playing Geography anyway."

"Fine," Mommy says. "Laura goes first."

We're on our way home from visiting Grandma. It's winter, and Laura, Beth, Max, and I are ten, seven, five, and eight, and this ride lasts four hours. Home is this far now because we've moved to the mountains in Pennsylvania, the first time our family, including Mommy and Daddy, has lived outside New Jersey. It's cold every night in our split-level, especially downstairs, where Laura and I sleep, so we make up reasons to sleep in the warm upstairs with everyone else. Sometimes it works, and Mommy lets me sleep in Beth's room, Laura in Max's. Sometimes when we're up there and I can't sleep, I hear Mommy in her bedroom, crying.

Last summer we moved to Pennsylvania for Daddy's new job as a college dean. In September I began third grade and Mommy became a librarian at Daddy's college and Daddy met a lady professor in the hall outside his office. Then the leaves fell off the trees and Daddy packed up the beige suitcase and Mommy stood next to him with runny eyes and he clicked the suitcase shut and he was gone.

In our bedroom, Laura whispered to me, "Maybe he'll be back."

And he did pull up in a truck a few days later, and we ran out to see him, all happy that he'd come home. But then he went inside and just carried out a cot and a rug and said he was sorry, he was so sorry, and we watched him lock the back of the truck and he hugged us and our faces got his shirt all wet, and then he climbed into the truck and drove down the road, and we were standing in the street waving bye and the wind felt cold on our cheeks and then the truck went over the hill and we couldn't hear it anymore. Mommy stayed in their room for a week. When she came out, her eyes were saggy and she burned all the dinners. Finally she said, "We're going to visit Grandma." We've been driving there every weekend since.

We like pulling into the parking lot of Grandma's white brick apartment house. We like the ride to the sixth floor on the elevator with the porthole window, and we like the echo our voices make in the dark halls. We like bursting into the living room, which smells of Grandma's matzo ball soup, and kissing her hello and dumping over the toy box and throwing ourselves onto the couch next to her console color TV and turning it up loud, so we won't hear the whoosh-whoosh-whoosh of the Garden State Parkway out the back window, and so Mommy can cry to Grandma in the kitchen in peace. For the longest time, that highway kept me up at night. I'd get up and tiptoe past Laura on the sofa, and Beth and Max on cots, and peek into the bedroom, but Grandma would be in one bed, Mommy in the other, everyone asleep, and I'd go back to my own cot and try to read a Peanuts book in the dark. But one night Mommy got up just as I was making my way to the bedroom. She came out and whispered to me, "Just pretend it's the ocean. That's what I try to do," and when she sat on the carpet beside me and I lay down and closed my eyes it did sound like waves after all, and then I fell asleep.

"All right," Laura says in the car. "Da da da DA dada da DA da."

"'See You in September,'" I guess right away. "That's the opening. Now my turn. Doo doodoodoo doo DOO doo doo."

"'I'm Henry the Eighth,'" Max guesses. We all know the same songs, so this game is easy. Then he says, "Dee dee deedee DEE DEE."

"'Hey, hey, we're the Monkees'!" Beth guesses.

"Great!" we all say. "Your turn, Beth."

Beth says, "DUH duh."

"*What else?*" *Laura says.*

"*Thaz it,*" *Beth says.*

"*There has to be more,*" *Max says.*

"*DUH duh.*"

"*But songs have more than two notes,*" *I say.* "*Do more.*"

"*Thaz all iz. DUH duh.*"

We guess "*Born Free.*" *We guess* "*These Boots Are Made for Walkin'.*" *We guess so hard we get that messy feeling inside that you sometimes get with Beth, where she makes you laugh but you get steamed up at the same time.*

Finally we say, "*All right, forget it. Just tell us.*"

"'*Hey Jude,*'" *she says.*

"*Aw, that's not fair,*" *Max says.*

"*How can we get it from two notes?*" *Laura says.*

"*It kind of makes sense to me,*" *I say.* "*It makes sense and doesn't make sense. Both.*"

Mommy says, "*All right, we're putting on the radio.*"

Ringo barks.

Mommy got Ringo after Daddy left. Dogs scare Beth and me, and Mommy said that's why we need one. "*You should look at what you're afraid of,*" *she said, her voice all shaky.*

Ringo's the size of a cat and he's black except for the tan rings around his paws, which is why he was named Ringo by the family that owned his mom. This is handy, since for a long time Ringo was our favorite Beatle. Ringo's readiness to play won us over the second we let him loose in our living room. We all like to hide him under the covers at bedtime and when Mommy comes to kiss us, we throw open the sheets and — surprise! — he licks her face instead.

Now Ringo is barking along with the music. There are songs we like to sing to and songs we like to hate to sing to, and the one we like to hate the most has come on. It's Jack Jones, and it's called, "*The Impossible Dream (The Quest),*" *and we think that title is stupid, but we know all the words.*

"*Now, no one act up this time,*" *Mommy warns.*

We sing along to all the words, behaving ourselves. But there's something about that song. It gets louder and louder as it goes, like a monster getting meaner and noisier as it gets closer in your nightmares, and the music starts pounding harder and harder, and we just can't help it. When we get to the end, we all hate it so much that Ringo is barking and our arms are out in the air like Las Vegas celebrities and Laura and Max and Beth and I are all belting out at the top of our lungs, "To reach the unreachable STARRRRSSSS."

"That's enough!" Mommy says, whipping around to smack anyone she can reach.

We're laughing, it's like the Fourth of July going off in the car, and Mommy says, "I can't take it anymore," as she snaps off the radio.

Silence falls. We didn't want to upset her. We can hear the tires moving over the road at the Delaware Water Gap. We look out at the icicles.

Then Beth says it. For the seventeenth time tonight she says it, twenty-ninth time this weekend, three hundredth time this winter. "Look!" she says, pointing out the back window. "Moon's following us!" We spin around as we always do, and there it is, high in the sky behind us, and we laugh when we see it, and even Mommy lets loose a little ha.

"It's not following us," Mommy says, her voice tired but nicer. "The moon's just there."

"Iz!" Beth insists. "Iz following us!"

We know the moon's the big thing and we're just puny underneath, but in Beth's head we're the big thing and it's the moon that's small, and there it is again, her makes-sense-doesn't-make-sense thinking. But her funniness wins out over our steaming up this time, the way it always does with Beth's moon.

"All right," Laura says. "Forget Alaska. How about Atlantic Ocean?"

"Newark," I reply.

"Kentucky," Max says.

We drive on into the night, doing the geography of the world, the moon hitching a ride above our bumper.

"Who wants to play Bingo?" Mommy asks.

"We do," we all say.

"Let's go down to your bedroom," she says to Laura and me, "so we can all sit on the beds together."

"It's cold down there," I say. "It feels like a basement."

"It *is* a basement," Mommy says. "But it's not good to have a whole part of the house that you never use." She picks up the dog, since he can't walk downstairs yet, and we traipse out of the kitchen after her.

We like playing Bingo, which is good because Beth is in special ed classes in school now, and they're teaching her letters and numbers, and Mommy tries to help her by playing Bingo.

At the landing, Mommy turns to us and says, "Let's let the puppy go pish," so she opens the door and he scoots into the snow outside. "This is why it's good to live in the country," she says, but her voice says she doesn't mean it. She misses New Jersey. With Daddy gone, we all do.

We get to the bottom of the stairs and go down to the North Pole of our room. Laura and I clear the Creepy Crawler kit off our beds and push them together, so our room becomes a nice soft Bingo palace. All four of us kids and Mommy get on the beds and sit in a circle and throw the blankets over our laps. She deals out the Bingo cards.

Mommy calls, "B3. N35." Beth marks the squares on her board.

There are two kinds of special ed classes, we've learned. They have big names: Trainable and Educable. Trainable is for kids who have lots of difficulties, Mommy says, like kids who can't dress themselves. Educable is for kids who can read.

Once, I found out that before Beth started school, a man at a big desk in a school office told Mommy that Beth should be put in Trainable classes. "According to her IQ score," he said. Mommy set her hand on the desk and said, "My daughter is going to read," and she put Beth into the Educable class instead.

"O72," Mommy says. "I22, G47."

"Bingo!" Beth cries out.

There's a noise outside, and we look up. Ringo is scratching his paw at the window above our beds. "He thought we were calling him!" Mommy laughs, bigger than her ha laugh. She opens the window and Ringo leaps in all wiggly and jumps on the bed, spilling the cards to the floor.

Mommy sits Max and Laura and me down in her room and closes the door. She tells us, "Beth needs a little extra help sometimes, and when-

ever you see that she does, help her. Don't you ever forget: it could have happened to any one of you."

Daddy sits Max and Laura and me down in his office when we're visiting and Beth is out with his secretary. He says, "When you get older, you'll have to save money for her, so when we're gone you can take care of her."

Mommy says, "People used to hide mentally retarded kids in back rooms. We will always have her as one of the family."

Daddy says, "Some people send mentally retarded kids away to institutions, but we'll never do that. Ever, ever, ever. We'll always have room for her."

Then when they get up and open the doors I think about how we just heard two words that they never say in front of Beth: "mentally retarded." We never ask why, we just go back to playing with her. But we know, too, not to say those words where she can hear them.

Mommy is away at her library job. The babysitter who has too much of a tan and a different hair color every time she's here is in the kitchen, copying the words to "I Am the Walrus" off our album. Ringo has been following Beth and me around all night, and today we're afraid of him all over again. First, because he's a dog with all those teeth. Second, because we've been teasing him with a sock and jumping around and now he's too excited and he's after us.

Since we know he can run up stairs and not down, we dart down the steps to the landing by the front door. Ringo flops to a halt at the top of the stairs and hangs his head down at us.

Beth and I hold onto each other, giggling with fear. "He gonna get us!" she says.

"No he won't," I say, but I'm worried he will.

We stare up at him, and he stares down at us, and we're squealing with fear till the babysitter comes out. "What's this?" she says.

"We're scared," Beth says.

"He's just a puppy," she says, pulling him back from the edge of the stairs. "I've got him. Come back upstairs."

"She's right," I tell Beth, even though I'm still nervous.

We're grabbing onto each other when we go up the stairs — one.

step. at. a. time. Ringo wags his tail as we come closer, and we relax. By the time we get to the top I realize two things: that Beth knows she's safe holding on to me, and that I kind of like that feeling.

Dear Mr. Simon,
     You don't know me, but I know what's best for you. I understand you have 4 great children. Your wife loves you, too. You could say it is not my bizness but I know that you will be happier if you go back to them all now.

I sit at Mommy's sewing table in her bedroom, trying to bang out this letter. She put her Underwood typewriter on the same table where she keeps her Singer sewing machine because we've just moved to a city apartment with no room for a desk. I'm nine, and we came back to New Jersey so Mommy could live closer to Grandma, because Grandma's her best friend. We live one block from the border with Newark, where Mommy and Dad grew up. Dad runs a mail correspondence school there now, but he lives in Greenwich Village with the lady professor, who wants to buy a farmhouse in upstate New York so she can turn it into a commune.

     If you go back you will make everyone happy again. The dog, Ringo, will like you too.

Mommy taught me how to press down on the keys. Every day I write letters and stories: a girl stows away on Columbus's ship, a girl obtains the knowledge that could stop Booth from killing Lincoln. I write fake newspapers. Beth still can't read more than the alphabet, so I write plays too, and then Laura and I put on a show for everyone, wearing costumes and using accents.
     Now I'm working on this letter, which I am planning to sign "A friend."

     So far you are only sepereted. You don't have to get divorced. Everything will be better if you give up that idea.

"Dad's here," Max calls out from the front of the apartment.
     Quickly, I whip the letter out of the machine and hide it under a book. Then I run down the hall, past Laura's room, my room, the back

door, the bathroom, and old Mrs. Vogel, the sitter with skin as white as her hair, drinking prune juice in the kitchen. I come into the living room, which is also where Beth and Max sleep. Laura's already in her coat. Beth and Max are kneeling beside their beds, showing Dad the Hot Wheels tracks. This is where I hang out mostly. We run the cars on the loop and play the Top Ten on 77 WABC and dress Ringo up in T-shirts.

We pile into Dad's blue car. We drive up past South Orange, past the hill where he used to take us sleigh riding when we were together, beyond the ice skating rink. It's nicer here than in the city where we live. Rats swim in the creek at the end of our block. The landlord downstairs cooks stinky food. Mrs. Vogel sucks on her dentures and serves us canned ravioli.

"So what have you guys been up to?" Dad asks.

Laura says, "I've been reading Nancy Drew."

Max says, "I've been watching this old show called Winky Dink and You, and, man, did TV used to be dumb."

Beth says, "I can sing 'Sugar, Sugar.'"

I'm trying to figure out how to ask Dad his work address so I can mail the letter, but then he sees a park he knows. "Shoot some hoops?" he says. We get on the court and dribble. Dad nails it, Laura bounces it off the rim, Dad sinks it, I graze the net, Dad shoots it backward over his shoulder and makes a bull's-eye, Max hits the pole. Dad says, "Let's have a few lessons here." Beth sits at a picnic table on the side.

At some point, after Dad explains what to do and says, "Verstehst?" and Laura and Max practice, and Dad and I are waiting at midcourt, he says, "And what's up with you?"

I say, "Well, I finally figured out the Big Dipper from the Little Dipper, and Laura and I read Betty and Veronica together, and Beth and I can sing 'Yellow Submarine' when the radio's on, and oh wow you know what I saw in the paper? John Lennon is leaving Cynthia for this other lady named Yoko."

I didn't mean to say anything like that, but it just pops out. Dad gets a surprised look and then turns his eyes back to Max and Laura on the court, and with this quiet voice he says, "Well, maybe John and

Cynthia just weren't the right fit. You know, sometimes a marriage gets so empty that people feel dead inside, and then one of them meets someone who makes them feel alive and . . . well, maybe that's what happened . . ."

Later, when he takes us home and Ringo leaps around and they click the leash on to walk him, I say, "I'm staying in." Then I go to the sewing table and lift my book. The letter's still hiding underneath. I go out the back door and down the two flights to the trash cans. I don't want anyone to find that letter in the apartment, to see how stupid I've been.

"Why?" we ask, sitting on Mommy's bed.

"Because," she says, putting on her lipstick as she looks in her closet door mirror, "I want to meet someone."

"But you don't have to go on a date. You can meet us when we go to see You're a Good Man, Charlie Brown *in New York next week."*

She combs her dark hair. "That's not the kind of date I'm talking about."

"But what about Dad—"

"This fellow seems like a very nice man. I met him in the library."

"We don't want you to date. We want you to stay home and watch TV with us."

She pulls at her paisley minidress so all the creases she got leaning in toward the mirror go away. "I'm sorry. I need to go out once in a while."

BREEK. The buzzer downstairs goes off.

"No!" we say, but she hurries through the apartment and down the stairs to the front door. We make our way into the living room and huddle by the beds, Ringo at our feet. Mrs. Vogel calls out from the kitchen, "Now you be good, don't give her any trouble." We hear talking downstairs, and then two sets of feet coming up, and then she walks in with a man.

He looks like Clark Kent, hat and all. She introduces us, and he shakes all our hands. We usually never shut up, but suddenly we don't know what to say.

Then they're out the door. We run to the front window and look down to the street. He's opening a car door for her, and she's getting inside. "She look nice," Beth says.

Max says, "I wish I had a water balloon so we could drop it on his dopey car."

A little before the holidays, Laura and I run into a sixth-grader named Chip. He's famous in the neighborhood because when the kids on our block play softball, using parked cars for bases, he always steals home. One day, we're in front of our house: I'm holding one end of a jump rope, and the other end is tied to the railing on our steps. Laura jumps while I sing: "Cinderella dressed in yellow, went uptown to meet her fellow. How many kisses did he give her? One — two —" But when Chip shuffles over and pulls a handful of candy cigarettes from his jacket, we stop and each take one. Then, while we're sucking in the fruity flavors, he says in this low voice, "I'll let you in on a secret. I've got ways to keep getting all the stuff I want for myself, and you could too. Want to learn how?"

"Uh, sure," Laura and I say. Because, after all, Mommy says that even with the child support and her salary, we don't really have much for Hanukkah, which she doesn't care about anymore anyway, but since we'd like some kind of holiday, she'll come up with something. Laura and I want to do our part, even if our allowance is too small.

"Follow me," Chip says, and he leads us over the rat creek, down to Madison Avenue.

Then he heads into Angelo's candy store, where we usually buy jaw-breakers and Bazooka gum on our way back from school. He strolls around, taking his sweet time. We're pretending to examine the pinball machine, but really we're watching. Bald Angelo is on a stool on the other side of the candy bars, a pencil behind his ear. The phone rings, and when Angelo picks it up, Chip snaps up a Baby Ruth and slips it under his shirt. Then he walks out.

We follow, and out on the street he rips off the wrapper.

"Aren't you scared?" we say.

"Naw," he says, chewing hard. "You just use what you got, and what kids've got is 'innocence.' If you play it right, no one will ever suspect you. It's a good scam."

"I'm too scared to steal," Laura says as we walk home.

"Yeah. But we need to get presents for Hanukkah."

"Stealing from Angelo's isn't even a good scam," she says. "Mommy wouldn't want candy anyway."

We walk along, trying to figure it out. Then we come up with a scam that uses what we've got.

The next night, Laura, Max, and I dress up a Tupperware container with construction paper wreaths and tell Mrs. Vogel we're going to walk Ringo. Then, with Ringo in a red T-shirt but without Beth, we go to Lenox Avenue and ring a bell.

An old couple answers the door, and the smell of meatballs comes at us. "Yes?" the old lady says.

"Collecting for charity," we three say together.

"Oh, how nice," the lady says.

"What charity?" her husband asks.

Laura says, "It's for retarded people."

I make my face look pitiful and say, "Our sister is retarded."

"Oh, we're so sorry," the lady says, and she goes and gets a big glass jar filled with money, and pulls out a dollar bill. She says, "How nice you are," and we try to look sad for our afflicted sister. Then they shut the door and we run back to the sidewalk, trying not to scream.

House to house we go. First night out, we get $26.45. Second night, $23.60.

I'm zipping up to go out for the third night and stick my head into Laura's bedroom. She's sitting in her pajamas.

"I don't think we should keep doing this," she says.

I walk to the living room and slump on Max's bed, my coat still on. I could ask him to come with me, but I just don't feel like it. I move down to the floor, where Max is building a Tinkertoy house and Beth is putting together a big puzzle. "Need some help?" I ask her.

"'Kay," she says.

I pick up some pieces and wonder what I'll get her with the loot.

All four of us are sitting on Mommy's bed, caught up in Green Acres. *She's supposed to be reading Agatha Christie, but when Arnold the pig appears I glance over and see her checking herself out in the closet mirror. Only it's not the kind of checking out she did last night, when she was getting ready for a date with a guy we called Jimmy Stewart. He's just like Clark Kent and the others. They all wear hats and shake our hands and then we never see them again.*

This time, she's got her hand on her face, running her fingers over her cheeks and lips, reading her skin like a blind man I once saw reading Braille. It's as if she's tracing the new lines pulling her mouth tight, trying to smooth them out.

She notices me looking and lowers her hand.

"I don't like it here," I say.

One night I'm up late in Mommy's bedroom, watching TV with her. Everyone else is asleep, and suddenly I see Beth in the hall. She never wakes up like this, so I think she needs the bathroom. Only she passes right by the bathroom and reaches for the back door.

"Beth? What are you doing?" I say.

She steps onto the back stairs and closes the door behind her.

Mommy and I hurl ourselves over to the staircase. "Beth!" we call, tearing down the steps. "Beth!"

Near the bottom we catch her, opening the door to the street. She is looking at us, but her eyes don't see. "Beth! Wake up, wake up!" we say.

She does wake then, all agitated. We walk her upstairs and tuck her back into bed. I go to my room so relieved that we'd been awake, but afraid she'll sleepwalk again. Was she chasing after something in a dream, I wonder, as I lie awake in a worry. Or was she just doing what the rest of us secretly want: trying to run away?

April

The Dreamer

9:30 A.M. In the warm breeze of this Easter season, the purple whirlwind of my sister sweeps down the sidewalk of tulips and cradle-shaped baby leaves, picks up speed around a corner, and, at the waiting doorway, leaps onto Rodolpho's bus and hunkers down in a state of rapture. Having shed my black coat for a lighter jacket, I follow in close formation, and propel myself up the steps to join her at her usual cruising altitude. Actually, I think, with Rodolpho in the cockpit, Beth is above the clouds. As she's made repeatedly clear to me: "Rodolpho's nice. He's neat. He's hot!"

Beneath his pencil-thin mustache, Rodolpho acknowledges us with a quarter smile. This greeting is notable, I soon discover, as he doles out smiles only when they've been earned. Then, with a quick hello, he pivots his gaze back to the sunny path before us. About thirty, small, lithe, and tieless, he has a shaved head and almond-shaped, osprey-brown eyes. Beth has informed me that his eyes are derived from his Arabic grandfather, his fine Mediterranean skin from his Italian grandmother, and, I see, he has the kind of symmetrically balanced face that would make a fetching *GQ* spread. Indeed, Rodolpho is exotically handsome, but it is perhaps because his features are combined with a reflective, reserved manner that Beth ranks him as number one on her Top Ten Driver Hit Parade.

Beth trains her gaze on him, holding her breath until he hovers at a red light. "What do you do while you wait for him to talk?" I say to Beth over the oceanic roar of the bus engine. "Do you look out the window?"

"I don't know."

"Are you just kind of drifting along in your own thoughts?"

"I don't *kno-oh*."

"Or are you not thinking about anything at all?"

"I don't *know*."

An eavesdropping young couple across from us gives me arched eyebrows, but I've now become sufficiently schooled in Beth-speak to translate this exchange for myself. "I don't know," with no stress on any word, means, oddly enough, that she actually does not know. "I don't *kno-oh*," with its combination stress-and-broken-syllable, means she does indeed have a genuine answer buried inside her, but she'll be damned if she's going to share it. Then, of course, there is the most mysterious "I don't *know*." In this variation, she might or might not know, but, for reasons you will never fathom, she is annoyed that you expect her to know if she knows, or, if she does know, to tell you what she knows, and would instead just like you to shut up.

So Beth fixes on Rodolpho, lost to me, and maybe to herself, in the labyrinth of her own mind.

I sit back and follow my own thoughts. So far, it hasn't been so difficult to attend to the good-sister obligation on these visits, simply putting off other obligations till tomorrow. *But you must admit,* the dark voice says, *it is wasted time, just spacing out here on a bus.* I snap back, But since meeting Tim, I have taken note of countless tiny details I'd missed before: the shadows of branches that lie like lace across the windshield, the wing-shaped triangle of Rodolpho's pale blue shirt where he would otherwise be wearing his tie. And since meeting Jacob, I have measured my actions against a new standard, asking myself which impulses are generous or selfish. No, this time hasn't been wasted at all. *Oh yeah?* the voice hisses back.

"Are you cold?" Beth asks.

"What?" I say.

"You're shaking like you're cold. I'm not cold. I'm *warm*."

"I'm fine," I say, hugging my shoulders.

Out the window I notice seagulls circling, and then I realize we're crossing a river. I peer down. Waves flicker like silvery pennants in the midmorning sun, as if hailing our arrival. Signs point toward an airport, and as my shoulders warm up, Rodolpho noses our bus onto that road.

"So how did you first meet Beth?" I say when we brake for an intersection, eager to re-immerse myself in my — in *Beth's* — journey.

Rodolpho glances at Beth with a should-I-tell? look. I detect a slight apprehension in her face, then a hey-the-truth-won't-hurt response in his.

"We met six years ago, on the Niteline," he says, as we sit at the red light. "That's the only bus that runs after seven P.M., and it makes all the major stops in the city. She didn't usually ride it —"

"And I don't now, either," she interjects.

"But then there she was, day after day, and she started talking to me. Always, the passenger starts talking to me. When I'm driving, I'm a stone-cold person. I take my job seriously, because I have a lot of lives in my hands, so I don't start anything up. That's why I didn't say much back, but I heard it all: stuff about Jesse, your family, her everyday life. Then I just let her ride my bus all the time. It just evolved that way."

He is quiet as he accelerates through the crosswalk, and I can tell, as the houses begin to grow sparse outside our windows, that six years ago Rodolpho hadn't realized what a crush Beth had on him, nor how minutely she had learned to read his emotions in the sliver of profile she could observe from her seat, in the smallest shifts in the nape of his neck. He certainly hadn't understood that in her letters to us, he was the only subject she wrote about, and, indeed, the only reason she was on the Niteline at all, and that his advice, which he offered casually at stop signs and which sometimes contradicted ours, might as well have been hand-delivered by a god.

Instead, as I learn at the next intersection, "She just kept riding and riding. And *riding*. So I put her on a schedule. And she stuck by those limits."

"Really?" I say, glancing at her with admiration.

"Well . . ." she says.

"But she found another way to test my limits," he says dryly. "She would talk about her love life with Jesse. Explicitly."

"And *loud*," Beth admits, no longer hiding this story from me.

"Too loud. I said, 'Beth, what you do with Jesse is your business. You shouldn't be telling people that. You got to pipe down.' I gave her warnings. Then I said, 'Next time you do that, you're off.' She did it again, and I said, 'That's it.' I stopped the bus and put her off."

He hits the gas. Miles with only pastures and stands of trees roll by; I note that the sprinkling of passengers with whom we'd begun has thinned to three solitary window gazers, perhaps wandering amid their own fantasies, perhaps trying not to hear a story they might have witnessed. I glance back at Beth. I feel for her; her hormones had flared so giddily out of control that she couldn't restrain herself, broadcasting soft-core porn on a bus.

"How long were you banished?" I ask Beth.

Without taking her sight off him, she says, "A long time. It was terrible." I try to reconstruct her life in that grim period: day after day, Rodolpho gliding along the streets, Beth perched on the curb as he sails by, longing for all the indulgences she'd raved about in her letters. I know that she pined for the way that he would keep the heat off in the winter until she boarded, and then, only for her, blast it on. I know that she missed his spontaneous quizzes: practical arithmetic problems, hard spelling words like "Mississippi." But her greatest hunger, I'm sure, was for those times when he would uncap a pen at a traffic light and compose poetry on the back of a transfer. His marriage had disintegrated, and he needed to write it down, and sometimes, when it was just he and Beth on the bus, he'd fish out a transfer, and read her his rhymes. She would glow the rest of the day, feeling deliciously privileged.

We crest a hill, and the sky opens wide. "Then one day," he continues at the next curb, "I saw Beth up ahead at one of my stops, and instead of passing by, I braked and opened the door. She was standing all alone at the foot of the steps. 'I told you you're off the bus,' I said. In a tiny voice, she said, 'I've learned my lesson.' I said, 'Once and for all?' 'Once and for all.'"

Beth's smile resumes, her eyes remembering.

"I wanted our little spat to be over, too," Rodolpho says. "'All right,' I told her. "'Come on.' She's been riding with me ever since."

"Not *evry* day," Beth quickly corrects him.

"She sticks to my limits: three days a week, with only one trip each day."

This diet seems too meager for her tastes, but, she tells me later, she can tolerate it, "'cause I get Saturday afternoon." That's when Rodolpho parks on a side street, unwraps the turkey sandwich he's brought for lunch, and allows her to sit in the empty bus, singing along to the Top Ten countdown on her radio while he eats. Then, when he's finished, he'll unfold a slip of poetry from his wallet, and she'll shut off her radio, and in the narrow luncheonette that's all their own, he'll read to his audience of one.

We park beneath the airport canopy as a Cessna zooms down the runway and lifts off. Rodolpho lets the last passengers out, but looks through the windshield, watching the aircraft rise.

"I got a surprise for you," Beth says to him.

He glances at her, then out the window behind her shoulders, where, I see, he spies a planter bursting with hyacinths. "Bet I know what it is," he says.

"Oh, you know, I know you do, you *know* me. Iz spring and you know what I want to do in the spring, 'cause thiz when you all take your *ties* off, yeah, thiz the *good* time, you know it."

She rummages in her Pooh backpack. A single-engine Bonanza bellies up to the airstrip.

"I wanted to be a pilot," Rodolpho says, his voice a murmur as he peers out to the plane. "I wanted to be out there, up free in the air, able to see everything."

"Why don't you *try?*" Beth says, her face in her bag.

"I did," he says. "I took lessons here. I even soloed a few times."

"So what happened?" I say.

He breaks the hypnotic pull that the plane seems to exert on him. "You know, I had a lot of plans. I was going to make money, and have everything that money could buy my wife and me: the nice home, the nice cars, the credit card. That was my idea of success. I worked three, four jobs, making myself rich. I bought a house. I had another house built for us. I got a Dodge Ram. I took flying lessons. I thought this was it, that I was going to get everything I want.

"But there was one problem. I worked so hard for all this that I was never home. My wife'd get upset, but I wouldn't give an inch. It was my way or the highway — it was just no balance at all. Finally, it all came crashing down around me, and when the divorce came, I ran out of money to pay for flying lessons."

"I'm so sorry," I say.

"Oh, it's all right," he says. "Because I met a woman after all this, and now I look at success a different way. It used to be just stepping out every morning and seeing my Dodge Ram sitting there, all shiny. Now it's making Sabrina smile. That's my idea of success now: not thinking of what I can get, but thinking of what I can give."

"Did you . . . did you ever try to fly again?" I say, my voice suddenly raspy.

"No, but I'm not sure I need to anymore." I nod, a gesture so politely forced that I briefly feel a crick in my neck. "I really don't need anything," he adds, "except to be able to come home, share my day, cry on somebody's shoulder, have someone I want to do things with. I still want to fly, but it's better to keep my feet on the ground if I have to pay that kind of price." I stretch my face into a smile but can't help wondering if I could discipline myself to reach this point in my own life.

"Do you think you'll marry Sabrina?" I ask Rodolpho.

"I hope so," he says. "But if things don't work out, at least I found somebody new. Somebody new within myself, that is."

"Got it!" Beth says, and extracts a Polaroid camera from her backpack.

"I knew it." Rodolpho laughs.

"Knew what?" I say.

Beth says, "Iz warm enough for *pic*tures."

Then Beth bounds down the steps to the curb, camera in hand. I expect Rodolpho to rise and pose beside his headlights, but he remains in his seat, cooperatively unbuttoning his driver's shirt, just enough to show a little chest hair.

"Thaz it," she says, pointing her lens up the steps toward him. "A little more."

"You got three buttons already," he says. "Last year I just did two."

"*Four* this year." She laughs, and he obliges.

She snaps a shot, then climbs back on the bus. As Rodolpho gives the engine gas and spins his wheels back toward the road, Beth holds the photo in her palm, watching the image emerge. Rodolpho's slim torso appears, then his arched, hollow cheekbones, and finally his solemn face.

"So many of you drivers," I say to him, as he slows to a stop, "seem to be philosophers, anthropologists, spiritual guides, commentators on what it means to be human, and how to be human a little better. It surprises me."

Rodolpho brakes, then turns back, and I see I've earned his pint-sized smile. "What do you do when you're a bus driver? You spend time with people and you sit and you think. I've thought all kinds of things in this seat. I think a lot in here about life."

I glance at Beth, who is not listening to us, but is gazing down at the image of her living deity, a person who not only imposes limits on her, but on himself, too. Both of them have learned the hard way. The bus suddenly seems chilly to me. I lean close as she presses a ballpoint to the Polaroid frame, her crooked scrawl coming out smaller than usual, and hence tidier, without spilling onto the photo. Her body warms me, as, slowly, the letters add up. *Number One DRiver,* they say.

The Drivers' Room

"Watch out," Jacob says. "It can be a soap opera in here."

Rodolpho has just deposited us at the bus terminal and pulled away, but as luck would have it — or as Beth has cleverly planned it — we happened to run into Jacob, who was just exiting his own bus for a break. Beth is again in search of a bathroom, so we are walking with him toward a glass door off an employee parking lot. "Thiz the drivers' room," Beth says, going in.

We pass from the windy spring morning into a coffee- and muffin-scented room of surprising serenity. Enclosed by the four corners of the bus terminal — garage, parking lot, dispatcher's office, and the bosses' offices — the drivers' room is, I've gathered, the inner sanctum. It's where the seventy or so drivers in this company secure their belongings, exchange tips and hard-luck stories, eat, read, lay down their heads, and have a laugh.

As a result, members of the public are viewed here as trespassers and immediately shown the door. Beth, however, perceives herself as more worthy than the rank of common folk, and the bosses, who have cast a kind eye upon her, agree. So when there are no curmudgeons who might ignore the bosses' wishes, Beth finds a bathroom here. Today there are no curmudgeons.

As my vision adjusts from sunlight to fluorescent tubes, I make out a rectangular space, with two walls of blue lockers — one of which incorporates an interior window to the dispatcher's office — another wall of vending machines, and one plate-glass window from which to scout out incoming buses. The four metal tables, each ringed by metal chairs, are almost militarily austere. Drivers cluster about, sipping from mugs, playing cards.

Beth emerges from the bathroom and glides up to me. "Thaz Perry, and Melanie, and Marco, and Rod, and Karl. And thaz Betty," she adds, pointing toward the dispatcher's office.

Nods and waves follow. Then Beth produces a birthday card from her pocket. It's for a driver whose big day is still months off, but why wait for the last minute? I am amused until I remember that, when I was a student, I handed in papers months early to avoid the suffocating feeling of deadlines, and as a college teacher, I write my syllabi half a year in advance. Now Beth carries the card to the dispatcher's window, passing it through for Betty's signature.

Everyone seems at ease, which makes sense. In the drivers' room, there are no rainstorms or demanding timetables or passengers squabbling about fares. "What soap opera?" I say to Jacob. "This place is pretty nice."

Jacob says, "Believe me, it ain't always so peaceful."

With an almost imperceptible nod, he beckons me into the corner. "If you knew what this room has seen. Guys come in here, they gripe about the union, they gossip about each other. Some of them can get pretty hot under the collar."

He talks about drivers attacking company policies, whispering rumors of their colleagues' infidelities and financial troubles. "But that's not all that gets folks going. Sometimes," Jacob says and sighs, "it's Beth."

"But she's not doing anything," I say, as Beth delivers her card to Karl for signing, asking him about his slipped disk.

"Well, some of us are her defenders, and some . . ."

And some, I know, thinking of the stories she's already told me, rail on about her when she's not here. They mock her chatter, get on a soapbox about her joblessness, and grumble about the way she, and some other riders, require extra personal attention.

Jacob's words, and Beth's stories, conjure up what I've learned is a typical scene: One of Beth's foes is grousing about her, casually stirring up others. The complaining escalates into a quarrel when one of her protectors speaks up on her behalf, then ratchets up even higher when, moments later, she is spotted shuffling off a bus toward their sanctuary. The angry guy bounds to his feet, fuming at the plate-glass window, and if that doesn't cow Beth into retreating, he seizes the door handle so she can't let herself in. At this point Beth sometimes does leave, but sometimes plants herself in the parking lot outside and heckles him back, until her enemy is enraged and red-faced, shaking his fist.

Clearly, not all the drivers are professors and dreamers. But just as clearly, it seems to me, Beth could handle her adversaries better.

Earlier, when she was gloating about a confrontation in the drivers' room, I'd said, "Maybe you could give them some privacy in here. It *is* where they relax during the workday."

"I'm not hurting *any*body. There's no reason I can't go in."

"Then maybe you could tell them you're sorry you've gotten them upset in the past, but you'd like to work things out now."

"I'm not sorry," she said. "They're *jerks*. I don't say I'm sorry."

So the bad blood goes on. In fact, about six months ago, a particularly stressful confrontation occurred.

A few new drivers had just come on board. For Beth, such events are momentous occasions. Throughout the weeks of training, she'll peer around corners to get a look, bursting with questions for anyone who's met the newcomers. Are they nice? Fun? Good-looking? The bosses, she knows, will be singing her praises during training, saying, "If you worry about making a wrong turn when you get started, there's this young lady who rides all the buses. She knows all the drivers, all the routes, all the times and checkpoints. She'll make sure you don't get lost." Beth will keep a vigil at the postings outside the dispatcher's office, and when they change every Saturday at noon for the following week, she'll run her small fingers down the list, searching for unfamiliar names. Finally, one will appear, listed beside the assigned run. The next Monday, she'll dress in her most glorious purple, paint extra layers of magenta and tangerine on her toenails, arrive at the appointed corner early, do a foot-to-foot shift in time to some inner countdown, until — there! Riding over the hill in a shiny silver steed, destination banner flying: a new face, a new voice, a new birthday card recipient waiting for her at the top of the steps, where this uninvited fuchsia squiress will assist him the rest of his way.

Beth may never have heard of King Arthur, but she understands chivalry. So as the weeks pass, she observes the new drivers' courtesy to herself and others. Then, the subject choosing her lord, she will adjust her travels accordingly.

But sometimes, these quests do not fare well. "New guys come in," Jacob confides, "and think they can look good, take her to dinner, be nice — and then they can't stand her anymore."

Six months ago, Beth became besotted with a new driver, Henry. He's a fortyish, broad-shouldered, broadly smiling guy, and, with his brown hair, bronze-tinted skin, and slight Hispanic accent, he reminds me of Desi Arnaz. After his bus training, Henry would walk with a sprightly step across the drivers' room, clapping other drivers on the back. Out on the road, he'd sweep up to a stop where Beth was waiting, proclaiming, "Beth, my darling!" He told her, "Me and you, we're like a stamp and an envelope, like peas in a pod. You're my riding buddy. You should win the Golden Steering Wheel Award." She instantly granted him a slot in her Top Ten.

Every day, Beth climbed bright-eyed onto his bus, primed for an hour of conversation, of feeling loved and indispensable. They were two loyal companions, venturing through the world, slaying dragons, or tilting at windmills, or whatever they pleased — what did it matter? They were filled with stuff and possibilities, and they were together.

The one hour on his bus slid into two, the two into five.

Maybe somewhere in their travels, Henry longed to say, "Hey, all's well and good, darling, but could you give me a breather now and then?" Perhaps he was too tactful to be as direct as Rodolpho had been, or felt guilty because he'd encouraged the collaboration.

Only after three months did he begin to object. He was in the drivers' room one evening, packing up to leave, with no one else around. Beth knew this; that was why she'd stopped in. As Beth tells the story, he said to her, "Beth, sweetie, the bosses just asked me into the office. They've been getting calls from some passengers who are complaining about you talking to me."

"They *have*?" Beth said.

"And," he went on, "the other drivers are growing jealous about how much you're choosing me over them."

"They *are*?"

"And a lady yesterday said, 'Every time your little missie gets on the bus, you never ask her for a pass. Maybe she doesn't have one this month —'"

"I *do* have one. And so *what*? Iz not her *bizness*."

"I don't understand why people do what they do, but I think you should know that people are talking." Then he got up and, with an apologetic smile, made his way to his car.

"Iz *wee-ard*," she mused to other drivers when she drifted onto their buses the next day. After all, even the surliest of riders were not routinely phoning the bosses about her conversations with the other drivers. And why would the drivers give even one thought to her time with him?

The drivers heard her out. Some said, "He's making up stories." Some said, "Henry's a good guy, so what he says must be true." Some said, "True or not, just lay off for a while."

"Well," she concluded, "if he wants me to stop he'll tell me to stop." By noon she'd jumped onto his bus as if nothing had happened, and didn't notice that she chatted more than he.

The rest of the story, I learned from other sources. One day, when Beth was elsewhere, Jacob entered the drivers' room to find, among the quiet crowd, Henry sitting there on break. Jacob called over to his table, "I hear you're having trouble with Beth."

Henry set down his newspaper. "I can't take it," he said.

At this point the truth is up for grabs. All I know from speaking with people who were in the room at the time is that Jacob and Henry briefly commiserated, then exchanged words, and then things somehow got so heated up that Henry jumped out of his seat and Jacob strode toward him and soon voices were bellowing and the other drivers in the room were saying, "Hey, guys, settle down, take it easy." The two moved closer anyway, glaring, jabbing fingers . . .

Another driver leapt to his feet, put his arm around Jacob, and then everyone calmed down. In the morning, both apologized.

Days passed. Unaware of the argument, Beth rode on, brushing off the quietness in Henry's voice and the distance in his eyes. But she knew something had changed. She wrote me letters about it.

> To Sis.
>   *Hi. Henry told me to Play it cool for aWhile that's what he said. No I said. some of it okay. I can't Wait to see you. I hope by theN Henry should be back. to his own self.*
>   *Cool Beth*
>
> To R.
>   *Hi. Henry told me agaiN. Henry is diffrnce. He will get Back to his own self. I hope soon.*
>   *Cool Beth*

But whenever we were speaking and the topic of Henry came up, her normally blaring voice would get slight and wispy, as if she was coming to the heartbreaking realization that someone who had once cared about her no longer did. I'd heard this bleakness in my own voice when I'd suffered some rejection, and I tried to tell her what I'd learned in life: how, just as she spots birthdays far ahead, so too can she learn to spot trouble before it arrives.

"Beth," I told her, "sometimes when we like someone a lot, we push harder than they can take, like you did with Rodolpho. Sometimes they try to tell us differently than Rodolpho did, but we just don't want to hear. This is why you might need to set limits for yourself with Henry."

In her small voice she'd repeat her refrain, "Henry will tell me when he wants to." I pointed out that he had, tactfully. But she insisted he had not. His wishes hadn't been blunt enough for her to hear, or accept.

I wanted to protect her. I wanted to take her by the hand and show her, as Merlin showed the young boy who would become King Arthur, that if you fly above the world like a hawk and look down, you will see that there are no boundaries between countries, and that might make you think that there are no boundaries between people. Yet there *are* boundaries between people, trust me, Beth: invisible lines that separate what you want from what they can give, borders you need to respect.

I imagined emotional devastation, Beth needing my support for months. I did not realize that she had other people who could take her by the hand, and that one of them would ultimately get through.

But that, I later learned, is what happened. Every night she discussed Henry with Jesse. In fact, for some time it was all she talked about during their nightly phone calls, and during the moments when they lay beside each other in bed. Jesse is an attentive listener, offering advice only when it's asked for. Whether this restraint results from his generally subdued personality, his slowness with speech, his southern gentility, or their trust in each other, I don't know, but for a decade Jesse has listened devotedly on the phone, and lain comfortingly beside Beth, as she has filled him in on the pinnacles and valleys of her life. There were a few occasions early on when her babbling and not-taking-no-for-an-answer manner got to him; he threw things around. Then his aides had long talks with him about controlling his temper, and ever since he has listened to and supported Beth, and when he's had his fill, he gets on his bike for another sixty-mile ride.

"Leave Henry be," Jesse finally advised in his drawl, "till he decides to come around."

So I received her final letter on the subject:

> *Dear Sis,*
>   *I give up. I don't know about Henry. Oh well. That's His lost. Not my.*
>
> > *Cool Beth*

Now, as Jacob and Beth and I stand at the plate-glass window, facing the yellow forsythia down by the employee parking lot, Henry rolls up in his bus. He jumps out with the engine running, and jauntily makes his way toward the drivers' room.

Beth regards him from our lookout. Then she pockets the birthday card and says, "I'm ready to go," her voice resonant once again.

Well, I think, maybe she arrived here slowly, but here she is, having survived the pain of a friendship that went bad, not dwelling on the past as she sets out into the future. Perhaps she is dreamily adventurous, sometimes impractically so. But Beth is no mere knight's servant. She is directing her own adventure. She might seem at first like Sancho Panza, but she is really Don Quixote.

We wave farewell to Jacob and the drivers, and she pushes open the door. Then we stride out, passing Henry, and mumble an indifferent goodbye.

The End of Play

Beth says, "Play it again."

I say, "You've already heard it fifty times. What's so special about Donny Osmond?"

"Play it."

"Which side?"

"One Bad Apple."

"That's not a side, it's a song. This is a forty-five, so there's an A-side and a B-side."

"Don't be mean. And do a puzzle with me, too."

"I don't want to do puzzles. I don't like puzzles."

"I like puzzles."

"I know. You're the Jimi Hendrix of puzzles."

"Who?"

"A famous guitarist."

"Donny. Play Donny."

I sigh and reach over to the portable record player sitting on her bed with us and pick dust off the needle. I know how to do things like pick dust off a needle now because I'm in junior high. I know how to roast a chicken so it's ready when Mom comes in from work because she says we're too old for babysitters. I know how to do a spitfire twirl with my baton (but I can't catch it as well as Laura catches hers). I know how to ride my bike to the five-and-ten with Max. I know that Beth likes "Puppy Love" while I like "People Are Strange."

"Look," I say, "you want to see how to put the needle on the record? It's not hard."

I put the tone arm in her hand. She grabs it as if it were a banister railing.

I say, "Lighter. Think of it like a tiny bird. You have to be gentle."

Her fingers do a little ripple, but her grip stays the same.

"Lighter," I say.

"Iz lighter."

I sigh, and steer her rock of a hand to the vinyl. It'll start spinning when I make the tone arm cross a certain spot, and here we go, the record's cranking up into its regular revolutions. "Now we're going to set the needle down," I say.

Gradually, I lower our hands to the wheeling record. Beth's tongue is out in concentration.

"Now, let it touch down soft."

She jams the needle down like an ice pick, so hard the record stops spinning.

"Beth," I say in that edgy tone I've had with her lately. She is too slow for me, that's what this little whisper in my head keeps saying. Though sometimes I wonder if it's just that my patience with her is getting too short.

"I didn't mean to."

"I hope you didn't break it," I say, pulling our hands off.

But then a funny thing happens. As soon as the needle's free, the record starts moving again. The music comes on in that muddy way it does when the speed's wrong, but then it gets faster and faster until the record starts playing normally.

"See?" Beth says. "Iz all right." Donny Osmond comes on and she leans back on the bed and starts singing along, "One bad apple don't spoil the whole lunch, girl."

I like it when she sings. She knows the tunes just fine but gets the words all wrong, and that makes us laugh, and then it makes her laugh.

I like helping her fix up her new room. We've moved again, to a two-story house on a lake in a farming part of New Jersey. Laura and I sleep in the attic bedrooms. Beth and Max and Mom sleep in the first-floor bedrooms. Beth's room is orange, thanks to me, because orange just became her favorite color, so I went to a store with Mom and got the most electric orange they had and painted Beth's walls for her. Then we pinned up posters of Donny Osmond — and David Cassidy, the Jackson 5, and Bobby Sherman. All her faves. She sees them in Tiger Beat. We got her a subscription for her birthday.

I like that she can read now. She reads picture books and TV Guide. *She writes, too, and keeps notebooks listing every card, record, and knickknack she receives, all of it in orange marker, all in chronological order.*

I like that Mom takes us to the library together. I pick up books like A Wrinkle in Time *and* The Hobbit *and* War of the Worlds. *Beth gets* Make Way for Ducklings. *I sneak a look at hers when I've had enough of mine.*

But I don't like it all. I don't like when we go to the lake across the street and she stays in the kids' swimming area. I don't like when she goes through my bookcase and finds the spelling book I've been saving since second grade, with stickers for all my 100s on every page, and she uses it like a coloring book. I cry when I find it. Mom says Beth didn't know it was important, I should be understanding, but now my prized book is ruined forever and I throw it away.

I don't like being bored by her puzzles. I don't like being bored by her music. I don't like telling her, No, I don't want to do that or that or that. I don't like that she doesn't get that I'm too old to play with her anymore.

But most of all, I don't like the way I feel when I'm walking down the hall at school around lunchtime, sticking to the walk-to-the-right rule along with a thousand other kids in their blue jeans and flannel shirts streaming to their next class, and the hall reeks of Herbal Essence shampoo and Clearasil and dirty bell-bottoms and Marlboros and pea coat wool, and all you hear is hollers and titters and grumbles echoing off the lockers, and everyone's secretly judging everyone else, and I'm staring straight ahead so no one picks on me, and ahead of me a wave of quiet starts rolling through the teenagers on my side of the hall and I know what this means. It means that when I get a few lockers closer I'll see the two special ed classes, the Trainable and the Educable, ambling on the left side of the hall toward lunch. I know that if I were to stand on my toes to peer over all the varsity shoulders and shag haircuts, I'd see that the cheerleaders from my history class would be gazing at their feet, and the Black Sabbath fans from my home ec class would be looking over with curiosity, and the chess club boys from English would be offering a quick look of pity, and the jocks from alge-

bra would be jostling one another with guffaws. But I just let the flow take me forward and then the two special ed groups come into view on the left, nine or ten people in each, walking out of step with us and one another. The Trainable students are in front. Led by their teacher, they grin and slouch, peering out at us with a kind of amazement in their eyes, as if they're surprised to see us. Then come the Educable students. I scan the bodies. There's Beth's school friend Billy in the striped shirt. She has milk and cookies with him. And there's Beth beside him, lumbering forward in her orange stretch pants and pink top, her frizzy hair almost the way Mom combed it this morning. We're a few feet from each other now, but she doesn't see me — no one in her class does. They're marching with their eyes on one another, but not giggling like my friends and I would. Instead, they look uncomfortable and walk in silence, as if they suspect they're being watched. And they *are being watched*: the teenagers around me are all quiet now, and walking stiffer and faster. To them, Beth's class is *different*. And they don't mean it in a nice way.

Then Beth and I see each other. I give a low-key wave, and she gives me a faint smile back. I hate how I feel then. Like yelling, "Hi, Beth!" real loud, so everyone who knows me will spin around to see her and understand that these two separate worlds aren't two separate worlds at all. But once again, as we pass each other, our shoulders almost touching, I don't yell anything. Instead I let myself be pressed along with the herd. A burn rises up in my throat, but I don't speak. I go into class and swallow my disloyalty and just feel disgusted for us all.

I hear the words people use.

I like words. At night I go up to my room, and after I've called my friends, I write lists of words as I hang out under this big blue clear plastic peace sign that I won at a county fair. It hangs from the sloped ceiling above my bed, and I put on the Who's *Tommy*, which Dad gave me during our last visit, and half lie down on my bed, and twirl the peace sign with my foot while the record sings, "Deaf, dumb, and blind boy, he's in a quiet vibration land." Then, on my bed, I write lists of words. I have pages of almost-synonyms in the back of my notebook:

PIG OUT, GORGE, WOLF, CHOW DOWN, CRAM IT IN, STUFF
YOUR FACE, LICK THE PLATTER CLEAN
WONDERLAND, NARNIA, LILLIPUT, OZ, SHANGRI-LA, NEVER-
NEVER LAND
BACKSIDE, ASS, BUM, BUTT, TUSHIE, TUFFET, DERRIERE,
CAN, RUMP, REAR END

But there's one kind of word I never write down. Kids in the halls at school use it, and teachers who talk about John Steinbeck's Of Mice and Men. *I don't need to write it because it bangs around every day in my head:*

DIMWIT, HALF-WIT, SIMPLETON, IDIOT, REJECT, SPAZZ,
IMBECILE, GALOOT, MORON, DEFECTIVE

And especially:

RETARD

They'll say these like it's nothing. Teachers will say, "Obviously in the childlike actions taken by the innocent half-wit Lennie, you can see Steinbeck's extraordinary literary blah blah blah," and you're supposed to go along. I go along because what else can you do?

But I can't go along when kids bungle a book report and smack their heads and say, "I'm such a retard." Or when someone messes up on the parallel bars in gym, and on the mats below someone else calls out, "What a retard."

You're supposed to agree that, yes, that would be as bad as getting thrown out of the human race. You're supposed to laugh.

I never laugh. I just stare sharply and say, "My sister's retarded."

"Oh, sorry, I didn't mean it," they come back.

They look away from me in the classroom after that, sometimes with their noses up, sometimes with their heads down. Either way is fine with me.

SMACK, POW, PUNCH, SOCK, BELT, BONK, BASH, BOX,
WHAM

Then I flip the notebook to the front and go back to writing. If "kike" and "spic" and "nigger" are bad words, why not "retard"? What makes that one okay when all the rest get you sent to detention? I give my peace sign a good, hard kick.

*We don't play together anymore, but Beth still wants to. I make ex-
cuses, which is easy because I have lots of friends. I can do headstands
in Susan's yard. I can make is-your-refrigerator-running? prank phone
calls with Marie. I can look at fashion magazines with David, or figure
out the lyrics to "You Can't Always Get What You Want" with Keiko.
Or I can just sit on the bed with any of them, and we can gossip and
eat chips and laugh our heads off until their mothers call out, "Will
you please keep it down?" and then we can laugh some more.*

*Sometimes when my friends aren't home, I boss Beth around. I
know she wants to please me, so it's hard to fight the urge. "Get me a
glass of water," I'll tell her when I'm in the living room watching* The
4:30 Movie *on Channel 7 and I'm in a bad mood that's come out of
nowhere, as it does lately. "Get it!"*

*She'll slink off to the kitchen to do my bidding, but glare at me every
step of the way.*

*Yet she keeps trying. She says hi to my friends when they come over.
She gets the mail every day and delivers it to me, telling me I got a letter from Kim, or my new issue of* Rolling Stone. *She'll draw pictures
and give them to me.*

A winter day. We are watching TV, and The 4:30 Movie *has just
ended, and Beth wants to turn to* Gilligan's Island.

"I want to see the news," I say.

"Don't want news."

*"Just for a few minutes. We'll leave it on Channel 7 until the
weather."*

*But the real reason I want to see the news isn't the weather or the
news, which is always about the war in Vietnam anyway. I want to see
the great-looking reporter they have on Channel 7, this guy my friend
Leslie has a crush on. His name is Geraldo Rivera, and all afternoon
there were commercials saying he'd be doing some special report on
Willowbrook at six o'clock. We go shopping at the Willowbrook Mall,
and I want to watch him go shopping so I can tell Leslie about it the
next day.*

*Beth sits next to me, and the news starts. Geraldo comes on, but he's
not in a mall. He's in a big, dark place where people are crying and na-*

ked, and some of the people look beat-up, and the rooms are all bare, and the walls are covered with icky stuff —

"Thiz gross," Beth says.

I don't know what it is, but it gives me shivers. I get up quick to change the channel, and just as I reach for it, a man with Geraldo says, "This is the Willowbrook State School."

I flick that channel and sit back down. It's the Gilligan episode where astronauts land on the island, and Beth falls into it, glued, while I wonder what I just saw. It couldn't be about anyone I know, nothing on the news ever is. But one face had an expression that Beth sometimes wears, and I shoot a look at her and wonder: Was this one of those institutions? The places where we didn't send Beth, and thank God we never will, ever ever ever?

It can't be, I tell myself. It's just too . . . it's too not human. It's as far away from me and Beth as Vietnam. I won't think about it. I won't.

But mostly, Beth tries to spend time with me, and I say no.

"No, I don't want to watch Adam-12. I don't want to sing to your dolls."

She gets a hurt look. "Call your own friends," I say. But her few school friends live too far away for her to reach with her oversized tricycle, which sits rusting in the garage. Or they have physical disabilities and can't get to our house without their parents' help. Beth is stuck, because there are no trains or subways or buses around here. And, as she puts it, she's bawd.

"Dominoes?" she asks.

"No."

"Go Fish?"

"No!"

"But we're twins!"

"Only one month a year."

She slumps off to her orange room, and I climb upstairs to my peace sign.

*　　　*　　　*

I guess she puts together a plan then. She will simply ambush me at the end of my school day. It's easy — she gets home before I do, and we

*have a park bench on the lawn looking out to the lake. She'll just sing
to herself, sit there with Ringo, and wait for my school bus.*

*The first time, I hear snickering in the seats behind me as the bus
pulls up. Snickering about her, I know. So when I get off and she's
standing at the bottom holding Ringo, grinning ecstatically at my
arrival, I usher her into the house fast, before they laugh any more.*

*The next time, the snickering is bolder. I run off the bus, telling her,
"Please wait inside."*

*But she does not wait inside the next day, or the next. I stop saying
"please" and just blow past her to get in quickly.*

*Then one spring day, she can't stand it anymore. When she gets
home, she finds her favorite water pistols. She slips on a pair of summer shorts and strips down to her undershirt. As my bus pulls up to
our house, there she is at the curb in seminaked cowgirl glory, shooting
off water double-handed, beaming up at my window.*

*The bus erupts. I seize my books and bolt down the aisle, my head
down. The laughter slams against my ears. I have never heard anything so loud. I have never felt such humiliation.*

"Get inside!" I blurt out in tears as I emerge from the bus.

*And they laugh and laugh. And don't stop when we get inside and
slam the door. Or when I run up to my room. I can hear it roll on and
on until I blast Led Zeppelin. Until I beat my pillow in despair.*

*Mom comes home late that night. She was out on a date. Not with a
Clark Kent who wears a hat and shakes our hands, but with one of the
surly types she sees now. They wear carpenter's belts or drive cement
trucks, and they never shake hands. They don't bother to learn our
names.*

*She tosses her pocketbook on her bureau. I tell her about that after-
noon, and I can barely keep from crying. "So please," I beg her when I
finish, "tell Beth not to come meet me at the bus! Tell her to wait for
me inside!"*

*Mom pauses a minute. Then she says, "I will not tell her that. She
has every right to wait for you on the lawn."*

"But it was terrible!" I say. "I was so ashamed!"

Her face gets hard, as it does more and more these days. "You shouldn't be ashamed. They *should be ashamed. I will not hide your sister from the world."*

I storm out, furious at life. It's not fair! It's not fair that, on top of being a teenager, which is bad enough as it is, I have this extra worry! It's not fair that I know — and Laura and Max know — that we can never think of a future that doesn't include Beth!

It could have happened to any one of you.

When you're older, save money for her, so when we're gone you can take care of her.

We don't believe in the back room. She'll be in plain sight, as one of the family.

Never put her in an institution. Ever ever ever. Make room for her in your own house.

That night, I sob at the injustice of it all. I know it's true, and I know Mom's right. But I hate it all so much that I decide I'll walk home from school from now on. This clears my mind but not my temper and doesn't lighten my conscience at all.

May

Lunch with Jesse

10:50 A.M.   "I've been thinking about love," I say to Beth, as she sails in her bumblebee yellow T-shirt toward Jesse's apartment building, her eyes shaded by sunglasses with psychedelic frames.

"You *have*? You got a *boyfriend*?"

"No, no."

"Oh," she says, disappointed.

"I've been thinking about *you* and love. Do you know what love is?"

"What? You talk *funny*. You don't make no *sense*."

"I mean, how would you define the word 'love'?"

"I don't know."

"No ideas at all?"

"I guess iz someone you *trust*."

"How do you do that? How do you love?"

"Why you need to *ask*? You got a *problem*? I don't know. I just do. It just happens. Ask Jesse. Maybe he knows. He'll know. He can *talk*. People think he's quiet, but he can talk, boy, can he talk, 'specially when we're alone. He'll tell you and then you'll know what to *do*."

"I'm not curious for myself," I say, a bit too tartly. Then, softening my tone: "Let me put it another way. What do you love about Jesse?"

"I don't *kno-oh*. Lots of things. Kissing him, I guess. That he's nice to me."

"That's it?" I say.

"You ask too many questions."

"I thought you said I could ask all the questions I wanted."

"Not *stupid* ones."

"Well, you said there were lots of things you loved about Jesse. So, like, what?"

"I don't *know*," she says, and, tsking away my interrogation, she breezes off the sidewalk toward his high-rise, her tiny sandaled feet splayed like a bird's.

"My sister has a boyfriend." When this information ends up making its way into conversation, it is usually in Conversation Number Two about Beth; Conversation Number One having foiled my friends' hopes of learning Beth's "mental age," a sequel sometimes arises weeks or months later, when I happen to mention her boyfriend. Often, my friends respond with a two-part smile. It's as if they initially think it's just so *cute*, but within seconds realize with a shock that Beth has womanly longings. "How did they, uh, meet?"

"She moved to a group home at twenty-eight, and he was living in a group home nearby."

"Oh, so he's retarded, too. But how retarded?"

Now it's my turn to sputter, as I've never seen the point in knowing *Beth's* exact diagnosis. Throughout my life, Beth has been, after all, Beth, just as Laura has been Laura, and Max has been Max. Not until this year on the buses did I cross paths with such information, when I peeked at Olivia's papers during Beth's Plan of Care meeting and learned that Beth's disability was classified as "mild." No doubt, my approach has complicated the task of translating my sister's life for my friends, but that has seemed insufficient reason for me to poke around in her medical records. So when Jesse came on the scene, I thought about his diagnosis no more than I'd ever thought about Beth's IQ, or, for that matter, my friends' IQs. It was none of my business; Jesse just is who he is.

I say, "You mean, what's he like?"

"Right," they say.

So I tell them about Jesse's Georgia accent, and inability to read, and how, beyond the walls of his apartment, he keeps to himself. At first, I say, I thought this reticence was run-of-the-mill shyness, but soon after I joined Beth on the buses, she suggested that it stemmed from his having grown up as an African-American in an impoverished rural town awash in prejudice, and from feeling self-conscious about his blind left eye. He lost the vision in it at thirteen, he once told me, when he was playing alone at an abandoned construction site and stepped on a pipe that swung up and slammed into his face. Although he had the wherewithal to stumble to a hospital (like Beth, Jesse is nothing if not resourceful), his sight was so damaged that he could do no more than sit, forlorn, beside the entrance. The wrong entrance, it turned out, because the hospital was a few buildings away, and he was in too much pain to judge. "A lady came out and tole me to move," he explained to me. "I tole her I can't move. She went in and called the cops, and the cops came and said I couldn't sit there, I was lottering. I told them some metal hit my eye, and I'm blind. So one of them took me by the hand, and led me to the hospital." I don't know if Jesse's tale is a story of racism or heartlessness, and he is too grateful for the compassion that ended it, and too polite, it seems, to speculate. All I know is that after weeks of agonizing operations, he learned to keep his smiles and words at home, where he and his big family would press the keys on the jukebox they kept in their living room, watch the forty-fives slap down on the platter, and dance along to Elvis, the Jackson 5, the Coasters, and the Drifters, while one brother would use library books to teach Jesse karate.

I tell my friends how he now spends his days: on endless bike rides and occasional odd jobs. He does lawn work for an old lady, couriers messages for one of his former aides, and helps a police officer who's asked him to bike up and down a misdemeanor magnet of a park path and radio in suspicious behavior. Every night he sets that yabbering police radio on top of his TV as if it were a golden statue on a museum pedestal. Beth hates having the static behind their talk, so he shuts it off during the four or five times a week when they get together. Then, as daylight spills through his windows, or as darkness gathers outside hers, they'll watch TV and talk. That is, if they're not, as Beth gigglingly puts it, "having fun," though these visits rarely culminate in their spending the night together. Both live in subsidized housing with no-overnight-guests policies, and residents continually glower at both entrances, quick to speak out at a violation of the rules.

Seldom do Beth and Jesse rendezvous in public, either, because in this city, a black man walking beside a white woman still seems to trigger hostility. When Beth and Jesse first took a shine to each other, tenants in neighboring group homes muttered epithets, and some bus riders who observed him talking to Beth on a corner would sneer at her, "Do your parents know about this?" "My parents don't *care*," she'd reply truthfully. Now, she overhears it in the drivers' room, from those who don't like her: "People should stick with their own kind."

I tell my friends I want to know what "their own kind" means. People with visual impairments? People who favor nomadic existences? People whom other people would like to label by their "mental age"? Okay, so she's a tiny, sassy, roly-poly, Crayola-bright, nonpracticing Jewish chatterbox, and he's a five-feet-four, bashful, sinewy, Lycra-clad, nonpracticing Baptist loner. Yet she makes sure he's safer by buying him a bike helmet. He makes sure she's prettier by shaving the hair that grows on her face. They scratch each other's backs, and they accept each other's moles. They argue over her queen bee ways or his reticence; they make up. He hangs his bike awards in her apartment. She keeps the redial button on her phone set to call him. They agree that they both want their own space and should remain unmarried, visiting in mornings or evenings, remaining alone with their dreams. I am still longing to meet *my* own kind, whatever that is, and I wonder who among these critics has met theirs.

That's often how I wrap up Conversation Number Two. My friends sit back, satisfied that they now know it all. They don't guess that there is also a Conversation Number Three.

A barefoot Jesse swings open his apartment door. He's wearing jeans and a white tunic, and knotted about his waist is a black belt.

"Hi, Jess-*eee*," Beth says, and in that run-on sentence way she gets when she's angry or excited, she adds, "Iz hot out, we're gonna have lunch, Rachel sez she'll pay if we go out, we can go anywhere we want, it won't be anything, it'll go fast, so please do it, you gonna do it? Please come, all right? Okay? All right?"

He eyes us, considering. Despite his social wariness, he's finally said he's willing to get together with me during one of Beth's bus days. So even though this get-to-know-my-sister undertaking requires an adherence to her routine (in this case, downing Ring-Dings on Jesse's sofa and charging back to the bus in ten minutes), I want to express my gratitude for his having drawn on some inner bravery. I also want to show my appreciation for his having found the time to admit me into their private territory. Besides, enough with apples stuffed in my pockets; I want to eat a decent meal.

"So you gonna do it?" she continues. "It won't be nothing, it'll be *fun*, please?"

He hesitates in his customary way, then turns to me. "Nice to see you again," he says.

I gesture toward his Asian-looking tunic and say, "Hey, you got all dressed up for us, Jesse," and as he nods, pleased that I've noticed, I reach out to shake his hand.

Handshaking is how we've always greeted each other, since he is even less fond of hugs than Beth. Our palms press together, as, behind him, the surfer bass line of the *Batman* theme song pulses on the television, and the police radio crows right along.

"So will you?" Beth repeats. "It'll be all right, no one'll be mean, it'll be okay."

"I . . . I'll think about it for a minute," he says, and he ushers us through his front door.

Without a pause, he and Beth enact a choreography as comfortable as any I've seen among couples. Beth produces a can of diet Pepsi from her pocket and lays it in his hand, then buzzes into his kitchen, waxing on about some bus intrigue, combing through his cabinet, and homing in on a pomegranate red glass. Jesse saunters behind, providing an ear for her bulletin, pouring her soda, closing the cabinet doors. She hands him a coupon a driver gave her for a free pizza, he turns over his latest bike racing certificate — Honorable Mention — which she will tack on her wall tonight. She opens his window, he shuts off the police radio and TV. She tightens his belt, he brushes lint off her shirt. It is the kind of dance I once fluidly executed with Sam, but not, I think, looking away, with anyone since.

Then Beth plops down onto the sofa, and, hoisting the red glass for a series of staccato sips, she asks him, "So, you gonna *practice* before we leave?"

"Practice what?" I say.

"Tae kwon do," Jesse says.

"He does this *sometimes*. You wanted to see what we *do*. *Thiz* what we do at *lunch*. *Some*times." She adds, "See his black *belt*?"

"When did you get that, Jesse?" I ask, knowing the drivers have been skeptical about the black belt since Beth first mentioned his skills.

"Oh, I got my black belt long ago," he says. He pauses, and I wait, having discerned that silence kindles his desire to speak. Then: "Well, first there was my brother's library books, and my cousin took karate classes, too. He tole me did I want to start karate, and he paid my way till I got my black belt. I could have went farther, I could have gotten the first degree, second degree, but that's with swords and knives. I just want the basic hand-to-hand stuff. It give me more confidence. I didn't used to have none of that."

I hear some rustling and turn to Beth. She's talking to herself, as, I'm realizing, she often does when she's alone or the conversation has strayed beyond bus topics. She catches my glance and smiles guiltily — it's clear that she was paying him no attention — and her lips stop moving. Except for her blush, it looks as if she's been interrupted while praying. I wonder if she was. She does pray, she's told me, when she wants things. "What were you saying?" I ask her.

"I don't *kno-oh*."

I glance at Jesse, but he's fussing with his black belt. Either he doesn't know or doesn't care that she has stopped listening. I think of how hard it is to understand her, with her roadblocks of *I don't knows*, how hard it is to understand both of them — and how much I wish I could.

I say, "So show us your stuff, Jesse. And then let us know if you want to go out for lunch."

His gaze tucks inward. As I relax into his sofa, and Beth's lips continue their soundless movements, Jesse reverently bows to the room, then to us. He kneels and seems to still himself inside. Then he rises, spreads his legs as if he's on horseback, and, crossing his left arm over his chest, he draws his right arm back, hands balled into fists. In a flash he turns his torso and punches straight in front of him.

And he's in it. Lunging into the downward punches of lower blocks, the skyward punches of upper blocks, inside, outside. He arcs his leg high in front of him — front kick, side kick — and, as I watch what I later learn is called the Way of the Flying Fist and Kicking Foot, I find myself feeling more alive in my seat, in awe at his agility.

Later Jesse tells me that for years he practiced so long and was so submerged in concentration that he saw visions when he got into bed at night: people in his bedroom doing karate motions. Sometimes he saw right through the walls to the snow or rain outside, and when he sat up to peek out his window, he found the weather exactly as he'd just seen it. And one time, when he'd just climbed beneath the covers, a wind blew in his ear, and it seemed that one of these visions must be trying to speak to him. He glanced out the window and saw God standing beneath the autumn trees. God was a white man with a brown mustache, curly hair, and dark eyes, and he just stared and stared at Jessë, as dying leaves drifted down around him. Jesse pulled himself together, and when he looked again, God had vanished.

, The visions gave Jesse a momentary feeling of safety. But although his mother told him she saw visions, too, they made him feel that he had to get a grip — "They're just not real, you know" — so he was relieved when they trailed off a few years ago. Instead, he's shifted his concerns of late to his dreams. Over and over, he'll dream that he's back in school, running as hard as he can; that somebody he can't see keeps chasing him. When he wakes up he'll remember where he is and laugh at himself. Nothing to be afraid of, he'll tell himself. I got my black belt, and I'm all growed up.

Now, in his compact living room, Jesse is flying. He's a blur of thigh and elbow. He's the Jet Li of his high-rise, twirling so fast he whips up a wind.

Then he is standing before us, breathless and bowing.

"That was great," I say, and Beth applauds.

"It's not hard," he says. "It's just a putting together of the mind, body, and spirit to give praise to martial arts. You don't think about nothing else while you do it. It's like saying a prayer."

I look to Beth, who has at last ceased moving her lips. "Lez eat," she says to Jesse. "It'll be all right. Iz early, no one'll be there, no one'll look."

He gazes down at his bare feet. "I don't know," he says.

"Don't worry," I say. "I'll be there. I'll make sure no one messes with you."

The skylit lobby of the sunny restaurant is empty; we have entered the front door an hour before the lunchtime crunch. Beth crosses the polished wooden floor toward the hostess, who stands before the room of pine tables, each already set for customers and adorned with a vase bearing a single carnation. Jesse, still wearing the tunic that I now know is called a dobok, ambles behind. The hostess glances up from her podium with a welcoming smile, then sees Beth approaching and her face falls. On carefully timed layovers between the Downtown Local and the Mall Express, Beth has asked to use the lavatory here, and they always issue a refusal — customers only — a policy I suspect that, were I on an identical quest in professional attire, they would not insist on. Now, from behind my sister, I say, "Table for three," and the hostess takes up three laminated menus and leads us to a table by the window. Beth struts into the deserted room, head held high in triumph.

We settle in. Beth opens her menu and, because Jesse never mastered reading, tells him what's listed for lunch.

We order drinks first. The hostess, who is also the waitress, has shed all traces of her earlier inhospitality, and she doesn't ignore Beth and Jesse, as some waitresses would do, waiting for me to act as the interpreter. Instead, she asks them what they want. It must be taxing for her, I think, as she pockets her pad and walks off; it's perplexing enough for me. And how *can* she assess the proper way to behave, when my conversations with friends have made plain to me how little even the most enlightened of them knows about people like my sister? After all, until Beth's generation, many people with mental retardation were shut away in institutions and attics, and, except for roles in a handful of movies and TV shows, which presented the trite image of the noble, naive hero, they have been almost entirely separated from the rest of us. This is why, I've come to think, some of my acquaintances feel sufficiently informed to declare about an entire population, "I think retarded people are God's true angels." Conversely, I also think this is why such a surprisingly large number of the elderly riders on Beth's buses simply can't tolerate her existence; if the Beths of this world were kept quietly out of sight for so long, why should they now be allowed to chatter all day on that most public of places: a bus?

As the waitress disappears into the kitchen, I notice that a bald white man has taken a seat at a corner table. He's holding up a newspaper, but it appears to be no more than a prop. He's glaring at Beth, then Jesse, then Beth, then me. With each second, his face clenches more tightly in abhorrence. It's the look of someone who wants his reality perfectly sorted, his whites washed only with other whites.

Beth and Jesse are preoccupied with pawing through our basket of rolls. I whip a scalding look at the bald man. He snaps his paper higher, obscuring his face.

Beth wipes a bread crumb from Jesse's small mustache. I bite into a roll, so frazzled that my hand is trembling. Now I understand that it's not just Jesse's blind eye or mental disability that discourages him from accepting my offers to join us in restaurants. There's so much separateness in this almost empty room that I can't breathe.

"Don't pay him no mind," Jesse says quietly, having observed more than I'd realized. "People is gonna look all day, and they might say that they don't think it's right, but it's not really for them to judge. As long as you be nice to a person, looks don't matter. You in this world, and you gotta accept it."

"*Yeah*," Beth says. "Sometimes people give us looks, but I don't *think* about it."

The bread feels thick in my mouth. Jesse blinks sloe-eyed at me as I swallow. He says, "You know, when I was younger, in Georgia, people always wanted to pick with me. I be out jogging, practicing karate on my front lawn, in special ed class, whatever, I got it from all sides. Black, white, it don't matter, they just see me and they say, You can't do this, you can't do that, and they treat me ugly. They don't care who you are, they just want to start with you.

"It just turned me to meanness. I was all anger. I broke a man's jaw once when he challenged me to karate. All I liked was being by myself. While everybody was out playing, I was in the living room. I had bought some toy army mens, and I just showed my meanness on them. My mom tole me you got to get that violence out of you. Then when I was getting up in age, twenty-four, twenty-five, she got me into classes for violence. It's like a round table, everybody talk about meanness, and a lady tell you the opposite, that people care about one another, and what to do when you have that real mean feeling. I saw I didn't want to live that kind of life.

"Now, I feel good every day when I get up. I feel good that I got into biking, and knowing Beth be all right. I feel good to be alive.

"That man over there, he just want to start something. He just don't know what's right and what's wrong. He just don't got nothing to do."

Our table is quiet for a minute. Then I say, "Does anyone want me to butter a roll?" They both say yes, and as I'm breaking the bread, I glance out the window to a granite building across the street. In one of the office windows, a spherical vase teems with a motley assembly of blue pansies and lavender irises and pink peonies and white poppies. I hand Beth and Jesse the bread, and we admire the flouncy blossoms and the pinstripe stamens basking in the sunlight.

Later, as Beth scurries off to the bathroom and the waitress hands me the check, I remember the conversation about love that Beth and I had begun earlier in the day. I glance at Jesse, who is sipping the last of his orange soda, and decide to extend my earlier line of inquiry to him. "What do you think it means," I say, "to be able to love?"

"You want to know 'bout love?" he says, lowering his glass. Then he sits up straight and says slowly, "Love is when you care for somebody, and you be willing to go out of your way and do anything for that person, and to take care of that person, and if they have problems, that you can help them out any way you know how. If they sick, that you can bring 'em medicine, or give 'em a helping hand. That's what love is."

I pause. "Beth was right," I say. "You do know."

I open my wallet to pay the check. "What do you love about Beth?" I ask.

"You got me stumped." He laughs, and then, as Beth blasts out of the restroom, he says, "Well, she's real funny. When I see her on the street, sometimes I wish I could stay talking to her forever. And sometime when I look at her or when she talk on the phone, I can just tell she feels happy or she feels hurt. I can just about feel it myself. I tell her, Why don't you be happy, because I can tell in your voice. And I try to make her happy."

He hesitates as we notice Beth rocking back and forth at the exit, gesturing to us to get going. "I guess I love her," he says, "just to be Beth."

I plunk down the tip, my hand shaking. He is so right, and for a second I think about Sam, and the way he used to say similar things to me, the sweetest look in his eyes, and for a long, terrible moment, I realize all over again how much I miss him. I inhale sharply.

"Now I got *you* stumped." Jesse laughs.

I try to laugh back, and I look to Beth, who's mouthing, Come on! Finally the laugh comes, and we make our way to the door.

A few days after the tae kwon do demonstration and the lunch, I receive a letter from Beth.

> *to sis*
>   *Hi. What I like about Jesse*
>   *is He is SExey and has Sexey legs and he can ride all over on his bike and he is Smart. and a great kisser. and he is Fun. to look at. too. all the time OK now you do have it. now*
>   *Cool Beth*

It has been a decade since I have initiated Conversation Number Three. Back then, I needed to talk about it, to question what was right and what was wrong, to receive a promise of forgiveness should I be influencing my sister wrongly. That winter is long behind us, but it is not the remoteness of the event that deters me from bringing up Conversation Number Three with new friends. It is that sometimes talking cannot provide the answer, nor can forgiveness always silence lingering doubts.

Conversation Number Three begins on an overcast afternoon the November that Beth is twenty-eight. She and Jesse have just begun keeping company, and our family is thrilled for her. At last she has met someone who will hold her hand while she watches TV, and enjoy her jigsaw puzzle masterpieces. This is how we see it at first.

It is a week into their courtship, and I am on one of my visits to see her. Jesse is out riding his bike, so I have not met him by the time she concludes that there are no television options for the next hour and walks me away from her roommates toward her bedroom. At the threshold she announces she wants to show me the latest Polaroids in her lifelong collection. I settle on her quilt, and Beth deposits her photo album on my lap with a grin and opens to the Halloween party the group homes threw the week before. I compliment wigs and capes and jack-o'-lanterns as we flip through, until she turns cheerfully to the final page. "Look at *this* one, what'dya think of *this* one?" she says. The planted evidence comes into focus: a man who is obviously Jesse, perched on the edge of her bed, beaming a snaggle-toothed smile. Not wearing a costume. Not wearing anything.

I don't know what to say. Beth giggles at my silence.

A day later, Beth phones Max. "Guess what *I* did last *night*," she says.

Max swallows. "How much did you do?"

"*Evrythiiiing*," she says.

A chain of phone calls follows, the family passing the news along like buckets in a small-town fire. Here it is, the moment we've dreaded since an eleven-year-old Beth first poked her head out of the bathroom and called Mom to come in to help. The moment bobbed into sight then, as Laura and I turned to each other on the sofa and said, "Some day she'll want to . . ." It receded for a while, only to pitch back up some years later when Beth would get goo-goo-eyed over David Soul in *Starsky and Hutch,* and then as soon as she left for the kitchen during a commercial, Laura would stop reading her mystery and whisper, "What's going to happen when she acts on this? She might remember birthday cards, but we all know the poor job she does brushing her teeth. I can't see her being conscientious with pills or foam or a diaphragm."

I would look up from my Kurt Vonnegut and say, "Well, it's not going to be an IUD, either. Remember how messed up my friend got from using one?"

Max would glance up from his San Francisco earthquake and Titanic books and say, "You want to trust that she won't be a klutz with a condom?"

Laura would say, "Maybe she won't become active."

I'd say, "She's human, you know."

Laura would say, "Maybe there'll be a perfect form of contraception by then."

Max would say, "Maybe there'll be peace in our time."

But now we feel an urgency; *evrythiiiing* had apparently not included *anything* for contraception. And the thought of Beth undergoing an abortion seems unbearable — not that she would anyway, as she is the one family member who objects to abortions. Yet now a man has entered the picture, and even if this romance fizzles in a month, Beth has learned how intoxicating it feels to have a person she loves in her bed.

In the single month in which I engage in — no, obsess about — Conversation Number Three, I explain to my friends that it's not sex itself that concerns us. Everyone's entitled to passion. And goodness knows it's not that her sweetheart is of another race; we do not even comment on this to one another. It's that Beth never passes an infant in the supermarket without veering close and gushing, "Aw, cute *baby*!" She has even speculated aloud about how much fun it would be to have a baby. But Beth needed over five years to take an interest in, and consistently perform, the steps necessary to deal with menstruation. She drops groceries; she can't hook her own bras; around her, things break. How long would it take her to learn bottles and diapers? Not to mention colic and teething and potty training and fevers and electrical outlets and terrible twos and lunchroom insults and orthodontia and facts-of-life talks and adolescent irony. We can see her loving a child — being delighted every minute by a child. We've read stories of people with mental retardation who've become responsible parents. But rightly or wrongly, each of us feels that parenthood will take a lot more than Beth can, or reliably will, give. Then what might happen?

Max calls Laura and says, "More government assistance is what would happen."

I call Mom and say, "Government or not, what'll probably happen is the family will have to step in to help. Maybe every week. Maybe every day."

"And it's not at all fair to a child," Dad says.

We hate to admit it, but we agree.

The day after *evrythiiiing*, our mother calls Beth. "So you really like Jesse?" she asks.

"Yup," Beth replies.

Mom grips the phone cord in her fist. "Can we talk about babies?" she says.

Then she renders pregnancy and infancy in detail, progressing from first trimester through bassinet. "Of course," she says, "it *can* be fun, but it's a lot of work. Babies are not like dolls. They get sick, and they grow."

Over the next week everyone else rings up Beth to contribute to her baby education, italicizing the unrelenting needs of a child through the toddler years, the grammar school years, and on and on. If she chooses to become a mother, she must accept that she'll have to be responsible all the time. *All the time;* none of us will be able to take on the daily needs of her baby. Then we address birth control. "Will you remember to take a pill every day?" "I don't *know.*" "Would you put a diaphragm in?" "I *might.*" "An IUD could make you bleed more, is that okay?" "*No.*" "But you have to do something, unless you want to risk having a baby. Do you want a baby?" "May*be*," she says during the first call. "No *way,*" she says in the last.

Finally our mother phones again, steeling herself to bring it up, the one form of birth control that none of us has mentioned. "It's called sterilization," she forces out. "It's an operation, and you have it once, and after that, you can do whatever you want. Forever. Without having to worry about it."

Beth listens hard. In a few days — one month from the moment I found Jesse's photograph — Mom calls back. "What do you think?" she asks.

"Okay," Beth says.

That winter ten years ago, with Beth having settled on a course of action, I abandon Conversation Number Three. I cannot translate it for friends. I can barely even speak it to myself.

Instead, I volunteer to be the one to accompany Beth through the process. Everyone is relieved to have someone else play the ambiguous role of parent and sibling, to balance the contradictions of right and wrong, so I call Beth's service provider and physician to set things in motion. Then I drive Beth to the preliminary appointments, hold her clamping fist when the gynecologist drapes the sheet on her legs for the exam, sit at her side in a darkened room during the hospital's required tubal ligation video. I get acquainted with Jesse after the doctor visits, as I chauffeur them around the valley. I hear about his sisters and brothers, his bicycle outings to a faraway amusement park, the janitorial job he keeps sleeping through. When I stop for take-out snacks, I learn his preference for orange soda. When I dawdle over goodbyes in their parking lot, I cheer at how well he can pop a wheelie.

Then, after I pull away, waving with a big, sunny smile, when I am too far down the road to glimpse them in my rearview, I weep. It is a terrible act to eliminate the possibility of children, to terminate a long march of futures.

I think, as I try to keep my blurry gaze on the road, that I still do not know when I might want a baby myself. So far, Max is the only one of us to have become a parent. It seems that I have not had the depth of longing for motherhood that many women possess. Perhaps my feelings about having a child resulted from my having observed my parents' efforts to rear children while striving to keep their own heads together. Perhaps it is a consequence of having parented Beth for much of my life — and fearing that I might give birth to a child with her disability. But my heart is still divided, and with relief I remember that I'm young; I don't have to make the decision yet. Beth, though, will have no more yets. At twenty-eight, her decision has been made.

The morning of the surgery, I pick up Beth and Jesse and steer us toward the hospital. It is a bitter January day, with a single ash white cloud staked to all four corners of the sky. Outside the car, the row houses seem swaddled in dimness. Inside the car, Beth stares out her window, nose and lips against the glass. She remains quiet except for fretting about the "knockout shot." When I make weak jokes, she manages a laugh, but it's as soft as a door hissing shut.

Assuring her that it will all be okay, I help her check in, and, when they call us, take her to the prep room. The doctor explains the surgery again, as Jesse sits nearby and listens. Then the doctor presents a consent form, and, without hesitation, Beth signs. She changes into her gown, and squeezes my hand during the shot. Jesse and I watch as they wheel her away.

We sit in the waiting room, and see through the window that a light snow has begun to fall. I stare at the crystals winnowing downward, melting at the touch of the earth. In the room, a family of five huddles in one corner, the genes of each rippling through the faces of the others. I look down at my hands, and find my fingers clenched tightly together.

Jesse wants to watch *Scooby-Doo.* I fiddle with the waiting room TV to find the program, though it's a rerun, and soon he is asleep. I try to read, but cannot concentrate; I have not eaten this morning, and my stomach has started to churn.

A few hours later, the doctor appears and motions for me to come speak with him in a corner. Beth has done fine, he says in a low voice. She'll need a week to recover fully, but soon you won't even see the scar. His voice is as hushed as the snow falling outside. I glance out the window and see the white tumbling down, and wonder what the hell we have just done.

The scarred flesh does heal, and Beth and Jesse grow into an unmarried couple. One with the same ups and downs as the rest of us. One that strangers gape at in restaurants.

Every January, Beth will mention the anniversary of her tubal ligation in a letter. *Its TEn years,* she wrote in the latest, *since I cant Have a baBy.* Then she'll switch to one of her typical topics, and I will muddle about for days, uncertain if I should mention it when I finally write back. In ten years, I never have.

Matchmaker

And now, Beth wants to fix me up with a husband. Not just any husband. Beth is drawing back her bow for specific targets, as I learn from her in a letter:

> Dear R,
>   *I wAnt to HavE a driver as a BrothEr in law.*
>   *Cool Beth*

I start my response. *Thanks but no,* I say. *I'm just not interested in marrying anyone right now.*

Though the truth is, I'm unnerved by the proposition. Last week when I made my usual ten-thirty P.M. foray into the produce section of my grocery store — no crowds, no lines, and, hurray, sixteen solid hours of work stacked up behind me before my usual late-night dinner — and was reaching for the kale, the overhead music cranked up louder. Or maybe I just thought it did, because suddenly I was listening to the same plaintive Nick Drake tune that Sam often put on when he came home from work, and thumbed open his tie, and he and our tabby and I would all collapse on the bed and I'd hear the chronicle of his day in the dusky light, or his soothing reassurances if I happened to be blue, or one of his silly accents when he wanted to make me laugh. In the refrigerated chill of the aisle I stiffened, clutching the leafy vegetable. What peculiar music for a supermarket, I thought, and then my mind sprang backward to all I had not said and all I had not done and the icy feeling in my veins when he drew too close, and then the produce sprayer was wetting my hand and I jerked it away, fearing I might never know what Beth and Jesse — and Sam — already know about love. I shoved my cart forward, so cold I shivered inside my cardigan.

I don't tell Beth that it's much easier to remain in my apartment with my books than to greet a date at my door. I don't tell her that I am afraid to care about someone who might back away and move on. Or whom I might never be able to let myself love.

So I write Beth that I appreciate that she cares. But no, I'm fine the way I am.

Okay, she scrawls back the next day. *I won't try to make that happen.*

"She's a writer," she mentions to one driver who likes to read fat library books.

"She's a vegetarian," she informs another who is inclined toward health food.

"Oh, yeah, she's single," she tells them all.

Absent from these particular exchanges, I do not know this is happening. I do not know I have a yenta for a sister.

I am on the phone with Rick, a driver about whom Beth has spoken highly, and often. An expert at pool, he runs a billiard school on the side, and, in the half year he has been with the bus company, has taken to inviting her out for milk shakes. I'm contemplating doing something more with the journal notes I've been keeping about Beth, maybe assembling an article about our bus adventures. So I've called him, along with other drivers, to conduct a brief interview. The sun has long since set, but I haven't bothered to lower the blinds. Leaf shadows shaped like small guitars flutter about my desk, dancing in the moonlight.

I begin, "Do you mind if I ask a few —"

"No, not at all."

I ease into it with small talk. He's cheerful and unassuming; when he tells me his full name, Rick Whitman Gulliver, he acknowledges with good-natured humility that it is absurdly literary. "But for years," he adds, "I've been saying, 'Ma, why couldn't it have been Minnesota Fats Gulliver?'" His gentle laughter pours across the miles. I can't help laughing back.

Then I steer us to the obligatory questions: How long have you been driving buses? Do you remember the first time Beth boarded your run? I check them off one by one until I say, "That's it." As I'm expressing my gratitude for his help, advancing toward the good-bye, he says:

"So maybe sometime when you're back in town, we can go to dinner."

A pause of several beats. He sounds charming and kind. Yet the receiver suddenly feels like a vise.

"Well," I say, "thanks, but I'm just so busy. Maybe someday I'll see you on the bus."

Three weeks later, I get a letter from Rick:

> *Dear Rachel,*
>
> *Beth gave me your address. When she rode the bus on Wednesday your name came up and I told her I didn't know what to say (in a letter). She said she would write some stuff down for me to use. I think I should find my own material, though hers might have been better.*
>
> *Last night I enjoyed my monthly fine-dining experience. During the meal it occurred to me that this may be a way to lure Rachel into a date with me. The place is the Kansas City Steak-house. Aside from the food being great, everything they do is up-lifting. I know you would enjoy it, and do hope you take me up on it. If you are interested, just say the word anytime.*
>
> > *Sincerely,*
> > *Rick*

I ponder what to say for a few days. Then I write him back. *Thanks,* I say, *but I can't,* and imply that I have some romantic drama in the wings.

The next time I phone Beth, she says, "I didn't know you had a boyfriend. I won't ask who he is, but maybe you'll tell me. But I won't ask. At all. I won't be *nosy* like that. I won't. Thaz not what I do. I could but I won't."

"Good," I say.

"I thought I could have Rick as a brother-in-law, but I don't think thaz gonna happen."

"Thanks for trying," I say.

There is a silence, and then she says, "Okay. I won't try anymore. I'll lay off. I'll let things go on for you just the way you want."

"I appreciate that."

I can't see her sly smile, but I have a feeling it's there.

The Pursuit of Happiness

We four kids sit in a diner with Dad. He's flipping titles in the jukebox at our booth.

Laura, lining up the salt and sugar holders, votes, "Three Dog Night's 'Eli's Coming.'"

"'Brown Sugar,'" I say, reading about New Jersey inventors on my placemat.

Max blows paper off his straw. "Ray Stevens's 'Gitarzan.'"

Beth draws a smile in the condensation on her water glass. "Partridge Family."

Dad runs his hand over his face. "Don't you guys ever agree?"

"No," we say together. Laura's eighteen, I'm sixteen, Beth's fifteen, Max is thirteen. We don't hang out together anymore; we hang out in our own rooms now, finding our own paths. Actually, Beth hangs out with Mom and Ringo in the kitchen, but Mom's so busy with her job and dating, and we're so determined to keep to ourselves, that we haven't had real family meals for years. Mom's crying has stopped. The long drives together have stopped. All she does is work late, date late, cook late, and lie in bed late reading spy novels and books on UFOs.

Dad fishes out a dime and drops it in. "Then I'll pick something you all like," he says, and presses the buttons for the crowd-pleasing "American Pie."

Every few months, Dad takes us to a restaurant and we order dessert while he asks how school is going. Today it's Christmas break, but he asks about school anyway while someone else's jukebox pick comes on — Jim Croce's "Time in a Bottle" — and we wait for our song's turn.

Laura says, "Finals are harder at community college than at high school."

I say, "We read The Odyssey*. I liked the story, but my English teacher's an ass."*

Max says, "School? Aren't we all in the school of hard knocks?"

Beth says, "I got new bankbook today."

Dad closes his eyes.

Our sundaes arrive. There's so much I want to ask Dad. I want to ask how to stop feeling so different from everyone in the world. I want to ask if Ringo still loves us because now when you pet him, he snaps. I want to ask why Mom always seems so bummed out. Dad still laughs his big laugh, though he and the lady professor have split up, and he doesn't laugh as much. But when I opened my holiday present from him, and it was an electric Smith Corona typewriter, I screamed with joy, and he laughed. Even when Mom vacations with a new boyfriend, or has coffee with Grandma, or helps patrons at the library research the history of horses, or wakes up to see the sun rise over the lake across the street, she's dragging.

But I don't ask. I'm afraid of not looking in control like Laura, or of getting hit with one of Max's sarcastic spitballs, or of boring Beth. Anyway, Max is talking about Patty Hearst, who got brainwashed by kidnappers and was just arrested as a criminal. I join in, my mouth moving right along, but I'm really thinking about last night.

It was late, and I'd raised my shades and peered down from my room. There was Mom, saying good night to a new man in front of the house — someone she hadn't endorsed too highly when she was getting dressed for her date a few hours before. Yet she'd pressed on as she had for eight years of dating now, just in case this was the one who might make her happy.

He leaned in for a kiss, and she complied. But when she turned toward the house, I saw the look on her face. It was the same one I'd seen after so many of her dates, or whenever she pulled into the driveway from work, or even just last week, when she came across a half-finished paint-by-number landscape and threw it into the garbage. Failure, it read to me, and terror.

I feel sorry for her, but I can't let her know. That would be like feeling sorry for Patty Hearst, which you're not supposed to do. "She made her own bed," my German teacher said and shrugged the day they caught Patty.

We're scraping the bottom of our sundaes when finally our song *comes on the jukebox. "A long, long time ago, I can still remember how that music used to make me smile."*

We all know the words, but we're too old to sing in a restaurant, so we make faces at one another while Dad goes to pay the check.

Happiness, I have grasped, is a destination, like Strawberry Fields. Once you find the way in, there you are, and you'll never feel low again.

I study the ways people try to get in. Flashy cars. Important jobs. Huge houses. Athletic trophies. Religion. Drugs. Beer.

Or the big one: romantic, head-over-heels love.

Many people believe in this. Just check out the Top Ten, or Love, American Style. *Just look at how people make eyes at each other at school.*

I believe it, too. Last year, I fell in love with a blond boy in my English class. We spent every afternoon together, and stayed out late together every night. When I woke up in the morning, I saw his face in my mind before I opened my eyes. When I talked to friends, all my stories were about him.

Yet I was always afraid that he would suddenly stop caring. This happens in the Top Ten. And it happens on back roads in Pennsylvania, where you stand at the door and stare at a truck hauling away your husband's clothing and a cot and a rug and there are your kids waving goodbye, and you go sit in your room for days. I lived for those moments when the blond boy called and visited as he'd promised, and I would know that it hadn't happened to me.

Then he did break up with me, as unexpectedly as I'd feared. He had his bellhop job to tend to, and his buddies to party with. Suddenly, when I glanced at the mirror, I saw a face that looked like Mom, wearing the same despair she wore all the time. Now, at New Year's six months later, I don't peek at mirrors anymore, and I don't look at her either. I don't want her to see that I haven't yet found the way. I don't want her to see herself in me.

"I met a new man last night," Mom tells me the day after New Year's. Beth is playing Chutes and Ladders with her at the kitchen table. Ringo is curled up on the next chair over.

I wonder why she's mentioning it. She never has before. I pour myself some orange juice.

Mom continues. "He doesn't seem to be much of a catch. He says he drinks two hundred dollars' worth of bourbon a week and smokes five packs of cigarettes a day."

I turn around but keep a glaze over my eyes.

"And," she goes on, flicking the Chutes and Ladders spinner, "he says he's an ex-con."

"Are you serious?" I muster.

"He's asked me out again." She sighs, moving down a chute on the board. "I don't think I'll go."

Three days later, I hang out at David's house after school. We stand on his bed with a lamp and a broom for microphones, and belt out songs from Ziggy Stardust and the Spiders from Mars. *Pooped and laughing, I go home long after dinner and walk into a wall of cigarette smoke.*

I follow its source to the kitchen. A scowly guy sits at the table between Mom and Beth, holding a filterless Camel. He looks like a scuzzy version of Moe from The Three Stooges. *There's a glass of amber liquid at his elbow.*

Mom says, "This is the man I was telling you about. He's living here now."

My chest feels like something just hit it. She has never moved someone in before. And she has a glass in her hand, too, even though she hates to drink. We all hate to drink, and we all hate cigarettes. Beth is holding a jack-in-the-box, her face down and hidden by her hair.

"Uh, I already had dinner at David's," I say, backing off. But that isn't true. I just want to get out of this kitchen.

"Can't you say hello?" she says.

"Hell. Low."

Then I charge up to my attic room, where I turn on my typewriter and drop the needle on Close to the Edge *and furiously pound out a letter to a friend.*

So I don't see Beth's confused face as she peers into the smoke at Mom and this man, trying to put all this together. I don't see the jack-in-the-box getting ready to erupt, in the room right underneath my feet.

June

The Earth Mother

11:45 A.M. "So is this your sister?" asks Estella. Her voice, issuing forth from within a tumble of thick, ginger-ale blond hair, is low and reedy, reminding me of the woody tone of a medieval recorder.

Panting, Beth and I throw ourselves into our customary seats. We've just descended from one bus as it angled around a corner, and then, spotting Estella drawing near, charged down the street to catch hers, Beth's sandals flapping, my gauzy print skirt snapping in the breeze.

I place my hand on my chest to still myself. Five miles a day on my treadmill at home, and here I am, winded. Estella swivels back to smile a benevolent greeting at me from behind her wire glasses. As I pat a sudden sweat off my forehead with the back of my hand, I take in her snow white complexion, unwrinkled despite her forty-odd years, her generous hourglass figure, halfway between maidenly and matronly, and her eyes — kindly, yet world-weary. I find her instantly likable.

"I've forgotten what Beth told me," Estella says. "Where're you from?"

"Philadelphia," I say, but there is something about Estella that makes me feel as if I've spotted the lights of an inn during a storm. So I add, "Actually, I'm from the state of confusion."

"No you're *not*," Beth says.

"Something getting to you?" Estella says at the next stop.

Before I decide how to answer, a gaunt woman with mousy, disheveled hair shuffles to the exit. Estella nods to her, "Tell your husband hello, Josie."

"Oh, Estella," Josie says, "he's feeling even worse than the last time I saw you."

"I thought the fever was gone."

Josie, having descended the steps, speaks from the curb. "The doctor prescribed some pills, and he took them and now he's in the hospital. Can you believe it? A prescription pill?"

"That driver Keith who was mean to me is talking to me *nice* now," Beth says, as she has said to every driver we've seen today.

"That's good, Beth," Estella says, still fixing on the woman.

"There you are —" says the woman.

"But I don't *trust* him —" Beth interrupts again.

". . . doing what the doctor says you're supposed to do —"

". . . and some drivers say to give him a *chance* and others say to watch *out* —"

". . . and you get hit with something ridiculous like a prescription pill —"

". . . and I don't know why he's so hot and cold, he's *wee-ard,* I don't know what to do —"

Put a lid on it, Beth, the dark voice inside me wants to say — the same voice that's been piping up since this year began, and especially in my past few trips to see her. *You've said precisely the same thing to every driver today, regardless of how the last one responded. Can't you get back to a sweeter mood? Would it be such a hardship to listen to someone else for a minute?*

Estella, hands on the steering wheel, focuses on Josie. "How is he now? Any better?"

"Well, you know what's happened because he's in the hospital?" Josie recites a chain of woes as Beth sits at her seat's edge, waiting eagle-eyed for Estella to turn back.

At length Josie's litany is exhausted. "It's some rough stuff, sweetheart," Estella says in a patient, compassionate tone, and adds, in a phrase that I later learn is derived from the Pennsylvania Dutch dialect, "Please tell him I asked about."

She draws the door closed, and, as Beth holds her tongue for just one more moment, Estella sighs and says to us, "Sometimes I want to move on from this job. There's a lot of stress. But I guess I'm where I'm supposed to be, at least for now. The people who go through big things, they're the ones that can help other people, and I think that's why I'm now here."

No sooner has she re-entered traffic than Beth leaps right back in with her broodings about Keith. "I think I should tell him *off,* I should tell him not to *mess* with me, I should tell him he's being *fake* and I don't trust him, Jill thinks so too, and Sal, and Perry, not Jacob, he don't ever say do that, but what do you think? Iz a free country, I should tell him like it is, right?"

Estella says, "Maybe he misjudged you, and you could give him another chance."

Beth pauses. I can't discern if this message is getting through, but I can tell she's pleased that Estella is now spending time on her troubles, and perhaps that's all Beth actually desires, as it seems to soothe her quickly. Estella must be familiar with the calming effect her concern seems to have, because after she quietly consoles Beth, I see that she seems to offer everyone such a haven, listening with gentle nods and encouragement to her next half-dozen passengers. At a lull, when I remark on her nurturing ways, she says, "They're my customers, and that means something to me. I try to make them feel at home before they get home." A block later a stoop-shouldered man with fleecy gray hair climbs aboard, delivering a linen-covered dish on his upturned palm. Butler-style, he whisks away the napkin to reveal a platter of his wife's special roast chicken: "And this batch is as good as I've been telling you." Laughing, Estella thanks him for letting her sample the famed dish. As he then sets it in a bag for her, he says, "A gift to the great sounding board. God knows, some days I need you."

On the last night of one of our visits in May, the pleasure I'd been deriving from our bus odyssey took a hit when I asked Beth for the first time if we could set out later the next morning. I needed to transport my sofa cushions and bedding home temporarily for a class I was conducting in my living room — a procedure that required some packing, several trips downstairs to my car, and the use of Beth's magnetic pass to fend off the glowering, self-appointed guards who would otherwise bar my way. I needed Beth's cooperation. "Could we try seven o'clock, instead of five-thirty?"

"I leave *early.*"

"Then can you leave when you want but come back and help me at seven? Just this once?"

"I *leave early.* There's nothing to do in *here.*"

"Okay. Can you lend me your front door pass, and I'll meet you later at the bus terminal?"

She looked away. "I don't *kno-oh.*"

In the dark that night, drifting between wakefulness and sleep, not to mention between sisterly affection and sisterly annoyance, I heard Beth rise and run a bath. My watch read four-thirty. Wondering drowsily about her decision for the upcoming day, I fell into a sound sleep — and then suddenly I jolted awake. She was perched on her love seat, staring at me.

"Beth, what are you doing!"

"I don't want to be *here.* I want to go." It was now five A.M.

"Then go," I mumbled in a stupor. "Just come back for me."

"May*be*," she said, jumping up and flying out her front door.

At six-fifteen she did return, grumbling, with Jesse pressed into service. In silence, we packed my car, and when she resumed her rounds — at seven — I joined her, as we'd previously agreed I would. But on every bus, she tilted away from me, not addressing a word in my direction. Then, just before the appointed hour for my departure, she bolted off two stops earlier than we'd arranged, vanishing before I could even call out goodbye. My throat tightened, and I blinked back the impulse to cry.

Did being a good sister mean having no needs of my own?

As we rumble along in Estella's bus, the midday sun casts its abundant light up the aisles of the streets. On either side, flowers seem to burst open; trees attend our march from stop to stop, resplendently green. In front of Victorian houses topped with witch's-hat roofs, young men in tank tops tinker beneath the hoods of Fords. Mothers lift infants from strollers. Children in shorts race about the fairy-tale castle in the park, calling out from its weathered blue turrets.

Some blocks later we find ourselves caught in a rare instance of gridlock. Everyone stays seated, except for a young, trimly dressed woman who has just angrily described being harassed by her boss on her early-morning shift, and wondered aloud how she can quit with two children to support. After she gets off, Estella, watching the woman let herself into her house down the street, says, "I hear hard things like that all the time. It's almost a given in this job. When people get a pink slip, or their wives throw them out, or the cops call to say that their son's in jail, I'm often the first person they see."

I'd long since grasped that the qualifications for a bus driver can and often must extend well beyond operational skills. But I had not realized that drivers might also be called upon to assume the role, at a moment's notice, of emergency caregiver — or bereavement counselor, confidante, inspirational speaker, and all-around healer of life's slings and arrows. The responsibility is so comprehensive; how, I ask Estella, does a person who has applied her efforts to obtaining a commercial driver's license possibly, when faced with everything from mild dissatisfaction to crisis-level suffering, know what to do?

"All my life," Estella says with a sigh, "I'd wanted things to be better for myself. When I was a kid, I had a stepfather who drank a lot. I got married at sixteen to escape that, but my husband wouldn't let me work. When my marriage fell apart, I just became involved with one man after another who was nothing but trouble. I had several kids by then, and I just thought I must deserve men like that because I wasn't a better person. But at least then I was working. I started as a call-taker for a tow truck company, and one particularly tough winter when they needed more drivers I asked to take the wheel. A few years later I started driving truck cross-country, the first woman in these parts to do that. I'd meet new people on the road and have adventures with sandstorms and twisters and you name it, all the way to the Texas Panhandle, but even that didn't show me that I could have a better life. I was with a very abusive man by then, and when you park your truck, no matter how far away you've traveled in this world, you still have to go home.

"Well, right after my last child, my fourth, I got very depressed, and went for help. I thought therapy might cure me, but it's not the waving of the magic wand — it really comes down to you. So there I was, and it was a true life-to-God moment, there was no one for me to look to for answers but myself and God. And I realized that I'd been with those men because I'd *chosen* them, and that I had to start making better choices. So I got the guy I was with out of my life, which wasn't easy, believe me. And I started working really hard on myself, with counseling, reading, digging into my past. Then I began to explore my spiritual side, and it all came together. I realized I would never be perfect, but that I was still a good person. My sense of self-worth began to come back. It's been so much better ever since.

"This is how I know to tell passengers what to do. I say that no matter what, there's nothing so terrible or that's gone on so long that you can't change it and look forward to a new tomorrow. I lost myself, but in the end that helped me find myself. You've just got to have faith and work at it."

"With anything?" I ask.

"Anything," she says, as a gap finally opens in the intersection. "As long as you accept the hardest thing of all: that you might have to lose to win."

I wish I could accept this myself. After that last visit, I so wanted to talk with someone about the dark voice, someone who would listen without judgment and suggest what I might do when I hear it. For days I could not dislodge the image of Sam from my mind, with his high forehead and goofy pirate accents, his ease with Chinese culinary skills and my self-doubts, his loving green eyes. Maybe I could tell him, I thought, remembering my exchange with Jesse at our lunch. Maybe his eyes would still be loving. I had not seen him for so long now, and, though mutual acquaintances told me he was not involved with anyone else and still kept a photo of me on his mantel, I trembled as I finally dialed his number in the city where he'd relocated for a new job. He had hung plants on his front porch, I'd heard, and was taking lessons in classical guitar; he had indeed moved on with his life. On the third ring, he picked up. "Hello . . . Hello?" I tried to speak back, but the words died in my throat. In silence, I hung up the phone.

We circle through the city, encountering rider after rider who offer Estella a hearty hello, rocking in our seats like children in a cradle. I close my eyes, letting snatches of conversation wash over me, wash my frustrations with Beth out of me, fill the desolation I've become oppressively aware of in my apartment, especially over the last weeks. It works, for a little while.

Then a woman with bobbed pumpkin-colored hair and a vinyl tote emblazoned with the words "Lucky Bingo Bag" asks as she climbs aboard, "My ex isn't here, is he?" Thirty years after their divorce, Beth fills me in, the woman's ex still sidles up to her on the bus to annoy her.

Beth says, "Don't worry, he already *rode* today."

"I tell you," Estella adds, "I could fix him up with someone and get him off your hands."

"I couldn't do that," the redhead says. "Pass him on to another poor sucker? Never."

A full-figured woman across from us makes a cynical quip about men, followed by Estella's gently humorous reassurance, "Come on, girls, you know they're not all that bad." But already her commentary is sparking others. I glance around, and realize with surprise that all the passengers happen to be female. Soon our chat in the front of the bus has rippled out to every unrequited teenager, too-young-to-vote mother, starry-eyed fiancée, common-law wife, football widow, three-time divorcée, golden-anniversary grandmother, and avowed single woman until the whole bus is talking together about men: the good, the bad, and their own choices.

I listen in wonder, and I think, watching these women confide and cluck and slap one another's arms with laughter, Beth contributing in her own way, Estella mothering them all, that maybe this is what it used to be like once upon a time. Maybe, when women gathered for quilting bees, or when men played checkers outside the general store, or when everyone came together at village dances and July Fourth picnics, this ease helped people feel less alone in their worries. Maybe, too, this was the swiftness with which neighbors became friends, and the simplicity with which one person's tale became another person's teacher.

I don't want to climb down to the ground and return to the emptiness that reclaims me at home. I want to stay up here, in this comforting place, harvesting the springtime light.

"There's Bailey," says Beth, poking my arm. "Lez *go!*"

She has already jumped to the top of the steps. I rise, and as I'm searching my fanny pack for my sunglasses, Estella draws Beth into a hug. Then, releasing my sister, she reaches out and hugs me.

I'm warm and sleepy and lightheaded all at once and I clomp down the steps to our next destination. Turning back to wave good-bye, dizzy from the scent of floral perfume in Estella's lush blond hair, I remember the call I couldn't complete, and think how nice it would be to have Estella's bus in my life, too.

Disabilities

"Where are we?" I ask.

"We're at Tenff and Main," Beth says definitively.

"We can't be. We're walking down a street, *between* two corners."

"Tenff and Main."

"But look: this is a street. The corner's up there. Maybe you mean *that's* Tenth and Main. If so, then we must now be on Tenth Street. Is that right?"

"What *diffrence* does it make? I get where I need to go."

"Because there's a difference between a street and a corner. You're smart. You can see that."

"Yeah."

"And we can't be at Tenth and Main until we reach the corner. Do you understand that?"

"I *guess.*"

"So what street are we on?"

Silence.

"Do you know what street we're on?"

"I don't *know.*"

"Yes you do. What *street* are we on?"

"Broad?"

For six months I have, for the most part, consigned my older, more disgruntled feelings about Beth to some remote corner of my heart. But now they are squirming out, as Beth's mood seems to shift toward being more self-absorbed and contrarian — or perhaps as we become so well reacquainted that she reveals these hidden sides and I, in turn, rediscover my impatience. I want to blurt at her, "Stop being so dense!" I want to shake her and cry out, "Don't close your mind so fast to every new concept just because it's new, or because someone thinks you might benefit from it. *Try* to get it!" I want to chase away what I increasingly suspect is Beth's habitual defiance or laziness.

I struggle to speak with kindness, but it's getting increasingly difficult. Why can she not learn the simplest things? Is it that she can't, or that she *won't*? Does the problem lie entirely in her disability?

And — while I'm railing on — why doesn't she notice that anyone else has needs? Lately, she's entered a phase where she won't listen to other bus riders, not even her most adored drivers, when they talk about anything not bus-related. Me, too: I always arrive in town with my own food, knowing it has never occurred to her this entire time to stock even a single slice of bread for my visits. I ask for nothing except to be part of her life, accept her *bawd* expression if I dare mention anything about myself, and affirm and admire and truly *like* her. Yet she still resents giving me any help at all, even in carrying my bedding to the car.

I don't get it. Especially because Beth is smart and acutely aware. She can also be outgoing and generous; she's started joining the retirees in her high-rise for Tuesday-night Bingo, and she routinely purchases and hand-delivers postage stamps to drivers with utility bills to pay. But every time she complains about the nasty drivers, sometimes even attempting to incite impartial drivers to war against their crustier colleagues, every time she pays no heed to a drowsy shift worker who has asked her to lower her voice, and every time she brags about how she barged into the drivers' room even though one of her enemies was there on his break, a feral feeling rears up within me, and it's all I can do to hold back my words.

How much is Beth, and how much is Beth's brain?

What *is* mental retardation, anyway?

I call Olivia at her office. We have been doing this every month; she brings me up to date on Beth's medical developments, I acquaint her with events on the buses. Sometimes, we allow ourselves to slide off course. We talk about long-beached romances; we offer wisdom from books. She refers to the Bible and Edgar Cayce, I talk about Toni Morrison and Benjamin Franklin.

This day, two beats before our goodbye, I try to sound casual:

"Oh, by the way, what, uh, did you think mental retardation was before, you know, you studied it for your career?"

She says, "People who couldn't do what I could do, because they were born that way."

"When did you understand . . . what did you learn when you entered the field?"

"Well, one of my big moments came during my training, when I saw this movie about babies with a type of MR. Their brain wants to process information about learning to crawl, but it doesn't coincide with how their body responds. Eventually it happens, but it takes longer than with other babies. That was when I saw that what I'd need to deal with these people is patience, patience, and *more* patience."

Good, I think. Perhaps she'll understand the return of my negative feelings and help me reach a calmer place. "Is that . . . what you find most . . . *difficult* about working with Beth?"

She thinks for a minute. "The worst part of it is the way the people *around* Beth deal with her: talking about her like she's not there, looking down their noses at her. I deal with this every day in my job, and not when I'm hearing about strangers, but sometimes families, too. One person I know was visiting her family, and became talkative during dinner. When the family got fed up, instead of saying, 'Can you give someone else a chance to speak?' someone actually said, 'Maybe we should stick a pacifier in your mouth,' and everyone laughed. It's so demeaning! People treat their pets with more respect.

"I don't have any trouble with Beth," she concludes. "I think she's a joy to work with."

"Me, too," I say, half-truthfully, and change my mind about asking my question. I hang up in a swirl of relief and shame. I have lived with mental retardation for thirty-nine years, and I have never asked anyone what it really is. In the interest of raising four equal children, our parents almost never uttered the words except in private and never added books about mental retardation to our shelves. In fact, I'd read about this disability only in works of fiction — *Flowers for Algernon, Of Mice and Men,* and *The Good Earth* when I was younger; when I was older, *The Sound and the Fury* and the Flannery O'Connor short story "The Life You Save May Be Your Own." And none of them answered the questions that I hadn't thought to ask. But why should it have occurred to me to do so? Mental retardation had just always been my sister, and my sister had always been it.

I am glad Olivia had to get off; I am not prepared for her to see my ignorance.

Then, on my next visit, which falls right after Beth's birthday, when we are now officially "twins," I drag through a day that sits especially heavy in my heart. On seventeen buses, over twelve hours, Beth's talk brims with spite about the brutes she encounters in the drivers' room. Her babble is unceasing, booming, and unvarying from bus to bus. People glare. An elderly man with a cane, who evidently assumes I sat beside Beth without knowing what I was getting into, leans close to me and says, "She sure does run her mouth, that one." While we're waiting at the terminal for a bus, I'm accosted on the sidewalk by a mother and her teenage daughter. The mother, who grasps immediately that I'm Beth's sister, ignores Beth while shouting at me that I need to control her: she picks fights with them on the bus, I'm told, as she's jealous when they speak with the drivers, and plays her radio because she knows it irritates them. Beth shrugs. Late in our day, when I suggest that she at least speak more softly on the bus, she says to driver after driver, "Rachel thinks I'm talking too loud. The last driver didn't think I was talking too loud, he sez I should do what I want, and thaz right, I don't talk too loud, do you think I talk too loud, do you, do you?" I tell myself to let it roll off me, that it's none of my business if she's as loud as a foghorn. I don't want to intrude like her nosy coriders. Live and let live. Right?

Then that evening, as we rest on her love seat watching *Diff'rent Strokes,* my head splitting despite my relief that I finally got to the end of this day, she gives me her slyest smile and says, "I'm gonna tell that fat girl off tomorrow. I'm gonna tell her like it *is.*"

I look at her. "Who are you talking about?"

"Just *somebody.* She wants everyone to treat her special, she wants the bus to leave her at her *house* instead of the *stop,* and the drivers are sick of it, and now she wants my *seat,* and I told her she couldn't have it, and she *yelled* at me. So I'm gonna tell her off. Now you *know."*

"What do you mean, tell her off?"

She laughs. "I'm gonna tell her that she stinks!"

In a different mood I might laugh, too, then calmly discuss civility. But I'm already too worn out and perturbed to control myself, and my feelings suddenly break loose. "Beth, why don't you try being nicer to people?!"

"I'm nice to people who are nice to *me."*

"Telling people they stink isn't being nice."

"It don't matter."

"It *does* matter. You don't need to be nasty to anyone."

"I don't *care."*

I take a few deep breaths; I know it's just a petty conflict. But it's at least the tenth one today, and dammit, I'm not just another busybody passenger, I'm her sister, and the bus isn't a military theater, it's just a city bus and she's just another rider, and — and — and I just can't stand it anymore! "Why can't you ever notice when you upset people!" My voice is rising; I can hear my angry, righteous tone. I look away, pretending I don't want an answer, telling myself that everyone has feelings like Beth's sometimes. *But,* the dark voice retorts, *most of us manage to keep them to ourselves.* I peer back at Beth and force my words into an approximation of composure. "Beth. Really. You could just keep your mouth shut."

"She'll get over it."

"But think about what Jacob says: do unto others. You could just share your seat."

"Iz not her seat."

"It's not *yours,* either."

"And she *does* stink. And I can say what I want. Iz a free country. Louie the driver sez so, and that new driver, Rita —"

"Sure, you can say what you want. But you don't have to say things that hurt."

"I don't have to be polite to *her*."

"Look, I don't have to be nice to everybody, but I try, even when people act badly, because there's no need to make bad situations worse. And if I hurt people's feelings by accident, I apologize."

"I'm not gonna apologize."

"That's what we do when we hurt people."

"Thaz what *you* do."

"But other people have feelings, right?"

"I don't *know*."

"What do you mean, you don't *know*!" I explode. "Other people matter! We can at least try to get along with each other!"

I flee into her bedroom.

Out in the living room, she turns her television up higher. I stay where I am, steaming at her window, clenching my fists. I will not go back out. I cannot. I breathe hard at my reflection, and past it, to the valley of row houses, their chimneys spiking up like fangs. I glance at her desktop and its feast of stickers waiting to decorate envelopes — teddy bears in tutus and smiling hearts and Beauty and the Beast — and I hate them all. I hate her Donald Duck sheets. I hate the Care Bear Christmas ornaments in the bathroom. This year is spreading out endlessly. Why bother? Why not just give up? I should just throw myself in my car and go home.

But she's my sister, I remind myself, closing my eyes, and under all this anger, I do love her. And I promised her a year. Stupid! A stupid promise! I am not up to this task at all.

I gaze out to the horizon, thinking, once again, How much is Beth, and how much is Beth's brain? Maybe it's time that I tried to find out.

Late one afternoon at home, seven hours before I will be leaving our annual twinness behind to turn forty, I shut off my fax machine, turn off the phone volume, close the computer file of my latest writing project, boil water for peppermint tea, and go online. Of course, I encounter many sites related to mental retardation. I wend my way through them, so caught up that I miss the sun's departure and the day passing into night. In the dark hours, I learn at last about my sister.

First I come upon The Arc of the United States at thearc.org, one of the leading advocacy organizations for people with mental retardation. I discover that 2.5 to 3 percent of the American population has mental retardation, which, based on the 1990 Census, means between 6.2 and 7.5 million people. That's a lot of Beths out there — twenty-five times as many people as those who are blind. One out of ten American families has intimate experience with mental retardation. That's a lot of me's.

I learn that my old nemesis, the term "mental age," does have some merit. "The term mental age," The Arc's site says, "is used in intelligence testing. It means that the individual received the same number of correct responses on a standardized IQ test as the average person of that age in the sample population. Saying that an older person with mental retardation is like a person of a younger age or has the 'mind' or 'understanding' of a younger person is incorrect usage of the term. The mental age only refers to the intelligence test score. It does not describe the level and nature of the person's experience and functioning in aspects of community life."

In other words, "mental age" does not mean, as some erroneously believe, that the clock stopped ticking in some people's minds when the hands reached two or seven or fifteen. Mental retardation is not a childhood that has simply gotten stuck.

I observe that I too must alter my vocabulary. No longer is it proper to say, as I have all my life, that someone "is mentally retarded." As I discover on other websites, by using the new "People First Language," one focuses on the person first, the disability last, as in "a woman who has mental retardation," or "a man with mental retardation." The analogy is that people with cancer *have* cancer, they are not cancer itself; the disability is only one aspect of who they are. In addition, with People First Language, one can avoid using the word "retarded," which is too close to the familiar slur. In fact, some websites minimize the use of "mental retardation" by using as synonyms terms such as "developmental disability," "intellectual disability," and "cognitive disability." As I scribble down this People First Language, I realize that many of my acquaintances might disparage such linguistic changes as mere nods to political correctness, and for a moment I do, too. But then I think, Look at how many cultural barriers Beth has had to deal with throughout her life — and how many physical barriers people with other disabilities experience: sidewalks without curb cuts, restrooms lacking accessible facilities, cabs that refuse guide dogs. Altering the way I speak is *nothing* compared to what she, and they, go through *almost all day, almost every day.* And it is such a simple way to help transform the cultural landscape that it seems arrogant and misguided to resist doing so.

Back at The Arc of the United States, I learn about the causes of mental retardation, a broad category that includes anything that impairs the development of the brain in utero, during birth, or in childhood. Among the causes that have been identified are fetal alcohol syndrome, childhood diseases, and genetic conditions such as Down syndrome. But, surprisingly, in one-third of all cases the cause of mental retardation remains a mystery, as it does for Beth. That figure swells to three-quarters when you're focusing on individuals with retardation that is considered mild.

Ah! Here it is: *mild.* I dig in deeper and turn up delineations so fundamental that I am embarrassed to be just discovering them. I learn that mental retardation is classified in four levels: mild, moderate, severe, and profound. Mild, which accounts for about 87 percent of all people with mental retardation, my sister among them, refers to an IQ of about 50 to 75. To supplement my understanding, I go to a psychology database. Among the books I am referred to is *Abnormal Psychology and Modern Life,* by Robert C. Carson, James N. Butcher, and James C. Coleman. The title is familiar; I turn to my dust-lined bookshelves and there it is, one of the textbooks I picked up at the end of a recent school year, on the "Take Me" shelf in the building where I work.

Here, I learn that people with mild mental retardation are considered educable, as Beth was, after my mother pressed the issue, and that "their intellectual levels as adults are comparable with those of average 8- to 11-year-old children." Wait a minute! I thought that whole mental age stuff was nonsense — but I read on. "Statements such as the latter, however, should not be taken too literally. The mildly retarded individual with a 'mental age' of, say, 10 . . . is not in fact comparable to the normal 10-year-old in information-processing ability. . . . The social adjustment of such persons often approximates that of the adolescent, although they tend to lack the normal adolescent's imagination, inventiveness, and judgment. . . . Often they require some measure of supervision because of their limited ability to foresee the consequences of their actions" (Carson, Butcher, and Coleman, Scott Foresman, 1988, p. 475).

I find this explanation wonderfully clear. Would that I'd had this textbook when I was in college. No — when I was in first grade. I'd like to memorize those lines so I could repeat them in any conversation I have about my sister.

As for the other levels, this book continues, people with moderate mental retardation, which refers to IQs between 36 and 51, were those I saw in the Trainable classes at school, and would have been Beth's classmates had the school system placed her where her IQ tests initially (and apparently shortsightedly) suggested she should go. Many cannot read or write, have very limited conceptualizing skills, and have poor motor coordination, which is evident in their clumsy movements; they can become partially independent in a sheltered environment. People with severe mental retardation, with an IQ between 20 and 35, have major problems with motor and speech development; and, although they can develop some hygiene and self-help skills, they will always be dependent on others for care. Lastly are people with profound mental retardation, which means an IQ under 20. Given their extreme deficiencies in adaptive behavior, their inability to master anything beyond the simplest tasks, their very basic verbal communication (if there is any speech at all), and their often severe physical disabilities, they need custodial care for life.

A charge races under my skin. I am a detective on a trail. I am amassing a profile of what might as well be a missing person.

Almost on a high as I pore over this book, and circle round and round the Internet, I lose myself for hours until — *how had I failed to see that?* — I spy the definition of mental retardation. It's right there, on The Arc's website. Not only that, but it is at the top of the very first page I discovered this evening; it was staring me in the face from the start.

There are three criteria:

1. IQ is below 70–75.

2. Significant limitations exist in "two or more adaptive skill areas," which means "those daily living skills needed to live, work and play in the community. They include communication, self-care, home living, social skills, leisure, health and safety, self-direction, functional academics (reading, writing, basic math), community use and work."

3. The condition manifests itself before age eighteen.

I find myself holding my breath in amazement, staring at 2: "adaptive skill areas." Shaking my head, I gaze at the list, as certain characteristics trigger specific associations for me:

Communication: The many times when "I don't know" indicates that Beth truly has no idea what she thinks; Beth muttering to herself during conversations.

Self-care: Her insistence on tempting pneumonia with shorts and sandals in cold conditions; her unbalanced diet, despite everyone's efforts to educate her about healthful eating and the harm that can come from ignoring it.

Social skills: The way she resorts to nasty verbal attacks rather than diplomacy with the fat girl on the bus; her inability to read Henry's nonverbal and even verbal cues.

Health and safety: Her reluctance to allow medical examinations; her denial of any possible medical consequences with "Thaz not gonna *happen*."

Of course, anybody could have one of these behavioral traits, but there have to be *two or more* of these adaptive deficiencies, *and* there has to have been a pattern of these from childhood on, *and* — though it can't be known definitively without a test — there has to be the lower IQ. Beth meets all three criteria.

I get it. This new information means that when I tutor Beth about street corners, or nudge her toward more appropriate attire for the weather, I should not expect instant assent or feel irate when

I don't receive it. Indeed, anger is a foolish and pointless response when I should actually *expect* limitations. Especially when I factor in her stubborn personality. And even more especially when I consider that she's in a society that careens between bullying her and seeing her as a perpetual child.

I look up. I am in my dark apartment, and it is midnight, and I think, how could I have known Beth for all these years, and just come to this realization now?

I stare into the unlit room. I still have not untangled how much is Beth and how much is Beth's brain, nor whether, when she does not welcome new conversations, fashions, manners, boundaries, or concepts of space, it is because she cannot, or will not, or is simply not in a mood to open her mind at a given moment. I also have not ascertained how much, if any, of her self-centeredness is a result of her mental retardation. And, given the inextricable weave of nature and nurture, of self and society, that exists in all of us, it seems unlikely that I ever will.

But now I do know that, like me, and the drivers, Beth is on a journey. It's just that Beth's bus chugs along a lot more slowly.

I am shaky with insight. I want to tell someone; I need to. The first minutes of my fortieth birthday have already ticked by when I call Olivia's voicemail and leave her a message. I confess my ignorance. I spill out my relief. I tell her I have chased my loathsome feelings back into their pit.

When I hang up, I expect to relish this triumph. Oddly, though, as I rise to microwave my late dinner, I feel only queasy. Yes, there was a missing person here; we were twins thirty-nine times before I even started to find out about Beth. I turn off my computer, and watch the screen go dark.

Goodbye

It is a sleeting February afternoon, exactly one month since Mom met the ex-con, and Max and I are hauling my trunk down the stairs from my attic room. He is bracing the bottom, I am clutching the top, and both of us are in shock.

I am leaving, I keep thinking. I am going away from all that I know.

When I glance down the dark stairs beyond Max to the first floor, I see fifteen-year-old Beth, standing with Ringo, looking up at us, her mouth agape.

We are leaving because Mom has made it clear that we must. She wants to be with this man, and he doesn't want us around. Four days ago she told Laura to leave, and Max and I know we're no longer welcome, either.

We are too numb to speak. The sleet outside seems to have moved into my heart.

Dad is waiting in his car in the driveway to take Max to live in his apartment a few hours away in Pennsylvania. Not the mountainous place where we lived long ago, but somewhere new, near factories. Laura will join them there after she finishes her semester at a local college. He will help her rent a room around here until then.

As for me, yesterday he drove to the boarding school that my friend Keiko entered last year and begged them for a scholarship. He was very persuasive, and they agreed. I am to move there this very night. My entire life is changing in one day.

No one made plans for Beth. It seems a given that Mom will continue to care for her.

Beth watches as Max and I lug the trunk across the living room toward the front door. Laura is gone, having driven off with her car packed to bursting.

We don't see Mom. After we put this plan to her an hour ago — a plan Dad and Laura and I came up with in the last four days, a plan

Max didn't know about until we told him this morning, and Beth didn't know about until fifteen minutes ago — Mom retreated into her bedroom with this new man.

"Beth, could you hold the front door open?" Max asks.

She shuffles forward in a daze. Her brother and sisters are leaving. She does not grasp why, and neither, really, do we. It is all happening too fast.

Sleet gusts in as she opens the storm door. Max and I cart the trunk past her, and I peer over at her face. She looks perplexed and alarmed, as if she's just dropped her biggest jigsaw puzzle.

Outside, Dad heaves my trunk onto his car roof and straps it down. "That's it," he says.

We sprint back to the house. Beth remains in the front doorway, Ringo at her side. Everyone says goodbye. I reach forward and do something I am not accustomed to: I hug her.

"See you soon," I whisper, keeping cheer in my voice. Though how soon it might be, I can't say. I haven't yet learned to drive.

She does not answer as we release each other. She cannot find any words.

We race back to the car. It is packed so full of our stuff that things start to fall out when I open the front passenger door: my turntable, my typewriter, my stuffed rabbit. I tuck them back and then get in.

Dad throws it into reverse, and I press my face to the window. Beth is standing behind the storm door, looking out, holding Ringo in her arms. I lift my hand and wave. Slowly, she raises one of Ringo's tan paws to wave back.

Then I turn away. I cannot look at her, alone in the doorway. We drive off into the February gale.

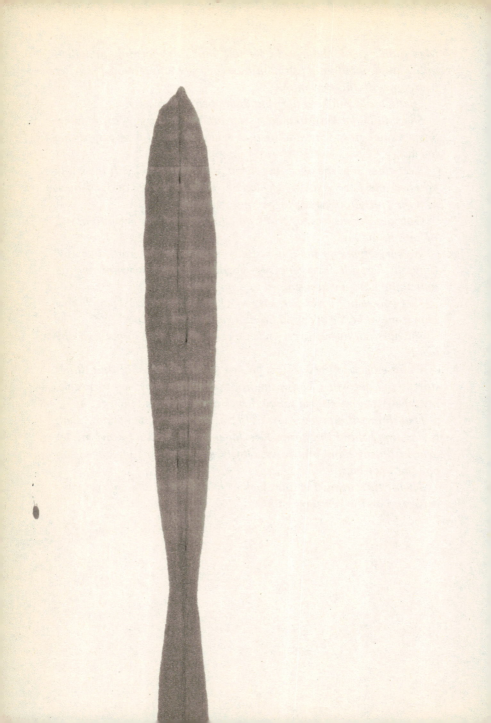

July

The Optimist

1:15 P.M. Bailey docks the bus outside Kmart and allows himself a restrained yawn.

"Number thir*teen*," Beth says in a teasing tone.

"No, it was not," he kids right back. "It was only eleven."

She shakes her head. "Thirteen."

Bailey waves his hands. "What do I know? I'm just the driver." He's an apple-cheeked, melon-bellied man of medium stature, whose bushy salt-and-pepper beard strongly hints that he's recently sighted forty in his headlights. His eyes, too, disclose personal information; although they spark with humor from time to time, there are pouches beneath his lids, evidence that he craves sleep. He reaches for his jumbo-sized cup of coffee, tips the rim toward his lips, and misses, splashing a brown stream down his blue driver's shirt. Dabbing at the cloth with a napkin, he steps out of his seat. "Okay," he announces, facing the aisle, "nobody sees that I spilled coffee on my shirt, right?"

Passengers look up. Some carry umbrellas, prepared for the summer thunderstorm that's been predicted.

"I don't see nothing," a man in a Hawaiian shirt humors him.

"What coffee?" a young mother in a sundress says, playing along.

"It makes a good *design*," Beth says. "Now you never need a tie."

"Why, you —" Bailey says, and she wards off any retaliation with a laugh.

She turns to me. "Thaz Crazy Bailey."

"Why'd you give him that name?" I say.

"'Cause he's *fun*. He counts my yawns. Sometimes I fake yawning to trick him."

"It's stuffy in here," a teenage girl applying lipstick says.

"We got five more minutes at this stop," Bailey says. "How about I open the sunroof?"

He positions himself beneath a hatch in the bus ceiling and pushes, grunting, until it pops up. In whirls a breeze, carrying the moist, earthy scent that portends a shower.

Bailey, Beth confirms, is indeed tired. His adolescent kids have grown fond of mischief lately — every day brings a complaint from a neighbor, a fresh variation on sulking from the accused — and last night being no exception, he found himself contending with one of his kids well past his desired bedtime. "I don't give up," he says. "I keep up the hope that it'll work out."

A few days every week, Bailey, like many of his driving cohorts, works a split shift. That means he climbs behind the wheel when the run first gets under way, often at four or five A.M., and parks back at the terminal at eight or nine A.M. Then he's off duty for a few hours, free to rest at home if he wishes. After lunch, he returns to the driver's seat, wrapping up by six or seven P.M., when most of the buses turn in for the night.

"Do you like that schedule?" I ask him. He is standing beside his seat, blotting the coffee stain, to no avail.

"Most of them do," Beth offers.

"You bet," he adds. "But one thing makes it inconvenient. It keeps me from being home in the morning when my kids wake up for school." Forgetting to contain his fatigue, or even clap a hand over our view of his dental fillings, he commences a lion-sized yawn.

"Number fourteen," Beth says.

"I've got an idea for you," Bailey said to Beth one day last winter.

"What?" A lady with a dowager's hump, who had kept to herself for miles, had, as she descended the steps to leave, suddenly leaned over the partition beside Beth's seat and screamed in her face, "Get a job!"

It is, as I know well by now, a familiar refrain. Why, some passengers think, should they labor for fifty years behind a forklift or cash register, why should they strive to get off welfare, why should they pay a cent of their hard-earned retirement savings for taxes, *if this woman can just sit on a bus all day?* It's a variation on what our family feels, though while we despair that Beth doesn't want more for herself, some riders seem to feel envy and outrage.

On that frost-speckled morning, as Bailey proceeded away from the curb, the lady still squawking up at the bus from the road, Beth drew on her usual resilience. "What's your idea?"

He said, "Maybe you can help me out."

At the end of that run, in the drivers' room, Bailey explained to Beth that he had a problem. His three teenagers, who all *could* rouse themselves, increasingly needed a nudge — or some days, he sighed, a cattle prod — to swing their feet from the bed to the floor on school days, and his wife's job now required an early shift, too. "I'm in a bind," he told Beth. "I need someone who can make sure my kids get on the school bus."

So Beth became, as he called it, his babysitter. Throughout the winter and spring, as dawn ascended over the mountain and Happy Timmy rhapsodized about the timelessness of the sunrise, Beth carried out a mission. She rode to Bailey's neighborhood, then hastened up a hill to his house. Into his unlocked back door she went, flinging off her coat, flicking on the kitchen radio, spinning from their evangelical gospel readings to her preferred Jammin' Oldies station, and settling down at the table for a few tunes. Often Bailey had set out a glass of orange juice for her, along with the Flintstones vitamins he kept hoping, in vain, that she would take. Instead, she extracted from her knapsack a baggie of M&M cookies. She stared at the clock over the sink, nibbling until the agreed-upon moment; then she bounded upstairs, planting herself at each of the three doorways in turn. Beyond them sleeping figures sprawled on beds. Using a voice louder than any bugle, she called out, "Time to wake *up!*"

Beth saw this arrangement as a worthy barter: all she had to do was stir Bailey's kids, and in return she received his guaranteed approval, as well as protection from cantankerous riders on the bus.

Bailey, though, had mounted a secret campaign. Yes, Beth alleviated his fear that his children would sleep through the homeroom bell. But he was strategizing for something beyond his own domestic concerns. He thought Beth might need some stirring, too.

As I learned at the annual Plan of Care, S.S.I., the governmental assistance program that pays Beth the money on which she lives, is for people sixty-five or older, or blind, or who have a disability, provided they have few possessions and little income, and that they cannot work.

And Beth does have difficulty holding jobs. Initially proud of herself for working and motivated to perform tasks well, she'll come to feel excluded from the social life in the staff room, or picked on for being told to wear a bra, or *bawd*. Next, she'll grow distracted by an *awesome* man in another department, or by Erika Kane's soap opera nuptials — far out of reach on her home TV — and suddenly instead of placing the required sixteen widgets in every bag, she'll put in twenty-three, or seven, and will scarcely contain her pleasure when the employer lets her go.

But her job loss does not essentially alter her income, since her S.S.I. benefits are cut back proportionally after she earns even a small amount of money. Thus, she need never experience the drudgery of a job. However, she also need never be exposed to the bonuses not listed in any employee handbook: fellowship, purpose, accomplishment, negotiation skills, or the satisfaction that can come from contributing to society.

Our conversation on this topic is an old one. Before I joined her on the buses, it typically went as follows: "You're so smart and fun and capable," I'd say. "You'd get to be with people and be really useful if you had a job, or did volunteer work, even for an hour a week."

"I don't want to volunteer. I don't want to do anything that won't make money."

"So what about a job?"

"I'd work if I had to, but I don't have to, so I won't."

When I started riding the buses, I was so enthralled by Beth's happiness and cooperative relationships with the drivers that I forgot about my wish that she would work. But in the past month, when Beth completely eschews the idea, a sourness burns in my throat. Not only does the rest of our family have a strong work ethic — ridiculously strong, in my case — but as I have come to see it, she is selling herself short.

As summer advances, my patience with this matter grows thinner, and I find myself slipping in the topic whenever I meet up with professionals in the field. A few confide that they know other individuals with developmental disabilities who've also found this loophole. Some professionals feel strongly, and one of them, a woman who once worked in a group home near Beth's, gets passionate about the subject when I call her to discuss it. "I think it's fine that Beth does her own thing," she tells me, "but it's not fine to thumb your nose at society. Beth thinks, I don't have to do anything anyone else does, but that's an immature, self-centered way of looking at the world. I'm not going to patronize her, and that's what I'd be doing if I believed she was incapable of holding a job.

"Many other people I work with — people like Beth — have jobs. They want the world to believe that people with disabilities can be productive, contributing members of society. That's why some of them are embarrassed when they see Beth spending her life on the buses. They don't think it reflects well on them."

Other professionals, though, defend the S.S.I. policy to me: "A lot of places wouldn't hire her anyway; how many businesses really want to deal with what it would take to keep her busy, even if she *did* want to be there?" They say, "No one in the field will criticize S.S.I. What if she didn't have a safety net?" They say, "If you don't like it, *you* pay for her."

As the days grow hotter and the conversations mount up, I feel guilty and pushy for wanting her to live a more responsible life and dismayed that anyone might believe that she can't develop further. But I feel enraged when I speak with people who don't know anyone like Beth and find it quite simple: "The buses are all she can handle," they'll say. "You should be pleased she can do that much." I want to shout back, "You're looking only at her disability, not her abilities!"

So, aware that Bailey's kids have finished the school year, I try introducing other options. I cheerfully offer to help Beth with applications at supermarkets. "Maybe in a year or two," she says. Okay, maybe she doesn't want to pack grocery bags; I can understand that. Thinking about the affection for animals she developed after we acquired Ringo, I volunteer us both for an hour at an animal shelter. We go into a holding pen of cages containing cats awaiting adoption, where the windows are too high to see more than a sliver of cloud. As the volunteer coordinator requested, I lift the cats out of their cages so we can cuddle them. But when I suggest to Beth that she show them attention, she gives a dutiful stroke, holds a cat I hand her as if it were a sack of potatoes, then fixes her eyes on the windows, and says, "How much longer till we go?" Fighting anger, I phone the head of the bus company and plead with him to find a way to employ her — cleaning buses, giving callers schedule information, anything, *anything*! "I can't," he says. "It's union, which means full-time. Your sister doesn't want full-time." This, Beth confirms as I seethe silently, is true.

One day, Bailey calls me, discussing the job ideas he has for her now that the school year has concluded. After all my futile conversations with others, I almost melt with gratitude.

"I'm trying to figure out her skills," he says. "She doesn't realize it, but I'm trying to see if she can memorize things. Maybe she can handle office work or a store. I'm also trying to build up her ability to take risks, so she can walk into a work environment with courage. It's a very lonely place that she's in now, a kind of rut. I want to help her develop more self-confidence. But I'm taking it one step at a time. That's why I started with her babysitting my kids."

"You are such a gift." I sigh.

"I'm just being optimistic that it'll all work out, same as I am with my kids, no matter what they throw at me. I want to see them — and her — do well."

"Oh, God, so do I," I say, swinging the phone cord.

But as I place the receiver in its cradle, the glow fades fast. Beth does not share our idea of "doing well," and last week Olivia explained to me that Beth's preferences are what matter most. There's a whole social movement, she told me, called self-determination.

The self-determination movement was triggered by news reports like Geraldo Rivera's many years ago. I had never forgotten the images from Willowbrook: naked children covered with welts, people in straitjackets, feces slathered on walls. The inhumane conditions at Willowbrook and some other institutions set off public outcries, lawsuits, and eventually the release into the community of many people who had formerly been confined. The concept of self-determination was born, though it drifted below my radar until this year.

Self-determination, I now know, is one of the most momentous civil rights developments in the history of mental retardation in America. It says that people with mental retardation should have the same choices as all citizens. If Beth wants to live on her own, go camping, register to vote, or raise a family, her provider agency will help. If Beth doesn't want to meet Olivia during the day, eat anything green, wear a bra, or get a job, the agency will not compel her to do so.

Instead, it might provide options. Let's suppose she didn't want to go to the Laundromat down the street. It might say, "Would you like to get some soap so you can wash your clothes in your bathtub?" It might also attempt creative solutions, such as, "Here's a map. Let's find other Laundromats in town." But it won't twist anyone's arm, and unless a person's health and safety, or the health and safety of others, are in jeopardy — someone refusing to take medication to control a psychosis, which then leads to violent impulses, for example — the agency won't take preventive action. In the case of neglected meds for mental illness, it would seek the support of psychiatrists and/or law enforcement agencies. But when major health issues and safety are not factors, it tries to help the individual understand the consequences of her actions, and allow her to learn, as we all do, from her mistakes. This is, in short, the main guiding principle that had so eluded me in Beth's Plan of Care meeting.

One day, Olivia tells me about a nearby conference on self-determination, and I decide to attend. On the first morning, two hundred professionals and I take our seats, and then the seminar leader, who has worked for three decades with individuals who have developmental disabilities, strides to the podium.

"In some areas," he starts, "people have been placed in group homes based on their diagnosis. But what if someone wants to live with a friend who has a different diagnosis? What if you don't want to eat exactly when you're told it's time for lunch? It's time that we listened to each individual to find out what's important to him."

I look around. The audience is beaming and, I think, it *does* sound right to me.

Then he says, "However, this can be challenging." He launches into several real-life scenarios describing individuals making choices that led to self-defeating or high-risk behaviors, or that could have been harmful to others, and asks the audience what we think should have been done in each situation. Hands go up, ideas pour out — and there is widespread disagreement. People have different values, or incompatible thresholds for intervention, or contrasting ideas on what it takes for people with MR to understand consequences.

When the audience files out for a break, I'm so confused that I'm practically tripping over chairs. "So how do you know what to *do*?" I beseech the people near me on the coffee line.

"There are no hard rules," one says. "You just do what seems best."

"We're still working out the snags," another offers.

"We just have to encourage accepted social norms," says a third.

"Society doesn't agree on its norms," a fourth says. "They have to be the individual's."

"I hate this crap," a fifth one whispers. "This is why I'm trying to leave the field."

"I love self-determination," a sixth one says. "It's time we respect everyone's individuality."

"But if you guys can't agree," I ask, "how can *I* figure out the right things to do?"

Bailey's run has funneled us into a traffic jam, and as he inches forward, talking at standstills about his children's latest scrapes, he does not become ill-tempered, as do so many automobile drivers in highway delays.

"Here we are, stuck," I say. "But you're relaxed about it."

"Thaz 'cause he knows we'll still get there," Beth says.

"Eventually," Bailey says. "Though we're falling behind schedule."

"But you'll still get us there, *some*time."

"Sure," he says. "I try not to worry about the schedule in a situation like this. I can't control it, and the more I get upset, the longer it'll seem to take."

When, I wonder, as he resumes his tales of teenage mishaps and we sit and sit, eventually not moving at all, will my sister stop being stalled in her life? Do I have the patience to work through the traffic with her? Do I even believe that we'll ever get there, *some*time?

"How do you stay so upbeat and positive about everything?" I finally blurt out.

Bailey looks surprised. "You just try to see that there's always the opportunity for things to get better. If you look on the negative side, you don't see that the opportunity even exists."

"But sometimes," I say, "there doesn't even seem to be a positive side."

"Good thing we're just sitting here, then, because I've got a story for you. It'll tell you what it means to be optimistic, and then you'll know forever." He glances at me. "And whatever's going on inside you that's making you ask about this? See if you can turn it off while you listen.

"There are two sons," Bailey begins. "One an optimist, one a pessimist. And their father is trying to teach them to round themselves out, to see how others think. He takes the pessimist, and locks him in a room full of brand-new toys. He says, 'I want to teach you a lesson. These are all yours to play with. I'll be back in an hour and we're going to talk.' Then he takes the optimist, and locks him in a room full of horse poop. He says, 'Stay here for an hour, and then we'll talk. I want you to think about what you see in here.'

"An hour passes. He comes back and unlocks the door with all the toys. The pessimist is sitting in the middle of the room, crying his eyes out. The father says, 'What's wrong with you?' And the boy says, 'I just know if I touch one of these toys, it's going to break!'

"Then he goes to the optimist and opens the door. And the son's jumping up and down in horse poop, giggling and screaming. The father says, 'What's wrong with you? You're in a room full of horse poop! How can you be so happy?' And the boy says, 'Dad, I just know there's got a be a pony in here somewhere.'"

Beth laughs, and Bailey says to me, "I don't know what's getting at you. But take my advice: just look for the pony."

I smile politely, and moments later the traffic begins to surge forward. Bailey turns back to the road and accelerates with the flow, and as we move ahead, many of the passengers nodding off, Beth holding her radio close to her ear and turning it on softly to catch a snippet of a song, I think: Ponies. How simplistic. How inadequate a parable when faced with the enormity of a situation like my sister's. Still, wouldn't it be nice, even liberating, if I could begin to see beyond my cynicism and resistance and controlling impulses? As we roll over hills and down country roads that I'd glimpsed but not quite seen from a distance, and as, mile after mile, I think about how so many of these drivers, at crucial turning points, learned to view and inhabit their own lives in fresh ways, slowly it comes to me.

Beth is living by *her own choices,* unfettered by the whims of an institution or group home placement decision; she travels according to the starred dots on *her* map; she eats what *she* likes when *she's* hungry; she boldly dresses in a fireworks display of ensembles that declare, Look at me, I count in this world. She is, in many ways, the embodiment of self-determination.

A tension that I hadn't even realized I'd been feeling — a tension that has possessed my body throughout this day — for weeks, no, for *months* — begins to ease.

"These drivers," I muse to Beth as Bailey pulls over to close the sun hatch, "seem just too good to be true. How did you find so many nice, wise people, all working in one place?"

"It just *happened,*" she says. "I rode, and I guess they were just *there,* and I saw them."

I look at her, her eyes milky from her corneal condition but also brimming with a response to life that I rarely perceive in the world or feel in myself, and I realize that nothing "just happens." Beth has sought out mentors in places where others might not look, and, moreover, taken the time, and endured the pain, to weed out those drivers who are decent and kind and reflective from those who are indifferent or hostile. The ones I'm meeting are, I realize as I quickly do the math, only about a sixth of the whole bus company. That took Beth a huge amount of trial and error — and, yes, determination. I shake my head, amazed at how much I'd somehow missed, and then, with a surge of optimism, wonder if one out of six people in *any* profession or community would also be exceptionally thoughtful. How could I really know? Have *I* ever spent this much time exploring the worldviews of my colleagues at school or the bookstore? Do I have a clue about whether my neighbors feel committed to the Golden Rule? I've never discussed anything with them besides trash pickup.

I look back at Beth. She's waving through the windshield to a driver passing in another bus, and it finally occurs to me that her invitation that I join her in her travels didn't "just happen," either. I realize, as the tightness yields in my shoulders and hips and feet, that Beth might well have wanted me to meet her drivers because I needed them, too.

I joined Beth on this odyssey so I could stop feeling like a bad sister. Perhaps on some level she is not aware of, some level that my own foggy vision has not allowed me to see, Beth invited me along because she wanted to stop feeling the same way about me.

Bailey positions himself once again before the wheel, and as softly as brooms sweeping the world clean, a summer rain begins to fall.

Break Shot

Among the fifteen or so letters I receive from Beth each week I find these:

> To Rachel,
>   Hi. Rick got a new hairdew. He looks great. I am So glad thAt he likes you a lot.
>
> *Cool Beth*

> Dear Sis,
>   Rick will take you Were ever you want to go out Eat. I said that diner I like has Good food.
>
> *Cool Beth*

> Oh guess What
>   Now Rick thinks the same way I do about you. now. I love You a lot.
>
> *Cool Beth*

Finally the day comes when she chaperones me onto his bus. I take my seat beside Beth — and am pleased to discover that Rick is attractive. In fact, he's burly and broad-chested, with a boyish, Warren Beatty face and laughing walnut eyes; beneath a full crown of richly brown hair, he sports a tan that, I learn, deepens on his days off, which he commits to the putting green during the warmer weather. He is, Beth informs me, about fifty, "only he don't *look* it." I have to agree.

But I have no intention of sliding into my sister's cunning little trap. I will simply be friendly but guarded, as I am with everyone I meet.

Yet, oddly, I find myself feeling a little giddy.

Rick tells me he's studied art history at a local college and that he is partial to Cézanne. He tells me he enjoys attending movies, especially films with real substance. He perks up when I mention that Beth lives down the street from a regional theater.

"And," he says at a stop sign, "I've gotten into crossword puzzles."

He produces one that he'd tucked beneath his side window. "I do a few of these a day, between runs. This one's not finished."

"I'm really bad at these," I say, though, despite my affection for words, I've never tried.

He waggles it in my direction. Beth takes it from his hand and passes it to me.

"No, I really can't do these," I say, reluctant to look foolish should I come up short.

Rick says, "Oh, come on. See if you can help me with the blanks."

He drives on, and the puzzle is in my hand. I read, "Fifty-four down: a recluse." I pause. "I know what it is. A hermit."

"Is that it?" Rick asks as we stop for a long traffic light.

"It fits."

"I'd have gotten it."

I continue. "Fifty-six across: snuggle. It's six letters, and D is the third one."

"Hug."

"Six letters. Cuddle? Hey, what about thirty-four down: a baby shoe. Six letters."

Beth jumps in. "I told her you want to take her out."

"Beth, please," I say.

Rick says to me, "What's this about a little theater near where Beth lives?"

"I just noticed it," I say. "Passing by in these buses. You get to notice every building from here. It's like you're Huck Finn and you're seeing America from along the Mississippi, and you get to understand so many things you'd missed when you were just standing on the shore."

He says to Beth, "Good-looking *and* smart." And to me, "You like going to plays?"

"Well, yes. I do."

"I sometimes do that. I like plays. I like pool, too."

"You sure *do*," Beth says.

"So, Rachel, you like pool?"

"Well, I've never even picked up a pool c —"

"Bootie," a passenger in a flannel shirt calls out. He rises to get off.

"What?" I say.

"Bootie," the man repeats, heading for the center door. And then he adds, "A baby shoe."

"Oh! Bootie!" Rick and I cry at the same time, and I scribble it in. "Thank you."

Rick winks at Beth as the man gets off. "Well, I think I've got some kind of chance now," he says, and pulls the bus onto the road.

Gone

In my first two weeks at boarding school, Beth and I write letters every day. Laura, who now rents a room near our mother's house, drives to see Beth every evening. She pulls into the driveway, and Beth runs outside. They sit in the car and listen to the radio, and after an hour or so, Beth goes back in.

Then right after Valentine's Day, I receive a letter from Beth. In it she says, I think Mom and That Guy. got MArried. I read it over and over, but it just keeps saying the same thing.

Laura tells Dad, who calls to tell me that it's true. Laura knows because when she stops by to see Beth, there is a babysitter who says, "They've left for their honeymoon."

But a week after the Valentine's Day wedding, when Laura stops by to see Beth, there is no babysitter. There are no lights on. In a panic, Laura scrambles around to the back door.

She finds Ringo, chained outside in the night. Shivering, he jumps up when he sees her, licking her hands. She glances down. His Alpo is frozen. He is alone in the cold, starving.

Dad calls Grandma. She tells him that she and Beth flew far away, to the place where our mother is spending her honeymoon. Then Grandma left Beth there and came home. We have no idea where that place is, and no matter how hard Dad yells, Grandma refuses to say.

Dad slams down the phone, and says, "Oh, Christ, where is she? Where?"

I don't understand what's happening except for one thing: my sister has disappeared.

August

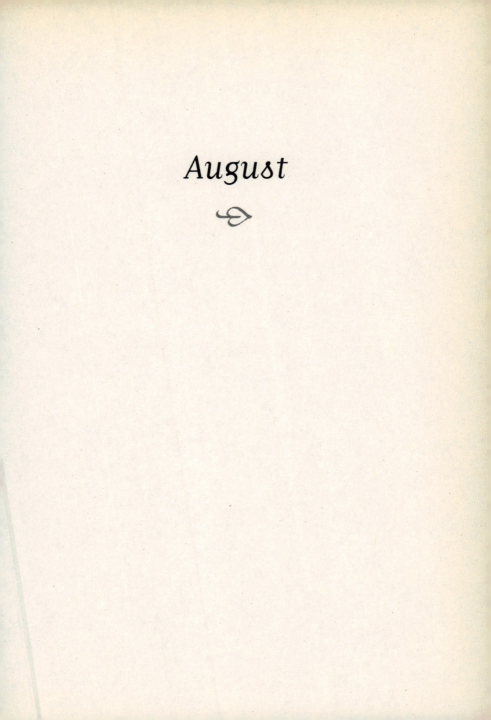

The Loner

2:25 P.M. "Just look at those children," a gap-toothed white woman mutters to her companion, who is probably, given their matching squints, her daughter.

"Disgusting," says the younger one, whose face is a shrine to aqua eye shadow.

We're standing a few feet from them at a bus shelter, peering up the street in anticipation of Jack's bus, but at this exchange Beth glances over. Monopolizing the bus bench, one in a faded denim jumper, the other in overstuffed capri pants, the women are sitting in judgment of a young family strolling down the opposite sidewalk in the blazing summer sun: white mother, black father, mixed-race children.

"It's a disgrace," Justice the Elder pronounces.

Justice the Younger opines, "Imagine a white mother raising her own babies to be nig —"

"You shouldn't talk like that," Beth says.

I hold my breath. The older one blinks. The younger one glares.

"They're just *people*," Beth says.

"It's none of your business what we —"

"What you're saying iz *wrong*. Iz not *nice*."

"How dare you interrupt us!"

Beth says, "You can't tell me what to do. You shouldn't tell them what to do, either."

Then Jack rounds the corner and comes to a stop at our curb. Beth turns away from this streetside court of opinion and, with dignity, marches toward his opening door.

"Sit yourself down," Jack says in his gruff voice, gesturing toward Beth's customary spot. "Them there seats're just open and waiting for you."

Chunky and pug-nosed, Jack has the kind of lived-in, seen-it-all face that looks made for chewing a cigar and a tough, give-'em-hell air that he might have picked up from Harry S. Truman, the first president Jack remembers. Yet Jack describes himself as a happy-go-lucky guy; his round, ruddy cheeks frame an easy smile.

Jack's run curlicues through a housing development on the periphery of the city, home to a substantial portion of the Indian and Southeast Asian communities. The bus bustles with colors beyond even Beth's visual vocabulary — mint, mango, emerald, periwinkle, ruby shot through with gold — and with conversations in languages from all over the globe.

Against this lively backdrop, Beth tells Jack about the toxic incident we just encountered. "They were gonna use a bad *word*," she says.

"I think it's really good you spoke up," I say. "Most people wouldn't."

"Beth's not like most people," Jack says, his short fingers gesturing. "Like John Wayne says in *True Grit*: 'She reminds me of me.' Beth and me, we're just independent-minded. If you think you should speak up, you do it."

"Yeah," Beth says. "You should say what you believe."

"We mingle with the crowd," Jack says, "but we also stand back from the crowd. We do what we want when we want, and we don't say, 'Do you think I should do this?'"

"Thaz right," Beth says. "They didn't think I should say that, but I don't *care*."

"Independence is a good thing. If people don't like you the way you are, you just go, Tough on them. I'm me, and Beth's Beth. After they made us, they threw the molds away."

Beth sits up tall.

"Know how I learned about being independent-minded?" he says. "My lessons started when I was six years old. That's when I started working."

"At *six*?" Beth says. "Why'd you do *that*?"

We're stopped at a curve in the development, a major hub on this run, I see, as a score of passengers parades off in their silks and crepes and jeans, and a garden of new finery breezes on. As Jack's expressive hands flit from fare box to transfer pad to fare box, he responds to Beth's question. "Both my parents died when I was still a baby," he says, "and I didn't have no siblings. So I went to live with my grandmother. All she got was Social Security, so when I had the opportunity to go with this Greek guy on his oil truck when I was a kid, I went, and then come summertime, he'd switch to a fruit and vegetable truck, and I helped with that, too. I worked with him every day after school, and then came home at night and helped my grandmother out.

"That's how I learned independence. I learned how to get along with everyone we met off his trucks, and there were all nationalities, and I learned to go among them all. No one could tell me I shouldn't talk to Thais or whatever. I listened to *myself,* and since I wanted to get along with them, I just figured out their ways. Clint Eastwood says in *Heartbreak Ridge,* 'Adapt. Overcome.' I wanted to adapt, so I did. I watched my grandmother cook, too, so I learned to cook all kinds of food. No one could tell me boys didn't cook — by the time I was eleven years old, I could cook a four-course meal. Now I can talk to anyone, and I can cook anything."

"Like what?" Beth asks.

"Everybody loves my chicken pot pie, red beet eggs, and chocolate mayonnaise cake, even though they're Pennsylvania Dutch foods and my friends aren't all Pennsylvania Dutch. That's because no matter how many differences there are among people," Jack says with a smile, "you *know* we all like to eat."

Jack's Chicken Pot Pie

"This comes out like my bus run, a big melting pot where everybody's mixing together. It's not like frozen dinner pot pies — it's a thick, gooey stew, with the dough mixed right in.

"I use lard, but it's okay to substitute shortening. But don't forget the yellow food coloring. It gives the chicken a golden yellow color, and that's what makes it really special."

FOR THE CHICKEN
½ split chicken breast
1 chicken leg

1 medium rib celery, diced
1 medium onion, peeled and halved
1 large potato, peeled and cut in half crosswise, then each
half quartered lengthwise to make 8 pieces
¾ teaspoon salt
¼ teaspoon pepper
5 cups water
¾ teaspoon yellow food coloring

"Place all these ingredients in a six- to eight-quart pot. Bring right up to a boil, then reduce heat to medium. Cover and simmer for one hour or until the chicken's thoroughly cooked. Then take the chicken from the pot, set it aside until it cools enough to handle, and scoop those onions out and throw them away."

FOR THE DOUGH
2 cups flour
¾ teaspoon baking powder
¼ teaspoon salt
1 tablespoon + 2 teaspoons lard or shortening
About ½ cup cold water

"Mix the dry ingredients in a bowl and cut in the shortening, like making a pie crust. Then add the water — just enough to form a ball of dough — and knead it a bit and let it rest for five minutes. Roll the dough out on a lightly floured board till you've got a square about twelve inches on each side, and about an eighth of an inch thick. Then cut it with a knife or a pizza cutter into a bunch of two-inch squares.

"Strip off the meat from the chicken, and toss the skin and bones. Set the meat back in the pot. Bring to a boil and add the dough one square at a time, stirring well after each addition. (The dough'll look like dumplings, not noodles.) Then turn down the heat to medium and keep cooking for about thirty minutes — but stir it real frequently. If it all gets too thick or the dough begins to stick, add more water, a quarter cup at a time. You know it's all done when the squares are cooked right through."

Enough for four hungry eaters, or six, if you serve with salad, rolls, and dessert

The humidity outside our air-conditioned shuttle engulfs the city like a steaming broth. Families lie limply in porch shade, their eyes glazed over, their skin sticking to lawn chairs like raw dough. Sidewalks simmer the feet of panting dogs. Wilted riders in saris and embroidered shoes press kerchiefs to their damp cheeks as they escape into the relief of the bus.

At a long red light, Jack says to Beth, "You don't know it, but you helped those people."

"They sure didn't act like it."

"Sometimes we can get through to people, and we don't even know it."

"I don't think I got through. They weren't listening to me."

"You never know. Let me tell you something that happened to me once: A woman got on my bus about six one morning. She said, 'Jack, they're following me.' I said, 'Who?' She said, 'I don't know.' I said, 'Can I ask you a question? Are you on any drugs?' 'No.' 'You drink a lot?' 'Yeah.' I said, 'Now I know why people are following you. You were drinking last night, weren't you?' 'Yeah, till four this morning.' 'I can't tell you what to do,' I told her, 'but you need help, if this happens a lot.' She said, 'I don't know where to get help.'

"Well, I'd taken this class to become a community service counselor. They tell you what to say if someone's in trouble, and then they give you this book that lists all the organizations that can help. I'd looked through that book — I call it the 'Help Anyone, Anytime Book' — so I knew right off what to do. I said, 'I'll tell you where to go, if you promise to get help.' And we were right there, so I just pulled the bus over and said, 'Go into this here hospital, and say you want to talk to someone in their detox program.' And she got up and went inside.

"A week later, I heard she was still there. A year later, she's still clean. I saw her one time on the bus, and she thanked me. So you never know when you can get through."

"That was a really nice thing you did," I say.

"I like helping people, but I feel like John Wayne — he's one of my heroes. He'll help everybody, but when it comes to him being in some predicament, he'll go it alone. That's how I feel. Helping people makes me feel good. I just don't want anybody helping *me*."

Beth doesn't say, "Yup, thaz the way I am." She says, "I'm cold. Will you turn the air conditioner down?" But I detect approval in her face.

To Beth, every day is Independence Day. This was not true for the first half of her life, and for the next quarter it was more of a rebel war, with its own versions of boycotts (particularly at meals), Boston Tea Parties (I shudder to remember her efforts to overturn the order in her classroom), and a one-woman Minuteman regiment. Since she has lived on her own, though, each day her actions declare anew that all men are created equal, and have the inalienable right to life, liberty, and, especially, the pursuit of happiness. I love this about her, and, now that I have come to see her as proudly bearing the torch of self-determination, I regard her as courageous, a social pioneer. However, sometimes Beth's assertion of independence can be at odds with what I see, and others do too, as her best interests, and I find this conflict to be as much of a challenge for me as her sometimes obstreperous ways on the bus.

This realization recurs at odd moments. One evening recently, Vera drove us to the supermarket.

"How much of your money do you want?" she asked Beth.

"Fifty dollas."

"You know you'll have to come back here pretty soon if you don't buy more now."

"I don't *care*. I'll get here on the bus."

After riding all day, I just wanted to be stationary. So as Beth hustled across the lot and Vera popped a tape of salsa music into her cassette player, we got to talking.

I'd finally pieced together that Vera, whom the drivers call Beth's aide, and who after a recent promotion became officially known as a team leader, works for a provider agency that oversees the work and home lives of people with special needs. Beth's first job out on her own was in their sheltered workshop, a section in the agency's headquarters, where, in a supervised production line, people with developmental disabilities perform low-tech tasks for local businesses, such as folding boxes or putting washers in plastic bags. When she wanted to move on from that, the agency trained her to get a job in the community. They also oversaw the group homes where Beth lived and now run the support program that sends Vera to monitor people who live independently.

"I used to go in there with her," Vera said, nodding toward the grocery store. "But I'd say, 'You need vegetables,' and she'd just walk by them, so to keep from getting upset I wait outside now. She'll take the bus here, but since you can carry only so much back on the bus, sometimes I drive her. Not that it encourages her to buy healthier. Though she did learn to cook real meals. I taught her myself."

I was surprised; I've never seen Beth do more than boil spaghetti. "When?"

"Oh, that was years ago, when I worked in her group home." She explained that they had two types of group homes then, one with twenty-four-hour care for people with severe and multiple disabilities, and the type Beth was in, with eight-hour care, for people who needed just some help. It was in that semi-independent program where Vera taught Beth cooking, "and fire safety, dealing with strangers, all that." Then six years ago there was a big push toward independence and the agency folded the semis. Beth and most of the others there moved into their own places. "She's happier this way, but I worry about newcomers. They don't have any intermediate step — it's either twenty-four-hour care or you're in your own place. It's like going from grade school to college overnight."

When the semis closed, Vera shifted to the Independent Living Program that oversees Beth now. Each individual can choose to see her for two to thirty hours a week. For Beth, the recommendation is seven. But she wants only three, so Vera obliges. "That's the way it works."

"Do you like it? Working with her?"

Well, she said, the job pays poorly; after thirteen years, she earns ten dollars an hour, and some other places pay less. "But I like Beth. She's got spunk. And she's a good person, too. If there's an emergency, no matter what time of night, I'd run over. This guy in her building was getting fresh with her in the elevator. How many times have I talked to him? 'Don't try that with her again!' Or people complain about her running around on her own. I stick up for her, I say, 'She has a brother who's a lawyer, people who care for her. She's not a nobody.'"

We heard the supermarket door open and Beth burst through the exit. "There's Miss Quick," Vera said. "Third song isn't even over on this tape. I don't know how she does it."

Her cart laden with Diet Pepsis and ketchup and macaroni, Beth charged across the lot.

"I'm supposed to teach her to be as independent as possible," Vera said. "That's not hard because she's a very smart lady and the most independent person I know."

She flicked off her cassette player. Yes, I saw, Vera shares my respect for my sister, but she also appreciates how difficult it is to balance her concern for Beth's well-being with Beth's unquenchable desire for freedom.

"Of course, independence," Jack says, as he munches on French fries during his lunch break, his back to the driver's side window, "can have its drawbacks."

"No," Beth says. I am spooning up fruit salad; beside me, Beth is nibbling on a slice of pizza. The otherwise empty bus is idling in the parking lot of a shopping center where we've just bought our food.

"Sure," Jack says. "I'll tell you, I love them lone cowboy movies, but sometimes independence makes loneliness hell. I've been single for twenty-two years, since my divorce. Once women start thinking they can possess me, then goodbye. I'm too independent. I'm always the oddball at parties, alone when people are in couples. That's no fun."

"Do you . . ." — I pause — "do you . . . *like* being alone? I mean, twenty-two years. That's a *long* time." I feel a pinch in my forehead.

"I like it, sure, but sometimes I want to be with someone — someone as independent as me. I've known only one person like that: a girl in high school. She was the only girl I ever truly loved. But at the time I was living with my aunt and uncle, and they pressured me not to see her. Too young, they said. Then I went in the army and lost track of her. I think about her a lot."

"Why don't you find her?" Beth and I ask at the same moment.

"Every time I go to high school reunions, I look around for her," Jack replies, "but she's never shown up. They say you have one true love in this life, and I believe that."

He gazes out the windshield at the shopping center, and his eyes fill with a distant longing. "Sometimes I wonder if I'd be a different person if my life had gone another way. I had a chance to go to a military academy when my grandmother died, and I would have learned a trade right off the bat, but I wanted to live with my aunt and uncle. And back in those times, you didn't have guys thinking of culinary school. Would I have been more satisfied in another life? Maybe I'd be a chef now, and make my specialties at a four-star restaurant. Maybe *I'd* be one of them cooks I watch on TV. Maybe I'd have that girl as a wife."

He sighs. "I now know that if you have a dream, act on it. If you love someone, hold onto her. Cooking got me lots of friends, and whenever they feel down, I just whip something up and it leaves them happy. So I'm not bitter. But this is what I learned too late: that you need to go for things when you can, because you might never get the chance again."

I try to come up with something to say in response, but I can't think of anything. I look at Beth, who, apparently guessing at my feelings of uselessness, turns her palms up in a gesture of *I don't know what to say, either.* We all sit there a moment, listening to the muffled thrum of the bus engine.

Then Jack clears his throat. "Well, like Walter Huston says in *The Treasure of the Sierra Madre,* 'Goin' through some mighty rough country, you'd better have some beans.'" With a small laugh he turns to his side, combs through a bag beside his seat, and produces a black, insulated container. "I was bringing these to a friend today," he says, "but want to help yourself now?"

"No *thanks*," says Beth, who does not stray from her familiar menu.

I generally share Beth's lack of interest in dishes outside my ordinary fare, but with one of the world's most enthusiastic undiscovered chefs sitting before me, his tough-guy face having just softened, however fleetingly, into vulnerability, how can I resist?

"Beans?" I say, walking over.

"Actually, *beets*. Red beet eggs."

I look down at a square Tupperware container of sliced beets and a dozen eggs — fat, plum-colored jewels suspended in a wine red sea. He hands me a plastic fork and napkin, and says, "Dig in."

Jack's Red Beet Eggs

"They're pickled, but you won't taste vinegar, because I balance the ingredients just right, so you get a sweet-sour taste. And I make sure the color goes all the way through."

    2 dozen large eggs
    4 14-ounce cans sliced red beets
    1 quart white vinegar (approximately)
    Sugar to taste (about 3 cups)

"First, hard-cook the eggs and run them under cold water real good. Then take a gallon jug, glass is best, and clean it. Then open four cans of sliced red beets, dump all the juice (but not the beets) and about a quart of white vinegar into a medium pot, and add enough sugar to give the liquid a sweet-sour flavor — that's right, right smack between the two. You have to do it by taste, but figure on somewhere around three cups.

"Bring that all to a boil, but don't let it boil too long. Then let it cool down to room temp, because if you add your cooked eggs to hot liquid they'll be so rubbery they'll bounce as high as balls. Then dump one can's worth of beets into the jug, shell the eggs, and layer eight or nine of the eggs on top of the beets. Do that over and over till the eggs are used up. You won't get all the beets in, but you layer them to keep the eggs from floating. Put on a lid and let it soak for about two to three days in the refrigerator. The eggs come out a real deep red-purple. Keep it refrigerated and serve it on a dish that's on ice unless you're eating them right away. And once you've opened the jug, eat the eggs within a week. That won't be hard, because they're just so good."

Enough to feed a party

Last week, Beth finally saw the ophthalmologist. He's one of the few in the city who accept her medical assistance card and who has experience treating people with special needs. Afterward, the doctor called me with the diagnosis: interstitial keratitis. Beth's corneas are, as we'd feared, scratched and numb, to the point where she is barely able to see. The eyedrops Vera helps her put in might be useful, but they will not eliminate the problem, and glasses will not make any difference, either. "This condition is rare in the United States," the doctor said.

"How did she get it?" I asked him.

"I wish I knew."

"How long has she had it?"

"I don't know. Her last eye doctor retired, and I can't get hold of her records."

I sat there on the phone, smoldering about all the things I can't control. It's not just her medical files, or her eyes. There are uterine fibroids, and how she bolted out to a bus right after her ultrasound, leaving her medical caseworker to discuss the results with the doctor. Bad teeth that she brushes too quickly. High cholesterol. Frequent colds.

"She also has a secondary eye condition," the doctor went on. "Her eyelashes are growing into her eyes, and scraping across her corneas. They're making matters even worse. I'd like to do something about this, to reduce the chances of her losing her sight even more: surgery. It's her decision, of course. Though if she wants you along, I hope you'll be able to help her."

What does help mean, I longed to ask, for someone who wants to do everything on her own, even if she does it badly? And who has too much pride to reveal vulnerability? But I stayed silent.

"I'll be in touch," the doctor said, and we hung up. I sat there, paralyzed.

After Jack's lunch is over, new passengers slump aboard, fanning themselves. Jack, who seems to have withdrawn into his own world, pulls out onto the road, and as he drives on, a loner once again, Beth turns to me. "I have a wish," she says.

"What?"

"I wish Jack would meet that lady again. The one that he loved."

"Yeah. He deserves it," I say, moved by her good heart. I want to remark on how thoughtful she can be, but am distracted by the white fog that's spread over her irises, which I now know might worsen without surgery. She has agreed to it, though not to spending two days afterward at home so that the stitches will heal. She wants to get back to the buses the moment the anesthesia wears off.

"I have a wish, too," I say, before I can stop myself.

"What?" she says.

"I wish I had a 'Help Anyone, Anytime Book,' like Jack's."

"Why?"

What I want is a guide to being a good sister, to doing well by Beth, and I would leave it propped on my lap all the time. There would be instructions on how to adjust my guidance to her self-reliance, and how to find the difference between caring and controlling.

But instead I say, "I'd like a book like Jack's so I could find you a new pair of eyes."

"That'd be nice," she says, and, only half joking, she adds, "Can you make them *purple*?"

I'm amused at the question, yet also saddened at how much it reveals about her "adaptive skill areas," and suddenly I wonder what kind of person she would have become had she not been born this way. When I was younger, friends used to ask me this question, though I found it ridiculous as well as rude, since the very thought seemed like a betrayal of some kind. Now I cut my gaze away from Beth, trying to form a picture, but, ensnared in shame and forty years of reality, I am utterly unable to conjure up a parallel Beth. She is the person she is — and, because of that, I am the person I am. Like Jack, I cannot know if I would have been more satisfied in another life, with a sister who wasn't *diffrent*. I do know I would not have been torn by these conflicts. But I also would not have watched two bigots on these streets get put in their place, nor learned the dreams of a John Wayne bus driver, nor eaten a red beet egg. I would not have the almost daily delight of opening a letter from Beth.

You need to go for things when you can, Jack said, *because you might never have the chance again.*

I turn back to Beth. She is still looking at me, awaiting my answer.

"Purple eyes?" I finally say.

"*Yeah,*" she replies, as if it's the most reasonable request in the world.

"I'll try my hardest," I say.

Jack's Chocolate Mayonnaise Cake

"My one regret with cooking is that I never watched my grandmother make her rice pudding. So that's lost for good. You know, I wish I'd written down *all* her recipes. But I was lucky with this one. Maybe she already knew you can't wait forever to do something important, and that's why she wrote this one down for me."

FOR THE CAKE
2 cups flour
1 cup sugar
¼ cup unsweetened cocoa powder
2 teaspoons baking soda
1 cup mayonnaise
1 cup water
1 teaspoon vanilla

"Preheat the oven to 350 degrees and lightly grease an eight-inch cake pan. Mix the flour, sugar, cocoa, and baking soda with a spoon. Add mayonnaise, water, and vanilla. Then take a mixer and mix it up like a cake mix and pour it into the pan. Bake for twenty-five to thirty minutes or until a toothpick stuck in the middle comes out clean. Some folks serve this just as it is with no frosting, but you can frost it like I sometimes do or make two cakes and layer them."

FOR THE CHOCOLATE FROSTING
1 8-ounce block cream cheese, softened
2 cups confectioners' sugar
1 cup whipped topping
3 tablespoons unsweetened cocoa powder

"Put all the ingredients in a medium bowl and slowly mix them together. This makes 2 cups of frosting — enough for two layers or one layer with some left over for cookies or cupcakes. It's real tasty this way, but if you use this frosting, keep the cake in the refrigerator. That's because there's the whipped cream in it, and when something's this good, you don't want to let it go bad."

Enough for eight small slices or six large

Nowhere

At boarding school, I sit late at night on friends' beanbag chairs, discussing my most feared scenarios about Beth's fate, keeping my listeners awake until they exile me to my room. I have no idea what is happening — there has been no word from Mom, Beth, Grandma, anyone.

I stop combing my hair in the morning.

Perhaps our mother is fitting mittens on Beth's hands. But perhaps something has gone terribly wrong, and now a mittenless Beth is forging through the snow on her own.

I stop sleeping at night.

I lie in the dark, imagining Beth wandering the streets in some strange city, kicking up slush in her sandals, searching through trash cans for food. I imagine her curled up at night, under fire escapes and loose newspapers and a pimp's appraising gaze.

I stop speaking in class.

One week passes.

One month.

Two months.

"She'll be okay," my friends say. "Be positive."

I try to be positive. Maybe she's stumbled upon a soup kitchen. Or found her way to a charitable family, the kind who take in babies left on their front porch. Or she's befriended a stray dog, and they're surviving together under highway overpasses.

But her image keeps slipping from my mind, and her voice is already fading away.

Be Not Afraid

At nine A.M. on an August morning, I step from the boardwalk onto the sand at the Jersey Shore. The beach stretching before me is bare except for five low chairs far off to my left, three girls throwing a ball, and Jacob the bus driver, now in bathing trunks, waving to me. "Come join!"

Two weeks ago he asked me, via e-mail, whether Beth and I would like to spend a day with his family at the ocean. He, his wife, Carol, and their twelve-year-old daughter, Grace, drive several hours to the shore every Sunday. They could bring Beth, and I could meet them there.

Although I was astonished and delighted by the invitation — one of Beth's bus drivers was asking us to spend time with his family off the bus, out of town! could there really be such generosity in the world? he truly cares about her! — I hesitated. I am not a beach person. I am a stay-in-the-shade person. Nor do I like the idea of bathing suits, tattling my imperfections to the world.

And God knows, except for the buses, I do not take whole days away from my work.

"But," Jacob e-mailed me, "isn't it time to start that second childhood? Isn't it time to be a little younger at heart?"

I surprised myself. For the first time in . . . I don't even know how long, the part of me that routinely answers "Sorry, I can't" fought a little less fiercely.

"Okay," I told him. "But I'm not wearing a bathing suit. I'll wear shorts and a T-shirt." Beth, perhaps not coincidentally, told him the same thing.

"I'm asking you to loosen up," he e-mailed back. "Writers need to experience what others experience to get a true understanding of life, correct? I want to give you more than a glimpse of fun — I want you to feel it. Don't worry about how you look, none of us are beauties."

Then he and Carol took Beth to Wal-Mart, after coaxing her off the bus one afternoon. "I don't *want* a bathing suit," she insisted, but once she was strolling along the aisles in the nucleus of a family, and once she saw the racks of swimsuits in her favorite tropical colors, she changed her mind. They applauded her when she selected one, a yellow neck-to-thigh ensemble.

"Let's go for it," Jacob wrote me. "Be not afraid."

So here I am, in a loose sweater and skirt over a one-piece black swimsuit, stepping across the sand, my head beneath a broad-brimmed straw hat.

The ocean glitters out to infinity, and sailboats glide across the horizon. I realize as I draw near that the three girls tossing the ball are Carol, Grace, and Beth. My sister catches with both arms and throws underhand into the sky. Carol and Grace laugh, and Jacob offers me a chair. Beth looks as happy as I've ever seen her.

As a school of dolphins arcs across the horizon, Jacob and I talk. We have recently begun swapping e-mail, initially so I could check in with him about how Beth was doing and so he could keep me abreast of major bus developments, but eventually this correspondence evolved into exchanges about what he calls the "Big Things": how to be good even when it's hard, why some people are not good even when it's easy, why it's important to keep trying. Now, as we sit on beach chairs and continue our dialogue in person, he tells me that, as careful as he is to treat his passengers and family well, and as faithfully as he tries to emulate Christ's selflessness, he still struggles to give himself to others.

On being critical: "This is tough for me, because I see every little thing that's wrong. But I work at it — all the time. So even though I see faults, I try real hard not to deal with other people, and myself, so harshly."

On why we're here: "We're here to learn, sooner or later, to surrender our pride and do unto others as you would have others do unto you. But most people don't want to hear this until they hit bottom."

On prayer: "It means so much more than what people think. It ain't just sitting there, mumbling things. My prayer has graduated from asking for things to downright praise and gratitude. And instead of wondering whether I'll get something I want, I pray for others. It's how I keep myself at peace."

Then Beth joins us and, without preamble, says, "I'm *afraid* to have my eye operation. But I have to, I know."

We talk about hospitals and healing. Jacob lifts his T-shirt to show us the scar from his liver transplant. Beth has told me he gets sick more often than most drivers. "Are you okay?" I ask, concerned. "Oh, yeah. It's under control." He smiles reassuringly.

The voices of children playing nearby rise and fall. Grace and Carol sit a few yards away, building a castle. Beth gets up and shoots a water pistol at me, giggling.

Later, along the boardwalk, we stop in shops with beaded curtains and seashell jewelry, watch hermit crabs crawl in wire crates and see the Ferris wheel rock to a stop, meander through an old-fashioned candy store, and ogle machines that make saltwater taffy. Banners zip through the air tied to light airplanes. We wave at a hot-air balloon.

Jacob takes pictures. We admire a miniature golf course with cartoon themes. Then Grace takes pictures. In a shop, Carol tries on a blue bathing suit that makes her look as fetching as a mermaid. Then she takes pictures: Jacob with his arms around Beth, Grace, and me. "Now you have *three* daughters," Beth says to Jacob as the shutter clicks.

I have not yet gone into the water. I don't care for being in over my head, or tempting the tides, or chancing across a rabid jellyfish swimming too close to the shore.

After lunch, we wind our way back through the sunbathers to our chairs. Jacob and Grace say, "Let's go in!" But I remain on the dry sand, with Carol and Beth.

"This is the beach!" Jacob says when he returns, dripping wet. He scoops up the ball. "Come on, you'll be fine."

"I'm fine here in my chair with my book," I say as he runs back in.

I watch him and Grace jumping about in the waves, tossing the ball. He returns one more time to say, "You drove all the way here and you're not going in?" Without waiting for an answer, he scurries back to the water.

Carol shrugs. "You're on your own."

Beth says, "I'll go if you go."

I pause. "Okay. I'll try."

I set down my book and remove my skirt and sweater and shirt and hat and sunglasses and wristwatch. An ocean breeze whistles past, pricking up goose bumps on my arms and legs. I feel as if I'm in my underwear, except that I can't lower the blinds.

Then Beth and I head past the many beach towels to the water's edge.

Jacob and Grace, happily tossing the ball in the deep, catch sight of us. "Hey!" Jacob calls above the breaking waves. "You're here!"

Beth and I put our toes into the foam. "It's cold!" we say.

Jacob reaches his arm over the water toward us, his fingers beckoning.

Beth and I linger on the shore, giggling, holding each other. He keeps on, finally throwing me the ball. I step out to catch it — up to my ankles. He throws it again, aiming deeper into the water. I move toward it — up to my knees.

"Come in!" he calls.

Beth, I see, has retreated to the beach. I throw the ball back. I am alone.

"You throw well!" Jacob says.

Grace joins in. "Come on out here!"

I let myself go partway in. Jacob is making his "come here" gesture.

The water is up over my knees. Over my thighs.

But then: "I'm cold!" I say.

"Just get in! C'mon!"

"I can't!"

"You'll warm up as soon as you get used to it!"

"No, no. The water seems warm, but the air is cold!"

He calls, "You know what that is? That's writer's crock!"

I'm suddenly shivering so hard I can't try any longer. I turn and run back up the beach.

Inside the Tears

Three months after Beth disappears, I am in class on a dewy spring morning when a student who works in the office comes to the classroom door. "Rachel has an emergency phone call," she says. I know, I just know, it has to do with Beth.

I tear across campus. It is a friend of Dad's, telling me that Mom's husband had called that morning and said he was about to put Beth on a plane in Albuquerque. Dad was told to get to La Guardia to meet her. Immediately.

Why so suddenly? Why didn't Mom call?

It is mysterious and frightening. When I step outside the office, I faint for the first time in my life.

I stay out of classes all day, waiting for Dad. He is supposed to swing by my school after he and Max have picked up Beth. I lie on my dormitory bed in silence, listening, telling myself my worst fears could not be founded.

Then I hear that cadenced, quacky voice.

I whip into the corridor. She is down the hall with my brother, grinning. She has the same heavy, awkward walk, the same body, the same laugh — though some of her hair has fallen out, her hands and face are grimy, and her all-yellow outfit is filthy beyond words.

I barrel down the hall and throw myself into her embrace.

Minutes later, we get into Dad's car, feigning normalcy. "So, Beth," I say, as Dad steers us down the country roads toward his apartment, "did you like the plane ride?"

"I liked Las Vegas."

"I thought you were in Albuquerque."

"Las Vegas."

Dad says, "Albuquerque was a lie. They obviously don't want us to know where they are."

"She has almost no clothes," Max says.

Dad adds, *"And what she has hasn't been washed."*

Hiding my dread, I ask, *"What happened, Beth? Where have you been?"*

She pours it out. Our mother and this guy — *"He was mean and he yelled. He was nuts!"* — have been running from what he said was the KGB and the CIA. They have been living in hotels under aliases, running from skipped bills, shoplifting. He beat Mom and once held a knife to her throat. He slept all day and drank all night. He wouldn't let them make calls except to Grandma, and they couldn't tell her where they were, and eventually they couldn't call at all. He wouldn't let them go out alone, or speak to anyone, even waiters or taxi drivers. Over and over, they left their luggage behind when they ran away from hotels in the middle of the night, except that he always kept his Samsonite, which was filled with guns and knives, and running away meant really running, doing it on foot, because they sold Mom's station wagon two months ago and she kept the money in her support hose because he didn't like banks and ever since then they'd traveled around Arizona and Nevada and New Mexico spending whole days on buses —

"Buses?" I say.

"Yeah. Long, long bus rides. They'd sit together in one seat, and I'd sit in my own seat and look around to see if anyone could help."

On a bus. Independent, yes, but not the way I'd envisioned it. She was on her own on a bus.

And all along, Beth kept planning to get away and call us to come rescue her. Everywhere she went, she looked for a pay phone. Yesterday she'd made her break. While he and Mom were in a casino, Beth sneaked out of her hotel room. She asked strangers in the lobby for their loose change and then she walked outside to find a phone. Showing a resourcefulness that had been incubating for three months, a resourcefulness she'd never shown before, she did find a phone. She figured out how to call the operator. She remembered Laura's phone number.

But Laura's landlady answered and said that Laura was away at class.

Moments later, when the man found her, he'd thrown himself, punching and raging, at Beth, saying he wanted to kill her. "Thaz when the crap started." He sent Beth to her hotel room, wouldn't let Mom come in, and held my sister at gunpoint all night, as she sat on her bed, staring at him in terror. This morning, at the airport, Mom kissed her over and over, and told her, crying, "I have to send you back, if you're going to stay alive."

Then Beth, in the car with us, begins to sob, and Dad does too. And then Max breaks down, and then me. In a cascade of tears we cruise down the road, not noticing the budding trees or the young corn in the fields.

So Beth also moves in with Dad, joining Max and Ringo, and, when she finishes the semester at college, Laura. In June, my summer vacation arrives, and I move into Dad's place, too.

We cannot begin to understand our mother, who seems to have gone off the deep end. We piece together that her new husband is a lawless alcoholic, for whom life careens between boredom and paranoia. But Mom went along with it all, to the point of talking her own mother into helping her. To the point of almost letting her daughter get killed.

Maybe, we think, our mother liked it. She must have. She must be a monster inside. Why else would she do that?

The sleet from that February afternoon has settled deep into my chest. I feel nothing for my mother. I lose myself in my homework and writing.

Laura and Max feel the same as I do about her. We dogleg around her name in conversations. We see only holes where she stood in our dreams. We try to forget with black humor, sundaes, new friendships, and scorn for phrases like "maternal instinct." Only rarely does anyone bring up what happened.

But sometimes in the afternoon we find ourselves in the living room while Dad is grading papers in his study and an old movie is on TV and feelings I don't understand poke out of the ice inside me. I'll be sitting on the wing-backed chair, writing to a friend in New Jersey, my pen going on about Richard Brautigan or the new Grateful Dead album, and then suddenly it'll veer off into a bold-letter marquee:

THE STORY OF THE DECLINE OF THE SIMON EMPIRE
WRITTEN, DIRECTED, AND STARRING
THE INCOMPARABLE RACHEL SIMON
(WITH ASSISTANCE FROM BLOOD RELATIVES)

Max and Laura don't know I'm spilling our tale to distant friends. It doesn't occur to them; they're hunkered down over the dining room table, each involved in a game of Solitaire. All the while, with their eyes on their cards, they talk. Laura says, "We just need to move on, forget it, begin a new life." Max says, "Life is a bowl of sour grapes. If I can beat myself at this game, that's enough for me."

But Beth sits on the sofa, staring at the TV. When the movie ends, she stares at the wall. I finish my letter and take a new sheet from the stationery box beside me to start another. Laura and Max start a game of Gin. Then, as dusk rolls in, Beth pulls herself to her feet and slowly climbs the stairs to the room she shares with me. I pause with my pen, Laura suspends her card shuffling, and we all look up to the ceiling. There're the feet, padding across the floor, one-two, one-two, one. There's the oomph of the bed. We keep looking up, hoping. Maybe this time she won't stay in that bed for twelve hours. Maybe her hair won't keep falling out every day.

"I wonder if she'll ever feel better," I say.

"I wonder if the Yankees are winning," Max says, but he's not wearing his joker face. "Just deal a new hand," he adds quietly.

September

The Jester

3:35 P.M. "Anybody have a birthday?" Bert bellows down the aisle in his New York accent as he positions himself like a comedian, the fare box area his stage.

We are stopped for a "time point" at a downtown corner. As distinct from a layover, which is actually written into the schedule, a time point means we've happened to reach a stop several minutes before our bus is due to depart. So, to prevent us from arriving at subsequent stops prematurely, he must take a recess here until it is time for us to move on. Towering, beefy, white-haired, red-cheeked, clownish, and in his late fifties, Bert is whiling away these extra minutes as he often does: "Getting folks going. Getting them to ease up a little."

Everyone looks toward the front of the bus: Little League boys, girls sucking Tootsie Pops, dreadlocked dads, one-kid-per-hip moms, leisure-suited retirees, the dozing, the listless, the fidgety, the gum-cracking, hand-holding lovebirds, sad-faced shoe-gazers. Beth and I perch on our front seats. Like the kids in the bus, she's laughing already, because she knows what's happening. Someone's bending the rules, someone so solid that he blocks the windshield and doesn't mind if he makes a monkey of himself if that's what it takes to get people relaxed and smiling.

"Anybody have a birthday or anniversary coming? Sir, you." He points to a young father halfway down the bus, a seemingly shy fellow who has hesitantly raised his hand.

Egged on by his daughter, who is leaning bright-eyed over the seat behind him, the man nods. His wife sits beside him, her lips curved in amusement.

"What's your first name?" Bert says.

"Domingo."

"Domingo. Domingo!" Then, as thirty passengers cohere into an audience, and kids slip away from their parents and gather around his feet, Bert lets loose with his song, breaking each note in two or three places, so his lyrics come out as a booming croak:

> *Happpppy birthday tooo yoouuuu,*
> *Happpppy birthday tooo yoouuuu,*
> *Happpppy BIRTHday, Dominnnnggggggoooo,*
> *HAPPPPPy BIRTHday TOOO YOOOUUUU.*

The bus, laughing, bursts into applause. "You sing *terrible*." Beth razzes him as she claps. "You need a tune-up." Domingo and his family are grinning, every child beams with delight, and Bert takes the applause like a pro, brushing away the praise.

"You do what you got to do," Bert says to me as the applause dies down. "You realize they need to smile, you go to work. You just get creative. There're no problems. There are only solutions." Mindful of his remaining spare minutes, he takes a breath and begins his next skit.

"Tell her about New York," Beth says to Bert earlier that day.

We're doing our stop-start bus dance down the city streets, which are, mercifully, no longer scorched by summer. Green leaves still flutter beside and above us, though the lawns have been singed to a lackluster brown, and in gardens sunflowers huddle over their shriveled brethren.

Before he retired, I learn, Bert had been a New York City bus driver for thirty years. He declares this history with a veteran's pride, then adds that when he relocated to this area, where the lower cost of living would allow him to spend his twilight years in more comfortable circumstances, he grew restless, searching for excitement. So now he drives part-time "just for fun." It's easier than in New York, since there are fewer pedestrians blocking crosswalks as his bus maneuvers through the streets, and only a handful of passengers, rather than a throng, flagging him down at every stop.

"But you know what I don't like about folks around here?" he says. "They're rude and crude."

"You *said* it," Beth chimes in.

"Like, people will get on Beth's case on the bus. I think it's so hilarious. Because she knows about four times as much as these people do. That's the truth, too.

"In the Big Apple, you get people like Beth on every bus, and nobody would say a word. You get races mixing, and it's no big deal. Old people, young people, everyone keeps their mouth shut. There's just more tolerance there."

"It's *here*, too," Beth adds. "For people that know how to be*have*."

"Not that New York was a piece of cake, believe me," Bert says. "And I'm not even talking prejudice or whatever. I'm talking the whole shebang, the whole grab bag of human actions. Because in New York, everything you can think of happens.

"Like when I started. Staten Island was more rural, more wild. And this kind of thing happened every day. I'm driving along at two in the morning, along swamps. Here comes this girl out of the woods with nothing on but shower slippers. Naked. Mud up to her knees. I'm all by myself. I pull over the bus — rrraahh! She gets on and says she and her boyfriend had a fight, they were parked in the woods there, and she left. She has no money, so what am I going to do? I let her on. She needs a ride! Rules don't mean anything in times like these. I mean, if someone gets on here with a dollar nine —"

"A dolla ten," Beth corrects him.

"Right. That's right. But if you only got a dollar nine, some drivers won't let you ride! But I'm not going to say no. I mean, what's she going to do? Naked, the middle of the night? Is it really that important to collect that fare? I think as a public service you're obligated to take the person if they have no money."

"Naked or not?" Beth asks.

"Any which way. Hell, I've given people money for breakfast because they just got kicked out of their apartment with no cash."

Beth says, "Tell her another naked story."

"Sure. Another time the only thing the girl had on was a bandanna — on her head. So I call up on the radio and tell my boss and he says, 'Tell her to take the bandanna and put it like a pair of underwear.'"

He cracks up. Beth follows his lead.

"It teaches you to be ready for anything. And to know that what-ever the problem, you'll figure it out. As long as you're not too rigid. There's always a solution."

I glance at Beth and am startled to remember something about her — no, about her and me and what we used to do together, in the days when we lay behind the lattice under the house, half mesmer-ized by the silvery threads of the spider's web. It rewarded us for ex-ploring in the diamond-shaped shadows, for surviving all those silly adult lessons on shoe tying and table manners; it threaded us together, too. I am saddened that I've forgotten it until now.

"What?" she says.

"Nothing," I reply. "Only, when we get home tonight, there's something I want to do."

"Okay, everybody," Bert says, standing in what I'm coming to think of as the Time Point Club. "Who's got a dime? I'll give you the time."

A boy in a Tommy Hilfiger T-shirt pitches a coin high in the air.

"Thanks for the dime. Four-fifteen's the time."

"Hey," says the boy. "You rhyme."

"I rhyme when I'm fine. It keeps my ears from getting grime."

The boy laughs.

"You, the girl in the pink sweater."

Bert holds his hand out toward an elderly woman. She blushes, flattered.

"Beautiful sweater. Beautiful hat. Tell me the truth, am I getting fat?"

"No," some adults call out.

"Yes!" the kids squeal.

"Hold it, hold it. We have another passenger here. Don't be shy, step right up. I don't bite, Beth don't bite, we don't bite, this bus's all right."

The whole bus has come alive. Bert is working the room.

"Any other birthdays?"

"Mine," says a little girl who's scrambled up to sit near him.

"And you have a tooth missing, right?"

She nods.

"Somewhere out there is a tooth fairy for you. She will have the money and put it under your pillow, too. There you go, I said it in a poem, so it has to happen. Requests?"

"Sing some more," Beth says.

"Well, it's not so far away that we have turkey day." Then he belts out:

> *Ovvvver the riiiivvver and throuuuugh the woooods*
> *To Grandmaaaa's houuuuse we go.*
> *Sheeee maaaakes the best cookies*
> *And sheeee's the best lookie*
> *And thaaaaat's whheeeere we'll goooo!*

"You sing terrible," Beth says again under the applause. "You need a tune-up real soon."

As Bert spins Beth and me through the city, he continues his tales at each stop. "In New York, on Halloween, they mess up the outside of the buses with eggs. They throw them onto your windshield. So it was a Halloween day, and I had maybe ten passengers, and I'm making this turn. It was in a bad section, and I see kids duck behind a parked car, then peek over the hood at my bus. I knew they were getting ready to hit us with a good dozen. So I turned the steering wheel hard and fast, hoping they'd miss the windshield. And as we swung past them, they stood up and I saw they didn't have eggs, they had *bricks*. I shouted, 'Get down!' The people went to the floor — and then it sounded like shotgun blasts — *bang, bang, bang* — and those kids took every window of the bus out! Finally, blocks away from it all, I pulled the bus over. There was glass everywhere. I went over to each rider and said, 'It's over now, you can get up,' but they wouldn't. They thought we got shot out, but I saw it coming, so we were safe.

"You got to look, and then you do a quick study, and then you act. The power to observe is the power to learn."

I click on my pen and open my journal. *The power to observe is the power to learn.*

"Why are you writing?" Beth asks.

"So I can remember," I say.

Bert waits extra long at a light, as a woman with a walker slowly crosses the street.

"Now that I'm older and getting stiff," he says, "I have more compassion for people moving down the sidewalk slow. I can't hustle myself across an intersection fast enough for the light anymore. When you walk in someone's moccasins, it gives you compassion. You can't figure out how to treat someone without a little compassion."

I write, *Compassion.*

"You with the Census?" asks a man with a Harley-Davidson tattoo on his forearm.

"No," I say.

"It's too early in the school year for finals," the man adds.

"It's not a test." I pause. "Not that kind of test."

We roll down country roads. I point out Jesse on his bike, speeding beside pastures off to our left. Beth moves to the window across from her and looks out. "He's going to the *high*way," she says.

"Jesse rides his bike on the highway?" I ask.

"How else can he get where he's going?" she says.

"Some places have buses everywhere," Bert says. "Or subways or cabs. Not around here. All we got is buses, and they don't go out to the distant towns. So we're used to seeing Jesse on the road. He's something you just expect to see." We watch until Jesse passes from view.

Minutes later, Bert turns the bus into a corporate parking lot: another time point. The bus has cleared out except for us. "Now I can tell you a few harder stories," Bert says, unfolding his large frame from his seat.

"When you first start, you think you got to do everything by the book. Like one time, I'm pulling away from a long ramp after I picked up about a dozen people. And just at the end of the ramp, a guy flags me down. So I let him on, and he immediately goes to the back of the bus, and he's got a *chain* in his hand, and he starts beating the heck out of a guy in the bus with his chain! Then he gets off, and someone says, 'He was chasing that guy before we got on.' So I said, 'Why didn't you tell me to keep going?' He says, 'Because you're supposed to stop, right?'

"It's ridiculous, you know? The rules got to have a little give. Jesse knows that, right, Beth? If there aren't buses, you find a way. You got to be willing to improvise."

Be willing to improvise.

He continues. "Then there's the school trips in New York City. And you learn, they'll pop this roof hatch, and the smaller and thinner ones'll climb out there onto the roof and run off. So what I did when there's school runs with a hundred kids on the bus? You drive as fast as you can and tap the brakes, right? That makes the kids standing up have to do this" — he grabs onto the straphangers — "and there's no time to climb out, because they're holding on for their life! See? That's the way you did it. Rock 'em all over the place.

"Once you learn it, though, you got to keep it in here." He points to his head. "So you don't keep learning the same thing every day."

Remember your lessons.

"But," Beth says, "iz not like that here."

Bert says, "New York's different. But one thing's the same. You still see how some people are lethargic and glum. Probably a lot of times they go through the whole day without laughing. That's why I do a little comedy, a little singing. If you can turn their switch from off to on, you're doing something right in this world."

His performance having successfully enlivened our excess minutes, Bert, emcee, headliner, and driver of the Time Point Club, flicks his wrist to check his watch. "Sorry, ladies and gentlemen, I must be going."

"Not *yet!*" a small boy yells.

"One more song?" Beth pleads.

"For you? Certainly," Bert says.

> *Somewheerrre over the raiiiinboooow,*
> *Waaayyy up highhh,*
> *That's where youuuu and I will goooo*
> *And eat a box of big French frieees.*

Then he returns to his seat and the audience disperses, cocking their faces toward windows and laps, isolated passengers once again.

"Bye, Bert," Beth says, jumping up at the last second, and scurrying down the steps. I grab my journal and follow, and at the bottom I look back up.

Bert is peering down to the curb. "Beth," he calls after us. "Beth." She stops her lunge for the next bus and glances up. And then, with an expression that manages to be both whimsical and sage, Bert pronounces the final and most important part of his code. "Beth, do the right thing," he says, flashing her a thumbs-up. Then he pulls the door shut and drives away.

"Beth," I say that evening as we're lounging on her love seat, feeling emboldened by Bert's master class, "remember how much you used to like having me tickle you?"

"Yeah?" she says.

"Do you want me to do that again?"

"Uh-*huh*."

She extends her arm, and I glide my fingernails over her skin. Then over her back. Then her calves. "So soon?" she asks when I inform her after half an hour that I've had enough. "Okay," I say, and continue. We don't have an argument all night. In fact, my dark voice seems to have curdled and died at long last, freeing me to enjoy my sister without reservation. Perhaps she feels the same, because when I put in her eyedrops she doesn't complain or push me away. Arm, back, calf: I tickle them over and over. "Dee-*lee*-shus," she says, just as she always did.

Surgery

Well, shake it up, baby, now, the car stereo blasts as we career down the city streets. Jacob, singing along with his tape as he floors his Nissan, shoots a look at Beth, beside him, and into the back seat toward me. Then he spins the volume off, fills in the lyrics, and whirls the sound back to high decibel level.

"Thiz what he did all the way to the *shore,*" Beth says. "Beatles. *On* and off, *on* and off."

"Sing with me!" Jacob hollers over the music.

Beth and I feebly mumble a line.

"Louder," Jacob says, circling the volume back off.

We up the ante a bit.

"Louder!" He laughs, cranking the knob.

The windows are open, our hair is whipping outside. Students on school steps with their book bags, touch football players in parks with their pigskins, grandmothers with overcoats and shopping carts — everyone on the street looks up as we blur past, twisting and shouting from our window.

It's fun, but we're not on our way to the shore. Today is the day of Beth's eye surgery, and Jacob, whose benevolence is inspiring me with awe, is chauffeuring us to the hospital.

I drove to Beth's apartment last night to keep her company and to ensure that she followed the doctor's instructions. She has a history of forgetting (or "forgetting") that when the doctor says not to eat or drink from midnight on, that means no diet Pepsi, no bagels, no chocolate pudding. And my presence was also likely to induce her to go through with the procedure and not decide the morning of the surgery that buses are more alluring than hospitals.

"You like this one?" Jacob says, screeching away from a stop sign, then amplifying the sound even more for "She Loves You."

Beth asked Jacob to come to the hospital. Incredibly, he agreed —

without hesitation. So we're flying down strips of row houses, almost like an amusement park ride at the shore, which is how Jacob apparently wants it to feel.

"I'm *scared* of the opa*ration*," Beth confided to me this morning.

Now she giggles beside Jacob in the front seat as we tear through the city. Then, louder than I've heard her sing in years, she yells with me at the top of her lungs, "Yeah, yeah, yeah!"

The doctor told me that it would take a corneal transplant to correct everything, but, since Beth's condition has left her eyes so scarred that her body might reject a transplant, and since she might neglect the crucial postoperative self-care, she really isn't a candidate for that procedure.

Instead, he's addressing the secondary condition by removing or redirecting her lashes so they will no longer grow into her eyes. This might, he says, ultimately help the primary condition.

It's an afternoon of surgery, after which we'll return to Beth's apartment. Then for the next two days, Beth is to lie down every two hours with ice packs on her eyes.

"But I *won't*," she announced repeatedly in the weeks leading up to the big day. "I want to ride the buses."

I could have been annoyed. Or I could have said, "Whatever you want," and stood back as she negated the operation with sloppy postoperative treatment. I suppose I would have, were I following self-determination to the letter. But I'm not convinced that Beth understands the notion of mortality or of *things going wrong*. I'm not even convinced that she sees time as I do, as she seems unable (or unwilling?) to acknowledge that the future could be drastically different from the present. This, in turn, might explain her dismissive attitude toward consequences. I don't know; but I emphatically do know that I do not want her to lose her vision.

I asked her, "If I hang out at your place for a while, will you stay inside for the ice treatments?"

"May*be*," she'd said, which sounded considerably better than "no."

So here I am, having shaken off my inevitable, irritable reaction: *I don't have the time.*

And here is Jacob. Not just lending support to Beth, but also, though I didn't speak up or even tell myself I needed it, to me.

I assume that after he delivers us to the surgical wing of the hospital, Jacob will say goodbye.

But he remains with us into the parking garage, onto the sweeping entrance steps beneath the clock tower, up the slow-moving elevator, down hushed corridors to the waiting room. So it is we, not just I, who shake hands with blond Mary, the medical caseworker from Beth's service provider, who rises from the tan sofa to greet us, paperwork in her shoulder bag. A licensed practical nurse, Mary maintains medical records and accompanies people to their doctor appointments. Today she's here for both Beth and an older woman with developmental disabilities, who sits alone across the crowded room.

"You don't need to stay," I tell Jacob as we all settle in beside Mary.

He says, "I don't have to get back home for a while, and it's my day off."

"I'm nervous," Beth says.

It's the second time she's revealed herself. I look at her, surprised and impressed.

"I'll be with you," I say. "Don't worry."

"Hey, you've got your whole entourage," Jacob says.

She still seems scared, but her body relaxes, as if reassured by having us all there. I explain to Jacob who Mary is, and to Mary who Jacob is, as Beth eyes the other patient across the room. I don't know what procedure she'll be undergoing, but I note that she appears anxious, too. As Beth, Mary, and Jacob discuss his new puppy, I wonder if this woman is part of a family, like Beth, or if she was kept hidden in the back of the house. And why is she here on her own — have all her relatives died? Or was she sent away to an institution long ago, and now, finally released, found no one waiting because they'd forgotten she existed?

I later learn that many years ago, Mary took in a small child whose abusive mother had shoved her head into a wall. The resulting brain damage left the girl with cognitive disabilities. Mary and her husband raised her as a foster child, along with their other children. Now she's doing well, living on her own like Beth. The birth mother has never tried to get in touch with her.

Every minute, it seems that Beth lets down her pride a little more. Not only does she swiftly execute any instructions that the hospital personnel give her, she also requests that I join her in the rooms where she answers medical questions, gets her blood pressure checked, and is handed her hospital gown. She even inquires if I can remain at her side as she undresses.

Though this desire for my company is hardly an indication that she has retired her usual willful ways. We pad through a hall to the ambulatory surgery unit, where Jacob and Mary are waiting for us beside Beth's gurney. "I'm not used to these *wee-ard* shoes," she says. "These clothes feel funny." And, as I draw the curtain around the four of us so she has a little privacy from the other patients in the room: "I need to go to the baffroom."

"You just went to the bathroom," I say.

"I need to go a*gain*."

"Okay," I say. "I'll take you."

She says, "I'm gonna run away when I go to the baffroom."

We all look at one another. Jacob says, "You can't run away. You have to do this."

"I *will*. I'm just *saying* I have to go to the baffroom. I'm really gonna run away."

But her voice is playful. I suspect she's expressing a wish, not an intent.

I escort her to the lavatory down the hall. She doesn't even look for the exit sign.

The next step is getting her to lie on the gurney. "You have to lie down to get operated on," I say.

Still playful: "I *will*."

"You need to do it now."

"I'll get *around* to it."

I climb onto the gurney beside her and lie down. "Do it like me."

"I'll *do* it."

"Now."

Finally, with Jacob and me coaxing, she lies down.

Then a man comes over with the dreaded knockout shot.

"You have to turn over so he can get to your butt," I say.

"I don't *want* to."

"You have to."

"I'll do it when I'm ready."

The man — a nurse, doctor, who knows? — gets that fuming look on his face that I've felt so many times on my own.

"Turn, Beth," I say.

"I'll get to it."

I look at Jacob. We seem to agree, without even speaking, and together we heave her onto her side as if we're turning over a boat. She's laughing, enjoying the attention. The man jams the shot in, and we let her roll back, and then her fight is over.

It stays over as they put up the gurney side rails and wheel her toward surgery, and I walk along beside her. It stays over as I sit on a stool beside her in the holding area, where the drug begins to take effect, and where I reach across the rails and tickle her arm while we wait.

There, in this quiet corner of the hospital, stroking her skin, I look into her eyes. They are so scratched and foggy, so hard to see inside. Yet in this moment, they are also stripped of all her defiance and foxiness and mischief. She looks at me with a fullness of trust that I seldom see.

And something happens: the ice in my heart starts to melt, and I feel a rush of love pour in. The sensation warms and surprises me, and I wonder if she sees astonishment in my eyes. She can't see much anyway and, besides, she's drifting off to sleep. But somehow I'm sure she knows.

Later, Olivia tells me, "As a professional, if I had been there in the hospital, and Beth had wanted to run away, I would have said, 'Okay.' And if Beth had said she didn't want the shot, there is no way I would have gotten beside her and pushed."

"Well, but . . . what would you have *done*?"

"Tried to convince her, and ensured and documented that I'd educated her about all the benefits of the surgery, and done everything I possibly could to inform her of the consequences. If this were a life-threatening illness, the CEO of my company would make a decision, which might mean that she'd get that surgery no matter what, even if it was forced on her. But since this particular medical problem wasn't life-threatening, if Beth didn't want the operation, she probably wouldn't get it."

I keep my mouth shut. I would like to be as laissez-faire as she is. And yet. That's all I can think. And yet.

For the required two days afterward, Beth agreeably does everything the doctor asks: Lies calmly beneath the ice packs. Accepts ointment in her eyes. Allows me to wash the caked-on blood from her painful lids.

Jacob stays with us all through the surgery and far into the night, driving us back to Beth's apartment, picking up dinner, keeping us company as Beth rests, eyes closed, before her TV. The next day, Rodolpho pays a visit. Rick arrives bearing a chocolate milk shake (Beth's request) and a bouquet. Betty, the dispatcher, sends flowers from the entire bus company. The day after, when I finally have to go home, Jacob invites Beth over to his house, so he and Carol can continue giving her the treatment for one just-in-case day longer.

During these two days, I learn, on the phone with Olivia, that this is how it's supposed to work. The system that supports independent living relies on it: the cultivation of friends in the community, who will, out of kindness and generosity, help out. Fortunately — amazingly — Beth has such friends, especially in Jacob. But it seems like a lot to ask, in this selfish, materialistic, inflexible world of ours, where so many of us are rocketing single-mindedly toward some personal vision of happiness.

I'm thinking about this rosy expectation, as Beth lies down on Jacob's sofa, and I explain to him and Carol how to take care of her eyes, then wave goodbye, and start my drive through the city toward home. What happened with the other woman who was waiting for surgery in the hospital? Did she have someone who looked out for her? Did someone bring her a milk shake?

I glance at the seat beside me. Beth asked me to keep some of her flowers. There were too many for her taste; she wasn't accustomed to having them around. So I'd taken the bouquet from Rick. Now the purple petals are my passengers, curling up like question marks in the sun.

Releasing the Rebel

"Okay," Dad says to Beth. "What size are you?"

"I don't know," she says.

Dad and Beth and I are standing before the women's fitting room in a department store. In an effort to welcome Beth into her new life with him — which means, among other things, getting her more clothes than will fit in one suitcase — he'd grabbed slacks and shirts and thrown them over his arms as we'd walked through the store.

"You must have some idea," he says to her, thumbing through the tags. "Don't you remember your neck size? Your arm length?"

"I don't think women's clothes work that way," I say.

He looks at me. "How *do* they work?"

Dad has never gone clothes shopping with us, so for him the tags might as well be written in Sanskrit. I am seventeen, and the last time I was in a department store with someone who could explain things — my mother — was at least five years ago, before she began her free fall. Since then I've worn bell-bottoms and T-shirts from the army and navy store, except for when friends and I ventured onto this foreign terrain to do fake shopping, trying on prom dresses and pretending to be movie stars. But we'd paid no attention to tags. "Beats me," I say.

We look around. Customers buzz by, but no salespeople. Dad rings the bell on the counter. "They'll know how to look at you and figure it out," he says, tapping his foot.

Beth shifts her weight. I feel stupid and useless. Dad rings the bell again.

"Hello?" he calls into the bowels of the fitting room. "Can we get some help?"

He turns back to us. Since we've moved in, he still laughs, but most of the time he looks torn up. "Go back there," he says to me, "and see if anyone's there who can help."

I start to walk, and then, perhaps sensing in my slow steps my vast lack of knowledge about shopping, or my unease about speaking to adult strangers, he says, "Shit," and takes Beth's hand and marches her into the fitting room. He moves fast, as if he's committing a crime.

Later, over pizza in the mall, when Beth gets up for napkins, I say to Dad, "I can't believe you went into the women's fitting room."

"She needs clothes," he says. "What else are you going to do?"

We try to settle into living with Dad, in the new townhouse he has bought in Pennsylvania. But it is hard because we are all so bitter about our mother.

Actually, the rest of us kids are. Once Beth gets new clothes and stops sleeping all the time and her hair grows back, she seems like Beth again. She draws sunny pictures with smiling houses. She takes over the dining room with her puzzles. She shadows Dad the way she shadowed Mom. She hangs out with Ringo in the parking lot that all the houses in our development share.

Then the summer she turns sixteen, she makes a friend, the best friend she has ever had. The friend's name is Juanita. We are pleased that Beth has a pal, but we are also worried: Juanita is four years old. She lives a few houses away, and every day she and Beth play together in the parking lot. They get silly and bounce balls and run around with Ringo.

Beth is beside herself with joy. But sometime, we whisper to each other with trepidation, Juanita will grow older, and she will look at Beth through different eyes. We brace ourselves for that moment.

Late that summer, I am in the bedroom I share with Beth when I hear shouting in the parking lot. I peek out the window. Juanita's older brother, who's seven or eight, is circling Beth on his bike as he shrieks at her, calling her stupid, a baby, a freak. Juanita is skipping along at his side, a savage smile on her face.

Beth stands horrified, her face burning red. Juanita dances about, hurling contempt. It's a spectacle of brutality, and Beth seems hopelessly tied to the stake.

Then they peel off, howling. Beth lumbers inside. She sits down on her bed and stares.

I look at her, tongue-tied. Finally I say, "Um, want to go out to a movie or something?"

"No." *She rises and clumps down to the living room, where she sits in silence all day.*

That fall is when it all comes out: the rage over our mother, over Juanita, over being in a world that hates her. With mixed feelings, we realize that a rebel is suddenly emerging.

Disdainfully, she throws aside her picture books. She teases Max until he starts yelling, then acts innocent when Dad comes to investigate. She invents her wicked "aaah-hah" laugh for when we drop things or trip. She consumes hot dogs and chocolate milk all the time and won't touch the fruit and vegetables that Dad begs her to eat. She spills our secrets. She tells us lies.

Dad calls her on all this, and she rolls her eyes, half closing them at the same time, as if she can't decide whether to sulk or fall asleep. He asks why she's lying, and she answers, "I don't know."

My feelings toward her become as complex as her emerging personality. I love her laugh, I cherish her affection for teenage music idols, I relish her originality (she collects and individually wraps coupons to give us for birthdays) and her pop culture expertise (in fact, I keep up with pop culture through her). I get a kick out of how she latches onto the word "cool" to indicate her highest praise. But at the same time I'm aware of her escalating self-centeredness and manipulativeness. Disheartened, I confide to friends that my sister is becoming a bitch.

Dad, irritated but hoping it's a phase, enrolls Beth in special education classes. But Beth acts up in school, too. Impertinent and pugnacious, she ignores Mr. Laredo's instructions, insists on calling him Mr. Ray-do, goads him, keeps her distance from other classmates except when she's provoking them, and does everything she can to incite glares or pouts from everyone.

When Dad goes to a parent-teacher conference, a beleaguered Mr. Laredo, sitting across the desk, unloads "I'm almost at the end of my rope." Dad lets out a sigh. "I love my daughter," he says, "but I know just how you feel."

After a year, Dad takes Beth out of school. He tells us it's the best thing, hiding his feelings of defeat.

But what then? Upholding the family policy, he declares he will not put her in anything that smacks, even remotely, of an institution, which he feels includes group homes as well. Instead, he decides he will bring her to work at the office of the mail correspondence school where he's been employed for years and which he now runs.

Every day they drive there and back. It's seventy-five miles from our house, a long, dull ride of almost two hours. He hasn't minded previously because he's spent the time listening to classical music on the radio. But now Beth babbles endlessly over the music. She tries to change the station, and when he says no, she gripes. Her voice, loud and centered on the Top Ten or office gossip, goes on and on and on.

He struggles to tolerate it, but after an hour or so it gets to him, and sometimes he snaps, "Stop talking, I'm trying to think!" Then she shushes up. But her restraint lasts only a moment before her chatter revs up again.

Happily, the owner of Dad's correspondence school accepts Beth's presence, so Dad sets her up with simple clerical jobs. She gets a little office area, where she plugs in her radio and learns the routine: these papers into those cubbyholes, alphabetize here, count there. Then she brings certain stacks out to the young man who runs the printing press in a building in the back, others to the salesmen. She sorts and delivers with virtuosity, singing most of the time. She's like a choreographed Motown show in one corner of the office.

But just when we think we've found a place in the world for her, things start to get misfiled.

Dad'll bring home a box she alphabetized — "Will you guys double-check this?" — and at first we'll find a few understandable errors, and Beth will say oops, she'll try harder tomorrow. Only tomorrow there are more mistakes. Soon everything she does must be checked. We agonize: Is it that she can't, or won't? It is true that she sometimes has trouble with communication; once, for instance, she goes out to pick up two slices of pizza for lunch and comes back with two whole pies, because the guy at the counter mistook her "pieces" for "pizzas." Yet as she flubs her official duties more and more, until every task she completes must be redone by others, we suspect that what's going on is that she simply does not want to work.

Eventually, no one at Dad's place will ask her to do anything. So Beth does what we suddenly realize she'd secretly wanted all along: she spends every day, from the moment Dad parks at dawn until he warms up the car at dusk, hanging out with the printer in the back.

The printer is a very competent worker, a soft-spoken family man who doesn't mind having company while he churns out booklets for the school, but to her, he's everything. She sits at his side, laughing at his jokes, hanging on to every word he says. He's the subject of every sentence she speaks and the antecedent of every "he." She lavishes on him records and personalized mugs and T-shirts. She draws cards for his kids' birthdays. We half joke that if we changed our names to his, she might at least give us something besides coupons.

Not just at work does she make sure she gets what she wants. Elsewhere, too, every time you turn around, she's making her will known.

"Turn here! I want to eat right here" and "I'm watching this and you can't change the channel, nyah nyah" and "I told him to name his new baby after me, and he will, you watch."

One day on their ride, Dad jokes that she wants to run the show so much that he now has a new name for her: the Sheriff.

She is flattered beyond description. "The Sheriff wants a better song on the radio. The printer likes Donna Summer so now the Sheriff does too and the Sheriff says we have to change the station so I'm gonna change the station now, see, I'm doing it now, see?"

Dad listens, but an hour later he's wishing he'd kept his mouth shut. Nothing's getting better. In fact, in addition to the printer, she's now taken a shine to a salesman for the school who lives in Queens. Just yesterday, she instigated a fight with Max and when Max predictably blew up, she took off into the frigid winter weather, completely underdressed. By the time Max ran to get Dad and they threw open the front door to look for her, she was long gone. But Dad spent so much time with her every day that he figured out that Beth might head to the far end of town, to where they merged onto the highway every morning, so she could walk along the interstate from Pennsylvania, across New Jersey, to Queens. A place she'd never been, but which she understood is on the other side of New Jersey — however far away that might turn out to be. He aimed his car toward the highway.

There she was, on the local road near the highway, about three miles *from the house. Just as he'd suspected, she was moving fast. He pulled up beside her. "Get in," he said.*

Now in the car with Dad again, Beth lunges for the radio. "The Sheriff says no more of that dumb music you like. The Sheriff wants the good stuff."

Dad tries to keep his laugh alive, but she is shattering his peace of mind.

But sometimes on their rides, Beth isn't demanding or maddening. Sometimes she speaks, in her own way, about the experience with our mother. She'll talk about the lights of Las Vegas and how she never wants to see a gun again. She'll talk about the bad man's wild temper, and how he threw a phone book at Mom's head, and how scared she was waiting at the airport for Dad. She'll shudder.

For a long time, though, she doesn't talk about the bewildering turn of events that occurs a year after she comes to live with us. We keep wondering if she will, despite our not talking about it, either. We cannot bring ourselves to discuss it. Indeed, we cannot cope with it at all.

It begins one Sunday, right around the time Dad has started bringing Beth to work. He is reading the local paper that morning, and by some fluke he glances at a section he has never paid attention to before: the bankruptcy notices. To his shock, he sees a notice for someone with our mother's first name and the bad man's last name. Neither is common, but it can't be her; she never lived in this part of Pennsylvania.

He tries to call, but the operator says the number is unlisted. So he drives to the address in the notice, thirty minutes away, just to see.

Mom opens the door.

In the living room squabble that follows, Dad learns that the bad man is gone. He also learns that Mom is a librarian in a nearby college, that in fact it was the job that brought her here, but that she has not tried to reach us.

He leaves, livid and speechless.

When he tells us, we all feel a fury too huge and confusing to face. Laura and Max vow never to think of her again — she is dead to them. As for me, I just bury my fury inside a layer of ice. I tell myself that I *will get such good grades that I won't see my anger or pain, and I do get good grades, and most of the time I don't see it. I just feel bereft and numb, and I continually fall for guys who won't return my affections. I also make a lot of friends and sit in their dorm rooms laughing about our difficulties with calculus and relationships. But at night the fury unleashes itself inside me, pounding and yelling. I wake up every few hours and cannot shut it up. When I go home for holidays I watch Beth sleeping and wish I could forget things the way she seems to.*

For a few weeks after this new development with Mom, Beth looks overwhelmingly perplexed. Then that stops, and for one year, two years, three years, as we say nothing about it, she says nothing as well. Or almost nothing.

One evening, she is driving home with Dad when a terrific thunderstorm hits. It washes out their usual route, and they get detoured onto back country roads. Driving on through the darkness and the downpour, swerving around fallen trees, and finally so far behind other traffic that they have no taillights to follow back to the highway, Dad realizes they are lost.

"I don't know where we are," he admits, squinting through the blackness.

"Will we get home?" Beth asks.

"Somehow. I'll get us there somehow."

She's quiet for a minute, then she looks at him. "At least we have each other," she says.

October

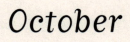

The Hunk

4:50 P.M. "Cliff races *cars*," Beth almost squeals. "He has a Mustang named Sally and he takes it to the track on Saturdays and drives it real fast and I like him a lot, a lot, I mean *a lot*!"

We're stationed at a bus shelter, a week before Halloween. In her lime green Tweety Bird T-shirt and purple jacket, she's hopping about at the curb, craning her neck to look down the street. The surgery has not improved her sight, but at least with the lashes retrained, her vision is not deteriorating further. I'm collapsed on the bench, adjusting my cream-colored shawl over my black coat to stay warm, hoping to revive; her aerodynamic pace is once again exhausting me.

A recent rookie at the bus company, Cliff entered right at the top of Beth's Top Ten chart, with Rodolpho bumped to Number Two. "He looks like Ro*dolph*o," she goes on, as we wait for the light down the street to turn green, "'cause they both shave their heads."

"Why's Cliff your new favorite?"

"Because he has that car. Because he's a decent person. Because he's *fine*-looking."

I sit back as she goes on about him and, as spooky recorded sounds waft from the five-and-ten behind us, I think about the crushes she's had. The pop stars. The printer in the back building, the salesman in Queens. Jesse. Lorenzo, a weight-lifting driver of her early bus days, who was generous with her until he tired of her obsession with the buses and with him. They had a falling-out and, though they'll kid around if they cross paths, she does not ride his bus anymore.

Then there was Rodolpho. Now Cliff.

I know just what will happen. For the next month or year, the Cliff saga will duplicate all those that came before: she'll chatter endlessly about him while he drives on, unaware of the enormous responsibility that she has thrust upon him.

For instance, in September, Bailey decided that his children didn't need a babysitter anymore. Since then, many of the drivers have begun to feel that it would be beneficial for Beth to spend less time on the buses, and, at least now and then, to pass her time more productively. The most outspoken of all was Claude, the main driver in my *Philadelphia Inquirer* article. He has driven Beth for almost seven years, and his patience with her bus routine had begun to run thin. One day when she took her seat, he declared that she was capable of holding a job, and, moreover, that it was time for her to get one. For the next several weeks, he bargained, he bribed, he appealed to her sense of equality — "Almost everyone works." He tried to simplify the circuitous connection between his taxes and her S.S.I. payments, he grumbled about fairness. Finally, he said, "If you don't even try, you can't ride with me anymore." Although at the time Beth had been Cliff's copilot for a scant two months, she sought his counsel, and, despite a less than full understanding of the particulars, and undoubtedly not realizing that her questions were a setup, he casually replied with precisely what she wanted to hear. "Cliff sez he wouldn't work if *he* didn't have to," she reported back to Claude. "He sez I should do what I *want*, so *thaz* what I'm *doing*." With that, Beth's partnership with Claude came to a close, and these days, when they end up in the drivers' room at the same time, each steps silently, with eyes averted, around the other.

Now, as Beth prattles on and on about Cliff, the loudspeaker switches from ghostly sounds to "The Monster Mash," an inane song I have heard almost every Halloween I've been alive. Beth starts singing along, getting wrong the same words she has always gotten wrong, and something about the song scares me for the first time.

Then Beth calls out, and I see Cliff rolling his bus toward the curb. "Come on!" she says, pulling a Mountain Dew out of her knapsack. "Iz his favorite drink, so I bought a case and now I give him one *evry* day and here he iz so come *on!*"

"The Monster Mash" ends as the bus door opens, and suddenly I see why I'm scared: the present looks just like the past and exactly the same as the future.

"It's a grudge-type race," Cliff says at a stop. "That's what I do on Saturdays." Cliff, a good-looking, lantern-jawed, George Clooney look-alike, has slightly more hair than Rodolpho — maybe a plush quarter-inch rather than a spare eighth — and, though he's past his mid-thirties, the hair on his head, and the five o'clock shadow on his face, are the same shade of bronze as his eyes. He also differs from Rodolpho in being taller and more muscular, and he seems considerably more inclined to chat.

I'm sure I haven't heard him correctly. "Grunge?"

"*Grudge.* If you want to race your buddy, or someone in your neighborhood — hey, my car's faster than yours — then instead of racing in the street, you go down to the track. It's a kind of drag race, a quarter of a mile, straight. Whoever has the quickest time wins."

Beth says, "You gotta see that *car,* iz great, you gotta see that. Iz a green Mustang. Iz really neat. I wanna *ride* in your car."

"I used to think you were harmless," he says, "till you started flirting with me."

She says, "I don't *flirt.* I have Jesse. I just like you. I don't do that."

"Ahhh, I know better than that, Beth."

"I'm not a flirt. I'm *not.* I want to fix you up with 'Livia."

She launches into a description of Olivia's beauty and kindness. Cliff, who is rolling away from the intersection, doesn't seem in the mood for dating, but persistence seems essential to Beth's matchmaking strategy. After all, she's still trying to fix me up with Rick. Just last week, she sent me a letter that said, *I gave Rick a pHOto of you. Now he can Freak out ☺ver it. now. Just kidding.*

"Look, there's the store that sells your favorite soda," Beth is saying to Cliff. "And thaz the house where that nasty driver Albert lives, he's a jerk, do you think he's a jerk? He put a sign on the ladies' room door in the drivers' room that said 'Only people who work here can use this.' I don't *care,* I'm going in anyway, as long as he's not there I'm going in 'cause iz just a *baff*room and I'm not hurting anybody, do you think iz okay for me to go in there, do you think Albert's a jerk, do you think iz right what he does . . ."

Damn it, Beth, shut up! my dark voice erupts. *Look at you — same expression, same seat, same stupefying conversation.*

"My mom," Cliff is saying to me as we pause at a light and as I try to still the voice, "used to race stock cars in powder-puff derbies before I was born. I must have driving in my blood. Even my grandpa was a mechanic. I still work in the same garage he did. It's attached to my house."

"Izn't he cool?" Beth says. "See?"

"So," I say, trying to will the discussion away from the fiftieth lap around the same old track, "you started driving because it's the family business?"

"Actually," he says, "I started out in shipping and receiving. Then I drove a school bus."

"Why did you change?"

"I'd always liked being behind the wheel. My parents took me to the races when I was eight or nine. I knew then that this is what I'd —"

"The people here are mean," Beth says.

"Beth," I say, trying to control my tone, "Cliff's talking about something else."

"They *are*," she says, "and so are some of the *drivers,* Cliff knows, you can ask him about how —" And then as he drives on in silence, she goes off on yet another story of how a passenger told her to quiet down and Driver X stood up for her, she told them off, they told her to stay at home where she belongs . . .

Passengers look at her severely, but she fixes her gaze on Cliff, avoiding their glares.

She goes on and on, and now the dark voice, which I thought I'd laid to rest last month, roars within me again. I squeeze my hands together. When I started riding the buses, I remember, I thought of the people who didn't like Beth as insensitive and narrow-minded. Now I find myself more sympathetic to their point of view. Yes, some of them are coarse and offensively vocal. But she *is* so loud. And she talks *all the time.* About *nothing.* I know many of us babble

on about nothing, too, but she does it over and over and over —
and over and over and *over* — and it's really eroding the limits of
my endurance. Dad used to tell us he came to dread their car rides
to work for precisely the same reasons. That was *twenty years ago.*

"Beth," Cliff says calmly. "Chill." Because he says it, she is quiet.
But only for a minute, and then she starts up again.

I stare at my feet. *She's driving me up a wall! When the hell will she
ever change?*

For the first time in our odyssey, I stand up, and, without even
planning to, retreat from her to the back of the bus, gritting my
teeth with shame for having these foul feelings all over again. But
I'm afraid if I don't pull myself away, I'll snap at her. No, I'll start
screaming.

We pass scarecrows on porches and black cats taped to doors. I
press my cheek to my window in the back of the bus. I can feel the
bus hum and the road rumble up through my bones. I close my
eyes and let it drown out the sound of her voice, far up the aisle
from me.

And I think: I wish I were a saint.

I wish I were a magnanimous sister who could feel compassion
for the way that Beth is re-creating a dysfunctional family environment on the buses.

I wish I had the serenity to accept the things I cannot change,
courage to change the things I can, and wisdom to know the difference.

I wish I could learn the language of Maybe It's Good Enough.
Maybe it's good enough that she can memorize seventy drivers'
schedules and stand up to racists and read. I wish I could be a realist
who could accept Beth's level of development and not long for
more.

I wish I were like acquaintances who think that people with mental retardation are "God's true angels." I don't want to think, "I wish
she'd behave a *little* more appropriately today."

I wish I could *change.*

Instead I peer toward the front of the bus. Beth must feel me looking, because she turns and squints through her scratched corneas, rooting out her sister from these strangers, until finally our eyes meet.

I'm sure I seem steamingly upset, and her expression registers her concern. We hold this gaze for a long time, as Cliff cruises down the potholed highway. The bus bangs with each imperfection, almost shaking us out of our seats, but neither of us breaks the look. It's a grudge race all our own; whoever holds on the longest will win.

Finally I feel sick and glance away. When I peer back, she's still staring at me. I'm so far away we can't speak to each other, though our faces are twisted with hurt.

Once, when Beth and I went out to dinner with Jesse, he tried to explain her to me. "You got to understand," he said. "Her mind is set like a clock. And no one can reset that clock. That's just the way she is."

How right he was, I think at the end of our run; needless to say, Beth has planned our ride so that we have the driver all to ourselves. Jesse's words return to me now as Beth asks Cliff if he would mind her getting off up ahead, "just for a *minit*," to use the bathroom, and elaborates on which pizzeria in this block has the clean restroom and just how long the owner's daughter — the one who accommodates Beth's restroom requests — stays on shift.

Cliff says okay, if she'll meet us within seven minutes at the top of the hill where he begins the next run. "I *will*, I always *do*." When we pull into a narrow city street, she jumps out.

As Cliff then chugs up a series of steep hills, I make my way toward the front of the empty bus. He pulls over at a corner, sits back to wait, and extracts a copy of a magazine, *Muscle Mustangs & Fast Fords*, from his bag. For a moment, as I stand halfway up the aisle in the now still bus, embarrassment courses through me. I realize how I keep turning to these drivers to help me steer my own life. But it has come to feel like a different world up here, with different rules, and, besides, I think, I am too desperate to remind myself that I should keep my mouth shut. I wait until I've calmed down, then slip into Beth's seat. I face him, as she always does, until he feels my eyes on him. He peers over at me.

I say, "Tell me, have you ever wanted something you couldn't have?"

He thinks for a minute. "I always wanted to be involved in sports when I was in school, and I couldn't because they found out I had scoliosis, which is a bad alignment of your spine. I was really disappointed. I couldn't accept it for a long time."

"What did you do?"

"I felt pretty bad, but eventually I thought, Maybe there's something else I can do, and I started bowling. The disappointment didn't disappear completely, but I was good at bowling, so it didn't weigh on me anymore."

Outside, a mom opens her front door and five little costumed kids dash down the steps to the street. "Or," he goes on, "let's say I want something for my car, and I know that I can't afford it. I look for something else that will be almost as good."

The kids tumble by us, a Teletubby, a princess, Batman, a firefighter, a hobo. The hobo drags a bit behind the others, not quite seeming to fit in.

Cliff says, "You just look at other ways to get the same results. Or other ways for *other* results. Like forget about football, which at some point a friend said to me, 'Get over it, look for something else.' That's the way you do it," he says. "Sometimes, you just have to change your goal."

"But how? How do you change?"

"When I was in shipping and receiving," he says, "I was always looking for something better financially. Plus there were times when I thought, I can't take this abuse on my body, lugging this stuff around. I had to change. It was hard for me, since I'd been in shipping awhile, and I liked it. But I just got to the point where I said to myself, You know what? I'm going to try something different. That's what I had to do to change, *really* change: be both at the end of the line with one thing, and willing to take a risk with something else. The two things together."

From the window I see a lime green streak in the street. It's Beth, flying along like the Road Runner. She blows past the hobo without a look and zips around the rest of the kids.

"I made it," she says, leaping onto the bus.

"Just in time, too," Cliff says, leaning in to look through his side mirror. "I was scared you weren't going to pull it off."

"Oh, you know I'd be back, you *know*."

I move aside, well aware that this is *her* seat. "Thanks," she says, and settles right in.

Then Cliff accelerates, and we head down the hill. A block in front of us, the street is swarming with kids: ten, twenty, all dressed up for a Halloween party, running down to a house that's decorated to appear scary. But the bats are made out of paper, the mummies are plastic. Fake tombstones sport bad jokes.

Beth is ignoring the parade of costumes in the street and gazing adoringly at Cliff — and with a jolt, I know what scares me.

It's not just the same old crush with a new face, or the same old song with the same wrong words. It's not just the pattern she doesn't see, or care about, and therefore cannot or will not change.

It's that Beth seems to need a cataclysmic event for her to change in any way — an event like our mother's complete abdication of her responsibility to protect her own child, Juanita's rejection, or Rodolpho's abandonment. This seems true whether she's being called upon to develop resourcefulness, assertiveness, or just basic self-restraint. I look at her and feel a clutch in my throat. What will it take now?

Is this all there will ever be to her life?

I stare outside, to the open row house door that is spilling light into the street, and to the kids crowding the doorway: the werewolves and ballerinas and pirates and the hobo. To all the sights I would be missing if I were at my desk, wrapped in my own pattern.

I suddenly realize that Jesse's metaphor applies to me, too. Whoa, I think, I don't want to be a clock that nobody can reset — not anymore, I don't. Especially if that nobody is me.

The Price of Being Human

"Here we are," Rick says, as he glides his car into the golf course parking lot. "Chip and putt."

In the chilly mist of an autumn evening, the golf green fans out to the left of his compact sedan, flags planted along its gentle hills. Before today, I had played only miniature golf with Beth. Now Rick is going to teach me the real game. "Sure," I'd told him when I called to say yes, I'd go out with him. But all day this Sunday, as a cold rain drizzled down and I loafed about with Beth in her apartment, I wondered if the weather would permit us to tee off. Now, though the rain has ceased, the leaves drip silver threads of water, and the fairway has become a sponge.

"So," he says, turning to me, "you ready to learn?"

"I . . . I don't think anyone's here," I say, peering through the windshield.

He glances up to the main building and then around at the grounds. Not a soul in sight.

"Oh no," he says. "I thought they'd stay open in the rain, but . . ." He sighs. Then he says, "But that doesn't mean we can't go in."

He smiles. Although tiny crinkles frame his eyes, his baby-smooth cheeks give him the air of a schoolboy, which is underscored by the kind of attentiveness and warm, ready laugh that I see on the faces of smitten youths strolling beside their sweethearts in mall corridors. This is not to say that Rick is shy. While it is true that he is adept in what he calls a lost art — the simple act of listening — he also talks easily, rolling out sketches from his life without egotism, reflecting knowledgeably on local lore. I am soothed, and stirred, to see that we have a natural rhythm to our conversation.

He hops out of the driver's seat, strides around to the passenger side, and opens the door with a slight bow. I climb out and look around. The golf course — smaller than a regular course, that's what a chip and putt is, he's explained — is but one feature of this sprawling, private park. There's also a baseball field, swing set, picnic area, and, in the distance, a stream with a footbridge.

We turned in here after a long country drive away from Beth's apartment, during which Rick told me that he used to be an over-the-road driver, as intercity, or Greyhound-type, bus drivers are called. The buses were far more luxurious, with restrooms in the back and upholstered seats, the works, but he couldn't form relationships in that job, with passengers keeping so much to themselves, the long hours, and overnights in distant hotels. He was still struggling with the disappointment of two divorces, and with pangs of loss and failure. He needed more interaction than four silent hours with a windshield.

He holds out his arm, and I rest my hand upon it. We walk down the sloping wet pavement, fallen leaves matted to the ground in the wake of the storm. A light breeze nips at his windbreaker, and at my raincoat and floral dress, which Beth convinced me to wear, saying, "You should look more *bright.*" Above Rick and me, the sky is still marbled with gray, but the late-day sun has begun to peek out, glowing gold and crimson along the horizon.

"Oh no, the gate's down," I observe sadly at the bottom of the hill, noting a waist-high metal barrier crossing the path in front of us. He simply climbs over it and offers me his hand in the misty fall evening. With his help, I step over the gate, too.

"You know," Rick says, as we walk along the path toward the ball field, "you have a lot in common with Beth."

I laugh. "Oh, yeah?"

"No, really. She's sweet, and sometimes very giving, and she has a kind of innocence to her. You do, too."

I am flattered, though I don't see myself this way, nor Beth, for that matter. "I think she's really streetwise."

"Sure she is. But there's also something else. You know, the way you're both shocked at the intolerance in the world. The way you both board these buses with such open hearts toward the drivers. It's a kind of innocence, seeing the good in humanity, and wishing for even more. That's too rare in this world."

I mull this compliment over. "But it can get us hurt when the bad stuff happens."

"Well, maybe that's okay," he says. "Maybe it's the price you pay to be more human."

We walk along, our backs to the rest of the world. In front of us lie picnic areas and patches of woods and, around the bend, the surging stream and the pretty wooden bridge.

We stop on the bridge. The water tumbles beneath our feet, and all around us grass sparkles from the recent rain. Everything smells fresh, and there are no voices but our own.

Lingering above the stream, we talk about love. The rocky love of fading romances and friendships. The distant affection of his grown son, who sometimes doesn't return his calls. The fondness I feel for my college students. The recently contentious love of his sister. The always complex love of my sister. The never-ending, hard work of love.

He is thoughtful and kind, and when I admit to my frustrations with Beth, he listens. "I understand," he says. "I can't make them go away, but I totally understand."

On the bridge, gazing down at the clear, flowing water, we trade anecdotes and advice, and ask ourselves how, and how much, to give to others. How, and how much, to ask from them.

The mist frizzes my hair, and the chill makes him button his windbreaker. But neither of us seems in a hurry. We may not be at the ocean, but I feel I've gone into the deep, as our clothes grow damp in the cool, humid air.

After the sun sets, we drive and talk. Then we eat and talk. We have Indian food, which this meat-and-potatoes guy tries because it's what I like, and he finds he likes it, too. He smiles all through the meal, and, with no hesitation, I smile back. Then we drive some more: "Here's a town I once lived in," he says. "And there's a garden I started years ago. Look how it's doing!" He points out the country bus stop where he used to pick up an elderly man who called himself a gypsy, and wore tattered clothes and lived in an unheated apartment, and rode the bus all winter long just to keep warm. "I'd talk with him. It's not hard to do that. If you don't want to, why drive a bus? You might as well be a truck driver." He nods toward a swinging lantern on the far side of a field, then slows down long enough for me to make out the farmer walking along toward his house. "That's probably an Amish family living at the end of some dirt road out there. Everyone calls them the plain folk. I think of them as dignified." I bring up the deceptively simple idea of self-determination, and we contemplate its intricacies. We then explore the intricacies of his own family, as he gestures toward the cemetery where he'll be buried beside his mother, who lives in a trailer near town. "Did you know bus drivers are deeply respected in Japan?" he says, steering us over the hills. He tells me how they dress in sharp uniforms, with white gloves, and are seen as true professionals, playing a role that's vital to the smooth workings of the community. "Isn't that something?" We talk about Thoreau, whom he's just begun to read. He makes little jokes now and then, and I laugh.

Then, heedful of the time when he has to get up the next morning — when the fleet rolls out of the terminal before dawn, there are no allowances made for late risers — he drives me back toward the city, and before I know it, he pulls up to Beth's apartment. Standing beside his car, I reach into my raincoat pocket and discover that I can't find her magnetic door pass, which I thought I'd taken with me, and since it's already eleven o'clock, she's sure to be asleep.

"I'll have to call her from my cell phone," I say, as her front buzzer is perpetually broken.

He walks me into Beth's vestibule, and I dial. She picks up in a stupor.

"I'm locked out," I say. "Can you come down and let me in?"

She agrees, half-asleep, and when I turn around to tell Rick, he is no longer beside me. I look through the glass vestibule doors, and he's leaning against his car, waving good night, saving us both from the awkwardness of having to figure out whether to kiss.

Then Beth comes downstairs, rubbing her eyes like a sleepy parent greeting her teenager after a late date. "Sorry about the pass," I say, as she opens the door, and behind me I hear Rick pull away.

"Iz o*kay*," she says, surprising me. There is no reproach in her voice.

Upstairs, she climbs back into bed without asking questions. I unzip my dress and turn out the lights and lie on my sofa cushions on the floor.

I don't know where it's going, but I have finally taken a step. For the first time in years, I sleep without waking once.

Come Home, Little Girl

I sit nervously before the therapist. I am a senior in college, and all the numbness and rage and ice inside me finally led me to confess my feelings to a friend who is a psychology major. "I think you're in a deep depression," she said, and gave me the name of this doctor.

"So, what can I do for you?" the therapist asks.

I take a deep breath. "I feel nothing," I say. "I'm one of the top students in the anthropology department, and I'm extremely conscientious with my office cleaning job, and I never forget a friend's birthday. Everyone thinks I'm totally together, a model student. But I can't ever really relax. I don't like myself. I'm scared of the world. I'm a wreck."

The therapist hears me out as I then go into the story about my mother. He watches me squeeze the arms of my chair. He watches me force laughter, and cry.

When I finish, he says, "I understand your feelings, but if you want to get better, if you truly want to get better, there is only one thing you can do."

"Yes?"

"You have to contact your mother."

"What?" I want to slap him.

"Just listen for a second," he says. "You know where she works. Look up the number in a phone book and carry it around with you. You might carry it for a month, ten years — but just hold on to it until you feel ready to use it."

"No. I can't, I won't. I would never do that."

"Okay, maybe not now. You've got your whole life to decide."

"I never will. No one in my family will. Ever."

I get up. For this crap I paid a week's worth of wages from my job. Thanks a lot.

*   *   *

But a few nights before I graduate, I'm chatting with a friend in the college library, and we're standing near the phone books, and well, what's the harm. Discreetly, when no one's looking, I page through until I find the number. I write it down and slip it into my pocket.

A few days later I put on my cap and gown and march down the aisle to get my degree. Dad, Laura, Max, and Beth wait outside the tent, and when I emerge newly graduated, I see them waving. The sun beats down as I make my way toward them, my diploma in my hand and the number in my pocket. A number that I decide, as I see Beth, not to mention. A number that means nothing to me.

Two months after my college graduation, a wonderful thing happens: I am sitting at my cubicle in the big Philadelphia law firm where I have my new paralegal job, loathing the stack of documents I am working on, loathing my life and everything about it, when a lawyer passes by carrying the newspaper. I glance up and notice an ad on the page tucked under his arm:

The Osmonds — Performing Live

I bolt onto the express elevator and run out to a newsstand. The performance will take place on a stage near Dad's house, and I do a little jump as I race back in.

I call Laura and Max. "I'm going to take Beth to this concert. Want to come?"

One month later, we four walk through the turnstile to an outdoor arena. Beth is wearing an orange hat, which we bought her for the occasion. She is carrying an Osmond concert book, which we picked up at the front gate. It's her first concert, and her smile is as big as the stands.

We sit, and then the Osmonds spring onto the stage and launch into their choreographed production. Dancing with their microphones, every word, gesture, and note chiseled to perfection, they do all the hits: "One Bad Apple," "Down by the Lazy River," "I'm Leaving It (All) Up to You," "Puppy Love." We're wildly impressed at how flawlessly they work together, each person necessary to the family show, each person a spark that keeps the energy moving.

All through the concert, Beth sings along — "Go away, little girl, go away, little girl, I'm not supposed to eat alone with you" — and she's so thrilled that we just have to join in. But even though I'm singing, and even though they're great, I can't keep my eyes on the stage. There's a much better show sitting right here beside me.

Ringo is old. For years, Max has been walking him, but now Max leaves for college, and since Laura has long been out in her own apartment, Beth and Ringo are the only ones at home. Dad asks the owner of the correspondence school if they can bring Ringo to work. The owner is understanding and says yes. Now, at work, Ringo sits in the back with the printer, too.

But one day, when we four kids all happen to be home for the weekend and Dad is out, Ringo starts coughing and can't stop. Beth bends down to comfort him and then looks up at us with horrified eyes. "Iz blood," she says.

I panic, we all panic, Ringo coughs and coughs around the living room, more blood spits out, and no one knows what to do. Finally someone realizes that we need to get to the vet, and Laura bundles him up and speeds him away. Later that night he dies.

We sit in the living room the next day, silent. There should be a barking furry presence in here with us, one we've known since he was so small he couldn't walk down the stairs. But there is only the sound of passing cars.

As we bury Ringo and that autumn begins, I settle into my paralegal job. I hate it. I should never have taken this job, or any office job, just to have an income. I hate offices. The other paralegals seem so fearless about walking anywhere, doing anything, but I am frightened of life. I have not been able to write anything creative for six years now, and I do not have the energy to make myself start. I am not ready to have a career. I am not ready to be an adult.

However, when the law firm assembles a team of paralegals to work on a trial in New York City, for some reason they include me. ("You're so reliable and efficient," a supervisor says one day, not realizing that I work late to avoid going home.) I'm relieved to get away from the of-

fice, but find that, as I am moved into a posh Manhattan hotel for the two-month duration, I am still prey to those same old depressive thoughts.

And there is another thing I cannot stop thinking about: I keep having memories of my mother.

Surprisingly, bizarrely, these are not the angry memories I've had since that sleeting February day six years ago. They are nicer thoughts, memories from the time before the divorce.

I remember her sewing Halloween costumes every year and executing paint-by-numbers in the living room. I remember her using Bingo cards to help Beth learn to read.

She taught me cursive writing when we moved before my second year of school ended and I missed those lessons. For years, my mother drove me weekly to the library to borrow books. She always kissed us good night, even when she was saddest, and if Ringo leapt up from our beds, she'd kiss him, too. She took us to planetariums and plays, to New York museums and the seashore. When I turned nine she bought me an astronomy book and then walked us all outside, even Ringo, and we stood in a field to look up at the stars.

Maybe, I think, startled, I don't quite hate her anymore.

Two weeks after the paralegal team arrives in New York, the case settles. One day we are racing around collating documents, and the next afternoon it's over. The lawyers inform us that we have a single night to celebrate. Then we are to pack our bags and go home.

In a wash of relief and disappointment, my team decides to take a few hours to rest in our rooms and then go out on the town for dinner. I retreat to my room, and the second I close the draperies and hit the mattress, all those memories start flashing once more against the backs of my eyelids. It makes no sense; what does my mother have to do with a settled lawsuit? What does my mother have to do with me? I roll over and over, unable to sleep.

Finally, I wrench myself up and find my hand reaching for the phone.

Her number is still in my wallet. I uncrease the paper, as soft as cotton, and make out the figures in the dusky light.

She won't be working at the library that evening, I tell myself as I dial. She must have quit by now, I think as I clear my throat. Or if she's there, maybe she'll hang up on me.

The phone rings on the other end. Someone picks up.

"Uh, reference desk, please?"

I am put on hold. Hang up! No, wait till someone answers. Just get a voice, to tell Max and Laura.

"Information services." It is a woman.

"I'm looking for —" and I say her name.

"This is she," she says.

I pause, and I take a deep breath, and then I do what may be the hardest thing I will ever do in my life. I say, "This is your daughter Rachel."

She gasps, and immediately begins to cry. "Thank God!" she whispers, and with a great rush I remember her voice and face. "Thank God!"

I feel dizzy, as if I've been turned upside down. As the room grows dark, and as I tumble through constellations of emotions, I fill her in on what has happened to all of us and ask about her life. I am curious, and she is still crying. I do not get angry, and she does not hang up.

"May I see you?" she asks at the end of the call.

"Yes," I tell her, surprising myself. "Yes. Here's my number. Yes."

I tell Laura. She feels betrayed.

Over the next year, I see our mother several times. I discover that she is not the cold-hearted, mayhem-loving monster I'd imagined, but a deeply unhappy and lonely woman who somehow got caught up with a violent con man, an event that fills her with shame. Like other battered and abused women I'd read about over the intervening years, she'd fallen into a trance of numb obedience and self-loathing and couldn't get out. She'd even let him manipulate her own mother, who grew ill from the stress and died. After Beth had been sent away, he'd almost beaten my mother to death — and only then, finally, had she fled, with fifty-seven cents in her hand.

I realize I need to learn forgiveness and compassion. Little by little, season after season, my days stop seeming so dark and my nights so scary.

I tell Laura how much better I feel, that my depression is lifting; I can even write again. I tell her that it may be the hardest thing she ever does in her life, but that if she can face it, she can do anything. She relents as she listens, and one day she too picks up the phone.

Laura and I tell Max. He is sickened.

But during the next year, Laura and I visit Mom. We learn that, from the time she played with dolls, she had always thought little of herself and struggled with feelings I now recognize as depression. She made few friends, and although she showed promise as a singer, she so lacked confidence that she never pursued a career. She tried to be a self-assured partner to our father, but a weariness enveloped her, and motherhood overwhelmed her, and she was devastated when he left. Recklessly, she sought happiness through other men — and an impulsive second marriage. Then, guilty and self-flagellating and consumed by a sadness deeper than she'd ever imagined, she had dreaded our rejection if she got in touch with us during those years.

As birthdays and holidays pass, we tell Max how much better we feel. Rediscovering our mother did not turn us into carefree Pollyannas, and it was hard to do, but it certainly has been worth it.

He asks questions as he listens, and one day he too picks up the phone.

At last we tell Beth. She is twenty-five now, still going to work with Dad, and we sit her down, all three of us, and tell her we got in touch with Mom.

"She wants to see you."

"Really? Where's the bad man?"

"Gone."

"No guns?"

"No. You're safe now."

We make a restaurant reservation for the reunion and drive there together. We hold Beth's hands as she walks in.

Mom is sitting at the table, rising tearfully as she sees us approach. Beth lets go of our hands and, a decade after their goodbye, she tugs at the hem of her new purple dress and tentatively steps forward.

November

The Girlfriend

6:15 P.M. "Ricky Martin," Beth says between giggles.

"Oh, *yeah*." Melanie laughs back, pulling to a stop in the November night. "He's hot."

"And Backstreet Boys."

"Which one?"

"*All* of them."

"Definitely. They are hot. Hotter than summer."

"Hotter than a *stove*." Beth laughs. "I want them to drive the bus."

I feel as if we're in a carnival fun house, partially because the inside of the bus is lit with blue lights. "To cut down on the night glare through the windshield," Melanie explains. At thirty-seven, she's tall, has an ample figure and auburn hair, a creamy complexion and a bouncy personality, and as she gestures to the window I marvel at how changing just one thing inside — adding blue lights — can make such a difference when you look out at the world.

But mostly our blue bus feels like a fun house because Melanie and Beth are cracking up. This is what they do privately, and what they're doing today, since, on this rarely used run, it's just them and me and a goofy stuffed turkey whose tummy plays "Over the River and Through the Woods" when you squeeze him. Melanie set him down on the dashboard as her hood ornament for the evening. When she grabs him at red lights, Beth breaks up all over again.

Melanie may be settled and married, with almost grown sons and a job that requires a level head. But when she's with Beth, they become teenage girlfriends.

"Oh, oh, I have another one," Melanie says. "Will Smith."

Beth squeals so hard she can barely get it out: "Oh, I'd like to have him here, all right, right here, and you know what I'd do, you *know*."

"How about that song?" Melanie asks.

"'Iz Raining Men,'" Beth roars.

They laugh so hard at the thought of men falling from the sky that they almost tip out of their seats.

I watch them as we pull onto a long, flat highway with almost no stops, mostly a straight forty-five minutes out to the remote country towns and back. They are having so much fun, and, sitting halfway back in the bus, at the far edge of their party — too distant to laugh along, yet close enough to wish I could — I remember how much I used to savor that feeling. It's a feeling I had almost forgotten until the night I went out with Rick.

But now a longing wells up within me, and I remember the days when I felt it, too: when a friend practiced cartwheels with me in our yard, or cheered when I tossed my spinning baton as high as the roof and caught it, or lay on her stomach next to me on a dormitory bed to analyze pop lyrics, or wiggled into overpriced gowns with me in department stores, pretending to have money and somewhere to go, collapsing on the fitting room floor in giggles.

Now, witnessing Beth and Melanie take such joy in making each other sparkle, mourning my own defection from such ready, easy pleasures, I appreciate anew how much having friends helped. Yes, work is a crucial part of life, but work alone cannot generate easy laughter, closeness, meandering conversation — and, best of all, the certainty that you belong right here, right now, because someone is special to you. I so took this feeling for granted, I never thought to name it. But now I think I would call it happiness.

"Cliff doesn't know why thaz so funny to us," Beth says at a brief stop, wiping her eyes.

"That's 'cause he doesn't know you wish *he'd* be raining from the skies!"

"He knows. I make sure he knows. That I want him and Jesse. Ten of them. Raining down right in front of me. Yum*mee*."

"Onto the roof of the bus."

"All over the road."

"All over the city!"

"Cliff's so fine-looking," Beth muses.

"Bet you think he's hotter than a heat wave."

"You got that right. Hotter than a stove!"

Envious, I turn toward the low-glare glass as we pull back onto the highway. I expect to see the nothingness of fallow fields in the night, but instead make out my reflection far too well, hauntingly blue and close. I cringe at the expression on my face.

Failure, it reads, and terror. The way my mother used to look when she trudged into the house after one of her dates. The way I used to feel when love withdrew. Though, no, I realize it is more than that, studying my face as if it were a student paper I'd been grading over and over all semester and suddenly understood. It's not only failure and terror I observed in Mom, and now see in my-self. There is self-pity, too.

That old darkness rises within me. *Don't think about this,* it says. *Keep telling the world, No, I can't, I'm sorry. Keep shutting the door.*

But I do think about it. Beth is in stitches along with her friend right in front of me, and I realize with a jolt that for all her failures and terrors, I have never seen self-pity on her face. Not even a trace. Not once.

Maybe I can begin to get rid of my own self-pity, I think. In the weeks to come, I tell myself, I will try.

Rodolpho admits that he'd like to explore new career options in his spare time. But he can't afford more pilot lessons and is casting about without direction, unsure what to do now.

"You're good-looking, you could be a model," I tell him. "Or an actor."

"Yeah, sure," he says. Then his eyes soften. "Well, okay. How?"

I think for a moment. "There's that community theater down the street from where Beth lives. Maybe you can audition for a play, to see how you like it."

"I've never done that before."

Without a moment of resistance, I volunteer to extend this visit a day longer and reschedule my student meetings. I say, "I'll help you."

We accompany him when he picks up the script for *Bye Bye Birdie.* Then we hole up in a pizzeria booth, and, as Beth sips her soda beside us, Rodolpho and I practice the lines. One minute he's Conrad Birdie, and I'm the what's-the-matter-with-kids-today father, and the next, we've reversed roles. We talk about stage fright. We talk about life fright.

We see him to the theater door. He gives us a high-five before he walks in.

Jacob has become fond of a particular rider: a young mother in an advanced stage of cancer. He tells me that she has a wisdom that life is to be lived to its fullest every moment, and a great love for her family. He says, "She makes me care more about people than I ever did."

He brings her homemade corn pie, her favorite. He speaks to other riders about her courage and he prays for her.

One day he informs me that she's back in the hospital because her liver has failed. I speak before I can stop myself. "I'll visit her with you," I say.

When we arrive, we see that the cancer treatment has stolen her hair and her energy. Her family is gathered around her. Within days, I realize, she will be dead.

We don't say much, just listen to them all, and to her. Her voice is so quiet that I can barely hear a word. When we leave the room, Jacob is weeping. I take his arm as we make our way down the hall.

In the blue bus, Melanie tells us that many years ago, she lost a close friend in a car accident. One minute he was on the phone with her, and half an hour later he was gone. She says, "You don't know what lies ahead of you the next ten minutes. I don't know what's going to happen when I turn this corner here. So why not be a friend? Why not give while you can?"

Soon it's as if word has spread.

In the drivers' room, James talks to me about his woefully unraveling marriage and his guilt over sending his son, who has autism, to a group home. "Can I talk to you?" he asks me.

Roberto asks my advice. Should he continue coaching his inner-city basketball league, or work up the courage to run for mayor? "Jacob says you have a good head on your shoulders," he says. "What do you think?"

Joan says she wants to return to school to get her G.E.D., but she feels insecure. "I know you're a teacher," she says. "Can you give me any tips on what to do?"

"Yes," I say, over and over. "Yes."

"You know what a friend is?" Melanie asks. "Someone you can tell anything and not worry that they're going to repeat it. Someone you can trust. Someone who's on your side."

Rick listens to me, and I to him, as we dawdle over dinner, as he demonstrates how to angle a pool cue, as we throw scarves around our necks to walk beside a pond filled with geese.

If I've gotten fed up with Beth, he lets me rant, and when I'm thrilled with her, he shares my excitement. When we're strolling on the grounds of the local art museum, we share jokes and worries. When we finish having coffee at a café and are walking back to his car, he sings old folk ballads to me.

But, despite all the time that has passed, there are days when I still long for Sam. So I tell Rick, "I really enjoy spending time with you, but I don't know that I'm ready for more."

He replies, "I like your company, and you can handle this any way you please. I just want you to feel safe with me."

Maybe this is how it goes, I think, watching Beth and Melanie, remembering the people I have loved, and the ones I wish I hadn't lost. Maybe we are all Beths, boarding other people's life journeys, or letting them hop aboard ours. For a while we ride together. A few minutes, a few miles. Companions on the road, sharing our air and our view, our feet swaying to the same beat. Then you get off at your stop, or I get off at mine. Unless we decide to stay on longer together.

The bus is still blue, I think, looking back at my reflection, but beyond the window, the world doesn't seem quite so dark.

The Eighteenth Hole

We are all in our twenties. I am trying to write a book of short stories, Laura is progressing in her career as an advertising sales executive, and Max is devoted to his classes at law school.

Beth sits in Dad's basement, watching soap operas every day.

"What are we going to do?" Laura says to me over the phone.

"She can't just stay there," I say to Max.

"We've got to think of something," Max says.

In a round robin of worries and complaints, we fret over her life. She is twenty-seven already; she shouldn't spend her life on the sofa. We dial one another late at night and mutter our fears into the telephone. In their bedrooms, with their new spouses, our parents agonize, too.

Dad turns to our stepmother. "I want to do the right thing for her," he says. "But, oh God, what'll be good for us, too?" Our stepmother is a cultured and poised college professor — not the lady professor at the time of the divorce, but one he met a few years ago. She explains Faulkner and Plato to me on holidays, teaches us backgammon, and brings home a film projector from her school to show us Casablanca *and* Citizen Kane. *She whips up gourmet dishes for dinner, while graciously making macaroni and cheese for Beth. At night, in the silence and the starlight, our stepmother and Dad go over it again. To be closer to her job, they've moved to a house off the beaten path in central Pennsylvania, even farther from Dad's job. It's a big house that they love, though too far from a downtown or even a store for Beth to take a stroll and enjoy a little distraction. A bus that stops a block away could carry her downtown, but she has never ridden buses alone before. Think of all that could go wrong on a bus — and that doesn't even begin to address what might hap-*

pen on the other end. For a while Dad continued to drive Beth to his office, and they stayed overnight a few times a week in a hotel. But with the longer commute and the nights upon nights at the Holiday Inn, he became so frazzled by Beth's talk and talk and talk, so vexed by her constant dismissal of his Beethoven or Upstairs, Downstairs *in favor of Madonna and* Three's Company, *so maddened by the way any office task dissolved into "Oops," so infuriated by her boomeranging any conversation back to the topics of the printer and the salesman again and again and again, that every time he came home he'd say to our stepmother, "I'm ready to blow my brains out." Besides, taking Beth to his office won't work anymore anyway; the business closed, and he's started a new career in real estate. He shakes his head at the thought of a group home, as she made few friends in her special education classes years ago and has seldom been drawn to people with mental retardation. He expects she'd be miserable. "I don't have any idea what to do with her." He sighs.*

Our mother, for her part, gets up long before dawn and, in the dappled shadows of her bedroom, sits on the edge of the bed. "Beth again?" asks her new husband. He's a gentle, industrious factory worker, nothing like her maniacal second husband, whom she never saw again and divorced by printing notices in newspapers around the country — which her lawyer recommended and the court agreed to. Not surprisingly, the notices were never answered, thus permitting the divorce to go through. She met this new man a few years ago, and he knows our names and knows how to garden and hugs us when we come to visit. "I don't know what to do with her," Mom says. Though her worries are different from Dad's. After their reconciliation, Beth visited often with Mom. They both looked forward to these get-togethers, when they'd shop and eat out and go to amusement parks and zoos. But soda by soda, and hamburger by hamburger, Mom grew distressed watching Beth's poor diet and surging weight. "Here, try this broccoli," she'd say at the table. "Don't tell me what to do," Beth would reply. "Beth, I'm just worried about your health." "You're being bossy." Then our stepfather got laid off from the factory, and Mom from the library, and new work took them to North Carolina. More letters, fewer visits. In the predawn light, our mother glances at the phone. She and Beth speak once a week. Or, really, they quarrel once a week. "I don't have any ideas." She sighs.

For a while, it seems that Dad has it figured out. He discovers something called a sheltered workshop, run by a local social service agency.

"There's more to life than soap operas," he tells her. "I want you to try this."

Every day, he drives her there, and though she is shy at first, she soon gets the hang of it. When she brings home her first check, she calls us all in delight.

"Maybe," I suggest to Laura and Max, "we're out of the woods at last."

But the feelings of glory fizzle as status reports come in from our father.

After a brief respite when she begins her job, she starts lying more and more. She routinely tells Dad that she did not lose the remote control, eat the cake, break the toilet — someone else did, though no one else but Dad and our stepmother live in the house. She pretends to be doing her chores, but really messes things up and hides the evidence, until eventually our father says, Please, don't bother again. She helps herself to cash from our stepmother's wallet. Okay, who took it, Beth? "I don't kno-oh," she says.

At work she meets Ron, who uses a wheelchair and lives a few miles away. She sneaks out to see him, walking along curved, shoulderless roads, then lies to Dad about where she's been.

She treats other people's things as worthless. Dropping the dry cleaning you asked her to hold, dropping the camera you gave her minutes ago as a present, leaving her radio in plain view in your parked car as she says, "If they steal it, they'll only break a window."

The sheltered workshop calls Dad. Beth is a discipline problem, they tell him. She keeps trying to get away with little stunts and doesn't listen to supervisors. She tries to incite others to insubordination.

"It's one thing after another," Dad tells us. "Each one adding to the feeling of water dripping on your head — constant, constant, constant — and it isn't going to end."

Increasingly, too, a smirk accompanies her misbehavior. As if she thinks it's charming to be bad, and she's certain we think her too incompetent to hold her responsible for her actions.

Or, I think to myself, it's as if she knew many holidays ago that we knocked on doors to collect for "charity" and decided at last that she'd exploit her disability, too.

"I feel so guilty," Laura says to Max.

"I feel so trapped," Max says to me.

"She's a dead weight," I say, shocking us all.

Although it is true that we care about our sister's well-being, secretly, slowly, our words show us that we care a lot more about our own. We know that if nothing changes, someday she will end up living with one of us. We are just getting established financially and professionally and hoping to find romances that will last. Adulthood is hard enough as it is.

"Did I say that?" I gasp in a fever of shame over the phone. I have become, it is clear, a bad sister.

One winter afternoon Dad drives the several hours to see me. Never before has he come without our stepmother or even Beth. Coat still on, he sits down on a chair, sighing deeply. Then he pulls out a piece of paper. It is a list of every weekend for the next year.

Quietly, he says, "I came to ask you to share in caring for Beth. I am asking you to bring her to your place here for one weekend a month. If you do this, and Laura, and Max, then we'll have her the rest of the time, and I'll feel a little more sane."

I take the paper from his hand and stare at it.

"Please," he says. "I'm begging you."

I sit there in silence. It is very little, compared to his burden: one weekend a month. I glance up at him. He is looking at me with desperation. I open my mouth to say the right thing, but instead I burst into tears. "I can't," I say. "I'm sorry. I just can't."

In a daze of disappointment, he says, "Max and Laura said no, too. And Beth refuses to live with your mother." Then he stands, unfolding himself as if every joint is painful. And as I watch him I know I will always be haunted by this moment, when I let my father — and my sis-

ter — *down so completely. I sit in a sweat of self-hatred as I watch him shuffle toward the door.*

Finally, feeling utterly crushed, he calls a social service agency.

"The waiting list for group homes is long," the first person he speaks with says. "Several years at least."

"I can't wait several years," he says.

The second person he tries tells him the same thing, and adds, "You don't have any choice."

"This is my daughter I'm talking about!" he shouts.

At his wit's end, he writes a letter to the governor.

Within days, he gets a call. There's a space open in a group home. Would Beth like to move in?

Far across town from Dad's house, I sit with Beth on her new bed in her new group home. It's in a low-rise apartment complex across a river, far enough from downtown that you can barely see the skyline, but close enough that shops and pedestrians still freckle the streets.

We're in that twin month, both of us twenty-eight. She slouches, forlorn.

"You'll get used to it," I say. "Look. There's a nice view from the window."

"Iz not nice. Iz a parking lot."

"Well. Still. It's . . . a window."

I feel bad for her, even though I know it was her rotten behavior that caused this turn of events. I feel heartsick that Dad tried so hard with so little success, finally moving her here a month ago and driving home without her. And though I control my expression so my feelings don't show, I'm profoundly relieved to know that she won't be a burden to me.

But still, who would want to move from a house where you have your own bedroom, bathroom, and TV, to an apartment with three women you don't know, a shared bedroom, bathroom, and TV, scheduled household chores, and your beloved stuffed animal collection confined to a dresser top?

This is the fourth week she has been here, and so far I have come every Saturday.

"You've seen me more this month than you ever do," she says.

I say, *"That's because I know how hard it is to live on your own all of a sudden."* Besides, I think, I have a little atoning to do.

A roommate walks in, and Beth lowers her eyes and goes quiet. Her housemates have mental retardation, too, and some of the people in the nearby units, also run by this agency, have additional disabilities as well. I've met a lot of them in the last month. Some say *"Thank you"* when you hold the door for them, others barge past you with a scowl. Some go outside every morning to thread a long string into the air and lift a kite into the sky, while others lounge about the front steps, grumbling about people with different skin color and smoking Kools. Some settle into the group sofa for an evening of The Sound of Music on video, others snatch the remote control as soon as the credits finish to click over to MTV. Some get into bed beneath posters of Miss Piggy, while others fall asleep beneath Dallas Cowboy calendars.

Beth isn't fond of any of them, or even comfortable in their presence. I watch her roommate retrieve something from a drawer while Beth keeps her gaze in her lap, her mouth tight. After the woman leaves the room, Beth says, *"She doesn't want me here."*

I have no idea what to do until my tongue suddenly finds the words that Dad used to utter when he'd come to visit us. *"Then let's go out for ice cream,"* I say.

"All right," she says with no enthusiasm.

We head out, and as we pass through the dining room, I notice that another housemate is vacuuming the carpet, clearly in an arctic mood. As Beth nears the door, the woman detours over with the machine and runs it *"accidentally"* over Beth's heels.

"God!" Beth says, running outside.

"Oh, God," I echo, running out of optimism.

We pick up the ice cream; Beth has abandoned the chocolate of her childhood for chocolate chip mint. As we lick our cones and get back in the car, I try to find a reason not to take her back right away. I pull over to a miniature golf course. *"Hey, let's play a round,"* I say, trying to think *Be cheerful* and *She'll adjust* . . . though never being able to eat when you want, or sleep in a room alone, or avoid people who vacuum your feet seems a kind of purgatory.

We stroll onto the course, holding ice cream cones and golf clubs.

The course is designed around a waterfall, with rock cliffs and tumbling streams. "Beautiful, isn't it?" I ask.

"Mmmm," Beth mutters, not looking.

She whacks away at one ball after another. Some spiral into the water. But some actually stay on the green. A few find their way to the hole. At the eighteenth, she even gets a hole in one.

"Hurray for the Sheriff!" I say, clapping my hands.

She smiles, but the ball gets swallowed up, and unlike the previous seventeen times, does not return. Her smile fades, and she stares too long at the empty hole.

"Game's over," I say. "The ball won't be coming back."

She keeps staring at the hole. "What happens to it now?" she says.

She does adjust, as best she can. At twenty-eight, she learns to ride the bus to and from the sheltered workshop. At twenty-nine, she develops a social life with people in nearby group homes, one of whom is Jesse. By thirty, she has adopted the grammar of this new world.

"That workshop place iz stupid. I know someone who don't go anymore."

"'Doesn't,' Beth. You know the right way to say it."

"Doesn't. He got a job working at a grocery store. But he don't like it there either."

I correct her until an acquaintance who's a sociologist tells me, "She's doing this deliberately so she can feel she fits in where she lives."

I understand that, but I wish my colleague could explain away the other things that are happening. Beth and I used to discuss family matters, sometimes the local news. But now — as she turns thirty-one, as she realizes she's unhappy at her job and leaves the sheltered workshop, as she begins and leaves jobs busing fast food tables and collecting carts at store parking lots, as she spends long sessions in front of the TV — all she'll talk about is the weather and sitcom stars, or she'll gossip about people I don't know. Our back-and-forth conversations end now, too; if I tell her that I just sold my first book or moved into a house with Sam, she glazes over. If I take her to a movie, she falls asleep. If I take her to a scenic park, "I'm bawd." So I sit with her in front of sitcoms, staring at the clock. Either I yawn all the time I'm around her, or she catches me so off-guard that I'm speechless. "I finally got back at my roommate," *she crows to me one afternoon.* "I gave her some Ex-Lax and told her it was a chocolate bar and she ate the whole thing and she was sick for three days! Aaah-hah."

"I can't figure out how to talk with her anymore," *says Laura.*

"I am so bored around her," *says Max.*

"She doesn't want to visit me," *says Mom.*

"She doesn't want me to visit her," *says Dad. The strain between them has gotten worse. He offers to take her shopping whenever she's willing, but she's rarely willing anymore.*

And as the years pass, a dark voice comes to life inside me. It finds fault with everything she does, and with myself for not knowing how to deal with her. Whenever we're together, it erupts without warning like a geyser. I hate it. Oh, how I hate it.

She is thirty-two when we all receive letters that say I wAnt To live. on my Own.

We call. "That address is downtown, Beth, in a kind of rough neighborhood."

"What if you get broken into?"

"Do you know not to let in strangers?"

"Fires," *we say to one another. Electrical shocks, hunger, mildew, muggings, too much macaroni, too little heat, loneliness, roaches.*

Dad says, "I'd much prefer it if you stayed in a group home."

"I'm moving out on my own."

On her snowy moving day, Jesse and her aides help her haul boxes up in the elevator. She brings her bed from home. The agency gives her other furniture, which she doesn't care for. "We could pawn it," *Jesse tells her.* "Whuz that?" *she asks. He shows her, and they make some money, and she uses it to purchase things more to her liking.* I want NEw things, *she writes me.* I Dont want LEFTovER.

I worry as much as everyone else about how she's doing, but not enough to visit. I am falling downhill in my relationship with Sam, as my fear of closeness increasingly causes resentment on both sides; now, when we lie on our sofa after work, we listen to Sam's records in silence. Knowing I must leave, yet desperately not wanting to, I am in a private panic most of the time. I rarely think about anything else, even my sister. Besides, whenever I call, her phone just rings and rings. Isn't she ever home?

"I think she's on the bus," Max tells me.

"All day long?" I say.

"You got it."

"That's impossible."

"Just call her at night."

I do, here and there. But I am breaking up with Sam and am too overwhelmed to cope with anything more. When I finally leave the house I share with him, I send Beth a letter with my new address, and I mention casually that he did not move with me. In her letter back, she does not ask what happened. I feel that she doesn't care, and with my need for more income and new work I conveniently don't have time to visit her.

So for years, every week I write her a card, festooned with stickers, and labor to come up with new topics.

Every month, Max brings his children to see her from their home a few hours away, and she sits on her floor and plays cars with them until he drives everyone to Dad's. There the Sheriff and her former driver give each other an awkward hello and focus the visit on the kids.

Every year, Laura flies east from her home in Colorado. She takes Beth to a diner, where they chew their meals in mutual resentment and, if they're lucky, make strained conversation.

Every few years, Mom visits from North Carolina. She tries to edit all the *you shoulds* from her vocabulary before her motor home gets within a hundred-mile radius. But inevitably she ends up in a mall with Beth, spitting out the forbidden words as Beth hurtles past displays of matter-of-fact bras or sensible shoes.

And every day, Dad sits at his dining room table, watching a bus approach the stop a block from his house, wondering if Beth just might get off for a spontaneous visit. Day after day, year after year, it pulls up to the curb and hovers for a moment, and sometimes he even recognizes her curly hair in the front seat, her toucan-colored shirts vivid in the bus window. He waits, trying to will the bus door to open. But in a moment the bus just rolls on down the street. Finally, he says "I give up" and keeps his back turned until the bus pulls away.

It is the middle of a December night. I am thirty-nine, and Beth is thirty-eight, and I am lying in bed in my apartment, staring at the ceiling. My editor at the Philadelphia Inquirer *needs a new piece from me, and I'm supposed to call tomorrow with an idea. I can come up with nothing at all.*

In disgust, I flip onto my side and find myself staring at the bedroom curtains. They are dark, as always, but a sliver of window that the fabric does not cover blinks at me. I expect to see only night beyond the glass, but then I notice a full moon.

It's too bright and, combined with the noise in my head, will certainly keep me awake, so I sit up to pull the curtains closed. But as I peer up to the light, I remember Beth turning our attention to the moon over and over as we drove to our grandmother's apartment so long ago. I think of what she used to say: "Moon's following us!" Suddenly I realize why this image has stayed with me all these years. It's not because the moon's the big thing and we're just puny underneath and she had it all reversed. It's because no matter how far you drive, or how hard you hide, you can never leave the moon behind. Perhaps this is what she meant all along.

I stare at that moon a long time. It is the holiday season, and we still exchange presents. I have shipped these gifts to Beth for years, or kept them around until I saw her again — the following spring, fall, whatever. But as the moon pours light down on me, I think, Maybe I should actually go to see her this year. Maybe I'll call my editor and put him off. It's time I went to visit my sister.

December

Swans and Witches

The beautician shakes open a purple haircutting cape. "Beth," she says, "you can sit here, okay?"

Beth, blushing with a rare case of shyness, plops into the salon chair.

Then the salon's best, Cindi, Marilyn, and Amy, flutter around her. Each looks as primped and radiant as a model, and each is wearing a Santa elf cap in tribute to the season.

I have taken Beth to receive one of her holiday presents: a makeover, courtesy of Bailey and Rick. Once again, her bus drivers have gone far beyond the call of duty, and, once again, I am astonished and moved. Not only that, but they purchased it for her in the most patient — and purple — salon in town. In fact, I pointed out the amethyst awnings, door, and front desk, as we walked in.

"Can we try some color in your hair?"

"Have you ever had a manicure?"

"Shall we remove some of the hair from your face?"

Bailey called me with the idea. Ever the optimist, he said, "It'll give her a whole new perspective. Once she sees how good she can look, it'll pick up her self-esteem, and that might motivate her to develop herself a little more."

She was not enthusiastic, as the appointment was scheduled for a weekday afternoon and hence would interfere with her time on the buses. But she consented anyway; as she told me, she didn't want to hurt the drivers' feelings. Now the center of attention in the salon chair, Beth fluctuates between looking giddy, overwhelmed, and irked, as the beauticians flip open style magazines and powder her up, admiring her small hands and her fine, curly hair.

"Look, Beth," I say. "Purple chairs. And rainbow-colored candy canes in the dish."

Marilyn approaches with hot wax, and Beth says, "I don't want that thing on my face."

"It's called waxing," Marilyn says. "It'll shape your eyebrows."

"But it *hurts*," she says, shoving Marilyn away with the force she reserves for dentists.

"Sometimes beauty hurts," Cindi says.

"No pain, no gain," Marilyn says, drawing near again.

Beth, with a second, determined push, propels poor Marilyn across the room.

"Well, you don't *have* to get wax to be beautiful," Cindi says, catching on.

"You'll look beautiful without it," Marilyn concludes in a sunny voice, putting the paraffin away.

They are real troopers. I decide to tip them generously.

Besides, Beth doesn't need the waxing. They dye and snip and style and blow-dry, they try to smear on lipstick despite her inclination to jolt back as if getting an electric shock, they transform her nails into canvases for glittery art, and a new loveliness emerges. Bailey has a perceptive eye; Beth now has the kind of sultry attractiveness that I've seen in glossy magazines.

"Wooo-hooo," Cindi says, like the admiring hoot of a cartoon train, though Beth does not bother to glance in the mirror.

When we finish up, Olivia stops by to see the results. "Gorgeous, Beth," she says in the lobby of the salon as Beth grabs for her coat.

"Spectacular," I agree.

"Yeah," Beth mumbles indifferently, and it occurs to me that, within a day, she'll probably wash her curls back to their familiar, air-dried style, and within hours she'll paint whatever five-and-dime polish she's got at home over Amy's careful designs.

The three of us walk toward the parking lot beneath a row of trees bathed in sunlight. Olivia lavishes praise on her, but all Beth wants to discuss are the reasons Olivia should date Cliff. Olivia responds sweetly, slipping in those monthly questions wherever the opportunity presents itself: "Are you obtaining the services you desire? Are you getting the help you need?"

I watch them go through this routine — Beth, looking as glamorous as she ever will, yet speaking as distinctively as always — and find it a bit unsettling, like watching an impersonation of my sister. Still, I must admit that she looks striking. I sigh, sad that her new appearance will be so short-lived.

Then Olivia pulls out a camera.

"Hey, Beth," I say, "now it's your turn."

She says, "Only if you'll be in the picture, too."

"Sure," I say, and Olivia nods. Then, agreeing to mail me the negatives, she sights the two of us through the viewer. As I follow Olivia's gestures and move closer toward my sister, I notice that Beth isn't smiling and I'm reminded of Dad's photo shoot that Halloween when we were kids. Suddenly I understand that Beth doesn't want to look like a swan any more than, way back then, she wanted to look like a witch. I feel a rush of respect and squeeze my arm around her shoulders. She still won't smile at the camera, but she lets me hold on, even after Olivia says "Cheese."

Still, this new look is so stunning that I can't help but admire her all evening, as we sit on her love seat watching *Facts of Life* and paging through her latest scrapbook. She doesn't seem to mind; as soon as we boarded the buses after Olivia's departure, Beth reverted to her usual self, regardless of whether the drivers gave her wolf whistles or expressed their appreciation in quieter ways. In fact, by the time we finished up for the evening, she had become almost silly with happiness; we laughed about nothing and everything, all the way back to her apartment. I'm glad that I am staying over tonight and that tomorrow I will be driving her to Max's house for our holiday celebration, that our time together will be extended.

Her high spirits seem related to more than our salon adventure, though; I think they are also the result of the season. Beth mailed a huge stack of cards right after we finished our last run this evening. She received several in her mailbox, too, and then, up in her apartment, eagerly showed me the many others that are displayed on her coffee table, since her dining table is piled high with the wrapped gifts she has been buying for months. She tells me she bought Brut after-shave for the male bus drivers, Christmas ornaments for the women, and toys for Max's kids. She's beaming about her purchases. And about something that's wrapped up for me, too.

"Open it now," she says, handing me the hefty, rectangular package.

"I'd rather wait," I say. "I'm planning to give you your present later on, at Hanukkah or Christmas, whenever I see you."

"So?"

"So I'd prefer to wait."

"Really?" she says, dipping a nail polish brush into a bottle of glossy shocking pink. "Why would you do *that*?"

In a playful mood, we go to bed, and, I think, Wow, everything's okay. I feel myself opening up to friendship and possibility, and she must be responding to that. I respect her for simply being herself. She can laugh with me. We are beyond conflict at last.

I sleep well, and when I wake at seven, I discover that she's been considerate enough to stay in her room, rather than bound into the living room and click on the TV. Groggy but with elevated spirits, I make my way into her bedroom, and find her already washed and combed back to normal, putting the finishing touches on her thank-you cards for the makeover.

I say, "It's so thoughtful of you to let me get an extra hour of sleep. And I'm so impressed that you wrote your thank-you cards already. You're more polite and prompt than almost anyone I know."

She says, "Well, there was nothing *else* to do, with you out there in the living room."

I look at her. She doesn't appear angry and in fact seems to be pushing herself to smile, but it is not the relaxed, warm smile I saw last night, and her tone is surprisingly cross. What could possibly have gone wrong since we went to sleep? Maybe if I remain kind and try to communicate more clearly, whatever's troubling her will fade. So I say, "What I mean is, I appreciate your waiting for me to get up before you turned on the TV."

"I only did that because Jacob told me I *have* to."

Her smile stiffens at the halfway mark and, as I stare at her, trying to grasp the source of this sudden hostility, the smile falls. She looks back at me, bright-eyed, clean-faced, and annoyed.

"What happened?" I say. "Why are you upset with me?"

"I don't *kno-oh*."

"I thought you liked having me over."

"I do. But I *like* it when you *leave*."

"I *am* going to leave. Today. With you. But I can't evaporate over-night."

"I *know*."

"So what do you want me to do?"

"I don't know."

"How could you not know?"

"I don't *know*."

I exhale and look away. This will pass. It has to; we've got too good a thing going. Just sidestep the friction, I decide, just get back to normal as quickly as possible.

I say, "Well, I think I'd like to take a shower before we get on the road. Can I use one of your towels?"

"If you *want*."

"Yes, I want. That's why I asked you."

"Well, I can't *stop* you."

I take another deep breath, and boom, the dark voice starts again: *After how hard I've worked to understand her, she resents my presence! All year long I've listened and tickled and eaten on buses and slept on goddamned sofa cushions on a dusty floor, and she can't give up an hour and a half of time and lend me a measly* towel? *She's a selfish brat — no, not a brat, she's not a child. She's an adult. A self-centered, obstinate — no. She's a damned-if-you-care-about-her, damned-if-you-don't, you'll-never-figure-her-out person.*

Stop it. I must be the big sister. The one who can make allow-ances. The one who has no needs. The one who must take the higher road. *Forever and ever and ever.*

Calmly I say, "Beth, that's not a very nice thing to say."

"Iz the *truth*. I'm just telling it like it *is*."

Restraining my anger so forcefully I hear a quiver in my voice, I explain what I know she was already taught by my father and Vera: that there are certain courtesies a host offers a guest. If a guest asks for a towel, for instance, the host says yes. "It's another way to show Jacob's do-unto-others idea. Do you understand?"

"Yeah."

"Okay. So, can we try it again?"

"I don't *know*."

I take a breath. "Beth, I'd like to take a shower. Can I use a towel?"

"If you *want*."

I put my hand to my heart. "I can't believe you're saying this again."

"Well, I can't *stop* you."

The darkness detonates in my throat, and I blurt out, "I hate you."

Her face contorts with pain and horror, as if something deep inside her has been shattered.

Immediately I regret it. I know I should apologize on the spot.

Instead I snatch a towel from her closet and slam into the bathroom. My heart is pounding hard as I get into the shower, and every breath I take slices through me. I close my eyes, and all I can see is her newly beautiful face as she proudly offered me my present just the night before.

When I come out, she stares at me with hurt and confusion.

I say, "I'm sorry. That was a terrible thing to say. I don't hate you."

"It wasn't *nice*."

"No, it wasn't. It was wrong. I hate your behavior when you're rude. I don't hate *you*."

"You said you *did*."

"I know. But I didn't mean it."

"What did you mean?"

"I meant . . ." — and I know right then what I meant — "I meant that I don't think I should come to visit you anymore."

"*Why?*"

"Because I don't think you really want me here."

"I *do* want you here."

"You don't act like you do."

"Well . . ." she says. "Well. . . ."

In silence we drive to Max's house. I don't care that the darkness has taken over. *Why the hell should I care about her when she doesn't care about me?* During the holiday meal, though she keeps giving me perplexed looks, I sit far on the other side of the table.

So that's it, I tell myself. I return my sofa cushions to my sofa. I leave her wrapped present to me in my car trunk. So my year with her will have a sour ending. So what. At least I can return to my life. Free at last. Back to the classes and papers and editors and phone calls.

Though something has changed. The next day, I reach into my mailbox and find an invitation to a party. I call the host. "Yes," I say.

And again the day after, a new business obligation swells beyond reasonable bounds: "Sorry, I can't put in that much time anymore," I say.

And the next evening, at the height of the holiday season, I am hunched over my desk and hear laughter outside. I peek through my blinds into the night. In front of my building is a cluster of people in overcoats, bending low to the ground, lighting matches. I look closer, and I see that all around them, lining the sidewalks, are small white bags, each holding a candle. Then I realize that the entire street is lit with hundreds of these flames, flickering into the hills that rise away from my apartment.

I turn off my desk light so I can see the candles glowing more clearly. I shut off my computer and sit for a minute in the dark. Then I grab my scarf and coat and go outside to join my neighbors.

Finding the Twin

Three days after our fight about the towel, I discover the first letter in my mailbox:

> To sis,
>   Hi. I love you. Sorry about Hurting your feelings. I didn't mean too. I Do care about you. So bElieve me.
>
> Cool Beth

Skeptical, I set the letter aside. The next day, I find two more:

> Dear R,
>   I wasn't mad at you. At All. Sorry if I hurt you. I had fun with you. now. I didn't mean to makE you mad.
>
> Love,
> Cool Beth

> Hi.
>   I will try harder to be a lot nicEr to you. You can use anything in my House. OK. I had fun with you.
>
> Cool Beth

Phone calls begin, too. I have been out catching up with old friends, but when I get home I have voicemail messages:

> Operator: It's a phone machine, miss. You'll have to call back.
> Beth: *(dejected)* Okay. I *will*. Okay.

Besides, one of her letters the next day says:

> To R.
>   Every night I bEEn calling you. But you are not home. OK so I try. I do care.
>
> Cool Beth

*   *   *

It is five days after our fight, and a light snow has begun to fall. I cut my car's engine in my parking lot, emerge into the flurries, open the mailbox — and discover a new quartet of apologies. I fan them out in my hands. Snow White stickers dance on the envelopes, Beth's irregular letters form the words, and smiley faces adorn the insides of random a's and e's and o's. And suddenly I am stricken with the grim awareness that I am being self-righteous and cruel. It's not making me feel better, and I doubt that it's doing much to help her.

I close my fingers around the envelopes, and the metal mailbox squeaks shut. In the cold silence of the night, I stand at the bottom of the stairs, flakes coiling around me, and know that I can try to get along with Beth, and I *must,* but that the dark voice will never go permanently away. It will keep billowing up inside me at moments when I least expect or want it, after I have tricked myself into thinking that we are over the hump forever.

Saddened yet also tremendously relieved, I carry her mail upstairs to my apartment. Before I can even brush off my coat, the phone rings.

"Collect call from Beth. Will you —"

"Yes."

The moment the operator disappears, Beth is off and running. "I'm sorry, I'll *watch* what I *say.* I'm already practicing. Really, *evry* day. Jacob helps me, and Rodolpho, and Cliff. Really, I *mean* it, I'm *sorry.* I'm really trying to *change.*"

I lean against my wall, moved and chastened. For fifteen minutes I watch the flurries turn to serious snow outside my window and listen to her, and think how hard this apology must be for her — and how hard all this is for me. I had always told myself that facing my feelings about my mother was the hardest thing I would ever have to do, but now, standing here after telling my sister that I hate her, and hating myself for hurting her so, I realize that being a good sister to Beth might be even more difficult. No one can be a good sister all the time. I can only try my best. Just because I am not a saint does not mean that I am a demon.

I look at all the letters piled before me, a small mountain on top of all my own notes and papers. In pink or green or blue Magic Marker, set in envelopes lavished with stickers of Snoopy or hearts, consisting of a one-carat sentence or a breathtaking nine, they all seem put together with a loving heart, honesty — and trust.

"So," she asks, "can you keep coming?"

"Yes," I say, "I can. I *will.*"

When we get off the phone, I open my front door. The snowstorm is sweeping across the streets as I run out to my car and unlock the trunk. In the darkness, I find her holiday gift to me, the one I threw in here and forgot. I rip open the wrapping paper and hold it in my hands.

It's a scrapbook.

In the gathering storm I turn it over and over. An attractive fake-leather scrapbook, with wide laminated pages and a stack of refills. Something she must have chosen with care.

Inside, like a bookmark, is a letter. I pull it out and angle it toward a streetlight. *N☺w. you Won't lose anything,* Beth has scribbled. The wind flutters the paper, and I look up into the sky, to the white flecks showering through the dark. Each one both like and unlike all the others.

Blowing the snow off the paper, I open the book and slip in the letter.

Iz Gonna Be All Right

I am driving on a long wooded stretch of the Pennsylvania Turnpike, about to visit Beth. I am coming to give her her holiday present: for the first time ever, I am coming to ride the buses.

I shoot past a certain apricot-colored outcropping, and I remember being on this same span of highway ten years ago. It was the night before Max's wedding, a summer evening shortly after Beth had moved into the group home and years before she discovered the buses. Sam and Beth and I were zipping along, listening to her tape of Neil Diamond's greatest hits, Beth nodding off in the back seat, when smoke suddenly poured out from under the hood of our car.

"Oh, my God!" Sam yelled. "Get out! Fast!"

He screeched over to the shoulder as Beth woke up. I jumped out, threw open the back door, and hauled my sister onto the gravel. The three of us ran toward a grass embankment at a bend past the rocks. At a safe distance, we turned back.

There was our old car, smoking on the side of the road, and here we were, stranded in the middle of nowhere.

Eventually three different truckers stopped to help us out, and a man in a tow truck drove us forty miles to a garage and then a motel, where we would wait out the night.

But before that happened, Beth and I plunked down on a tuft of grass somewhere deep in the Pennsylvania mountains, the nighttime wildlife behind us, the world whizzing by before us.

"Oh, no," I said. "What on earth are we going to do?"

Beth said, "Iz gonna be all right."

I think of that now, as I round that same bend in the road. I turn my gaze from my windshield and spy the very spot where we sat, ten years ago, as Sam ventured back onto the shoulder to wait by the car.

In the dark together, Beth and I were two sisters holding onto each other, both of us knowing that we needed help, one assuring the other that somehow help would come. I put my arm inside her elbow, and she leaned against my side. Then, in the night, under the stars, we named old tunes, and we sang.

January

Beyond the Limits of the Sky

I maneuver my Toyota off the exit ramp from the highway, then turn onto the outlying streets of Beth's city. Blankets of ice dot the shoulders, and I accelerate for the final fifteen minutes into the downtown. There's the scrapyard, the always vacant motel, the motorcycle repair shop, the topless restaurant. I've made good time, having left my apartment early for her annual Plan of Care meeting. I'd told myself that I wanted to get the highways behind me before I encountered the rain that I'd read about in the forecast, and, besides, I could use the extra hour to develop Olivia's negatives from our day at the beauty salon. Once in the car, though, I conceded the truth: I just wanted to drive here more slowly, so I could gaze out the windshield at the silos and rolling valleys and sleepy cows and forests where naked trees nod in the wind.

There's that hex sign on the old red barn. The acre-sized gas station. The Kmart where Bailey stopped. The city neighborhood where a six-year-old Jack sold fruit from a truck long ago.

And there, up ahead in my lane, as close to the icy shoulder as possible, rides a man on a bicycle. Cars arc around him as he pedals fast. An athletic-looking African-American man, I see as I come up behind him.

"Hey!" I wave at Jesse.

He looks over through my passenger window. For a second he strains to figure out who I am. Then he breaks into a wide smile.

I pull around him and, pointing, turn into a florist's parking lot.

He brakes beside the driver's window as I slow to a stop. I roll it down, and a January chill rushes inside my car.

"I knew you was coming," he says. "But you're early."

"Thought I'd beat the rain," I sort of explain. "Hey, I heard you're preparing for some big bike races this summer."

"I got a coach," he says. "My coach said, you should be riding with your stomach looking at the road. I'm trying to make it so I can do thirty times around a track. I'm getting there."

"You'll do it," I say.

"I know I will."

I remember my errands. "So what'd you think of Beth's make-over last month?"

"It's not her style. She's happier like she is."

"Well, I'm having some photos we took that day developed. Do you want any?"

"That's all right. I don't need none."

"You sure? I can easily get some extras."

He sighs, and his voice goes quiet, and he says, "See, I . . . I don't know if I can look at pictures about her. They make me sad."

I look at him and know he's serious. "Why?"

"It's like somebody being all by theirself. Even when the pictures of her are not that old, or even when your sister and brother're in them, too — it's just, they make me think about when they first put her where she lives now, and I visit her and then she takes me down the elevator later and I leave out. And what I do is I look back, and she's waving her hand, and it seems like a bye when the person knows you're not coming back no more. And I was coming back, but that's how she looked, and that got fixed in my mind. So now all pictures of Beth make me think of her being alone. She gives me photos, but I look once and stick 'em in a drawer. I don't know why. It's just a feeling I get in my mind that I got to overcome, I guess."

I don't know what to say. We sit in the raw January day, I in my car, he on his bike, clouds hugging the sky above us. "You're a good man," I say finally.

"Yeah? Well," he says, and looks down at the ground.

There is no sound but the fan from my heater. Finally he says, "I try to be. I don't like to be the bad guy. It cause too many problems. My mom taught me that you just do your best on this day, and then see what the next day be like, and keep moving like that."

"That's a good approach to life," I say.

"You can learn a lot in just one day," he replies.

"I'm seeing that," I say. "Look, I'll probably see you tonight, after we finish riding, okay?"

He gives me a funny look I don't understand, then says, "Yeah." I reach into the cold air, and we shake hands goodbye.

I drive toward downtown, thinking of all I don't know about Beth. After sharing bedrooms, buses, Donny Osmond, and thirty-nine years, I don't know the melancholy that Jesse sees. I've long suspected it, but she almost never allows it to show. She is my sister, and I remember tossing grass cuttings under the house with her when we were little, and singing about "The Impossible Dream" in the car with her when she was learning to name tunes. I remember the tearful ride home from La Guardia. I've always figured there must be some grief in her heart, but I don't see the things that she censors. What she *must* censor, I correct myself, as we all do when we grow up and make ourselves distinct from our families. I love her, and at last I believe that she loves me too, but I know that in her eyes I will always be the big sister. It is both my bridge to her, and the moat eternally between us.

I am coming down the mountain now, cruising past the row houses, the park with the fairy-tale castle. I must pass through the city to reach a mall, and when I take the left from the ridge, Main Street opens before me like the central aisle of a temple. I glide down its graceful slope. Past Tenff. The used furniture shop. Eighff. The farmers' market. I coast along until I must stop for a light. Fiff and Main. The eye of the universe.

I think about all the times we waited here, hitching ourselves to one of these shelters regardless of the weather. I look out, from corner to corner. Then I see Beth.

She is standing near a bus bench in her purple coat and orange slacks. Only, I realize as I focus, she's not merely waiting. Her arms are up, her legs are bouncing, her hips are shifting. She is dancing.

I roll the window down to say hi. That's when I hear that she is singing, too, accompanying a hip-hop song on her yellow radio. People in the nearby bus shelter ignore her, making it clear that they've already seen this routine many times. She ignores them, too. She's the Carmen Miranda of the corner, shimmying and shaking and spinning and stomping. She is Cool Beth, and I didn't even know she could dance.

The light changes and I roll up my window and move on without calling her name.

"Bagels, anyone?" I offer.

"Got another chair?" Mary asks.

"Man, look at that cloud," Olivia says, pointing with her chin toward the window in Beth's apartment. We turn, all five of us, as we continue peeling off our wet coats. The storm arrived just as I parked on Beth's block, and now I see its source: an enormous rain cloud crawling like a cougar down the mountain, pawing swiftly across the valley.

We are meeting for Beth's annual Plan of Care. Unlike last year, she's requested that we gather in her apartment, and also unlike last year she's sitting on the edge of her seat, already impatient to catch a bus. Vera is not with us; she had a minor stroke last week. Beth went to see her yesterday in the hospital, bursting in at seven A.M., handing the tired but pleased patient a card, then hustling back to the bus by seven-fifteen. In Vera's place we have Amber. She no longer works with Beth regularly, but is filling in for Vera as best she can.

Vera's absence concerns us all, and scares me. As we admire the photographs of Beth's short-lived metamorphosis over the holidays, I drift off into the maybes, the down-the-roads, the inevitables. Eventually, I know, these professional caregivers will all get ill, or promoted, or will burn out. Or they'll retire. As they set their paperwork on the table, I have a flash of panic. What will we do then? Where will Beth be without Mary taking her to doctors? Where will I be without Olivia to turn to?

I take a deep breath to calm myself. I will simply adjust when the time comes. It won't be impossible, because I now understand what they're doing, and I'll have the drivers to turn to. And last week I started seeking out some sibling support groups. There seem to be few out there, but the one I've found online, SibNet, includes people who share my feelings on so many levels that I know they'll help me sort through what to do when the what-ifs happen.

Then I think, I may die before Beth, and I shudder to imagine leaving her behind. If we are lucky, someone else in the family will

still be alive and will have made peace with her and her lifestyle by
then. If we're not lucky, Beth will be fully on her own. That is, on
her own with Jesse and the drivers and the system and whatever extra funds I've left for her in a special needs trust. It's a trust I finally
created last week, when I sat down with a lawyer and said, "I'm
forty, and I have this sister. I have to start planning for what-if . . ."

Now I think, What if she does outlive me — and outlives everyone we now know? What if no one is here to clean her eyes? What if
no one is here to tickle her legs?

But I know that Beth, in her own rebellious way, has spent her
life learning how to adjust. And I think, My death won't stop her. A
typhoon would not stop her.

"Finances," Olivia says, introducing the first topic.

The same.

"Teeth?"

Beth's new dentist, exceptionally experienced with patients who
have special needs, pulled two.

"Uterine fibroids?"

The gynecologist is still monitoring them.

"Cough?"

The doctor gave her an inhaler for this recently persistent problem, but when Mary asks to see it, we discover that Beth isn't using
it correctly.

"Eyes?" Though the operation was a success, there might be
more trouble to come; in one eye, a few lashes are stubbornly growing toward her cornea once more.

Throughout the meeting, there are again tense brows and exasperated slumps, and even though I keep looking at Beth and seeing
the joyous dancer on the street, I find myself sharing in the worries. Perhaps even more than last year, Beth seems to be neglecting
self-care and ignoring consequences. She says she doesn't want to
meet Mary at the pharmacy to pick up prescriptions anymore, even
though, Amber points out, that's why she's using the inhaler incor-
rectly. "I don't want to miss the *bus*." She insists she wants to take
care of her own eyedrops, though Mary notes she's been unable to
manage that before. "I do it when I re*member*."

This back-and-forth goes on awhile, Beth shooting looks at her

wall clock. I watch everyone, seeing that you can believe in self-determination, and offer choices, and point out the fallacies in her
reasoning, but if Beth doesn't want to be cautious with her meds,
her weight, her money, or even with giving this once-a-year meeting the time and attention it deserves, then all you can do is hope
her love of life will someday nudge her toward noticing there's a future, and hence altering her behavior accordingly. More than once
the three professionals disagree among themselves — "I won't let
her throw her money away on that," one says at some point, to
which another jumps in with "*Let* her? Whose money *is* it?" They
keep haggling over the details. She keeps inching toward the edge of
her seat. They keep negotiating about how to give her the assistance
she needs while adhering to the principles of self-determination.
She keeps asking, "Are we done?" And when they pose potentially
troublesome medical scenarios to her: "Thaz not gonna *happen*."

Yes, they are professionals, I see, but, as I deduced about Vera
months ago, they too are struggling. We are in an age of new rules,
and no one quite knows how to use them.

"Look," one of them says finally with a sigh, "I think we should
just leave things where they are with Beth."

Another responds, "It's her life."

They lower their heads to their papers and bagels as Beth steals a
glance at her coat. And though it pains me to acknowledge, I know
they are right. I also know that I will always wrestle with the notion
of self-determination, debating again and again when and how to
help — and even if I should.

"Okay, honey," Olivia says. And then, initiating an exchange I've
heard before, she asks, "Tell me, what are your dreams for the future?"

"To go to Disney World with Jesse," Beth replies, replicating her
response from last year. "To live with my niece and nephew for one
day."

"What about the coming year? Do you want to take any classes?"

"No."

"Do you want to join any organiz —"

"No."

"Do you want —"

"No."

"— a job?"

"*No.* I like not working. Thiz *fun.*"

Beth jumps up to leave — Melanie's bus passes by in five minutes, so the meeting has come to an end — and as we throw on our damp coats I know that, once again, the report will say: "Beth does not wish to change anything."

But that doesn't mean that nothing has changed, I think, as all five of us cram into the small elevator. Beth bangs on the button for the lobby, already giggling in anticipation of our rendezvous with Melanie, unconcerned about needing an umbrella, though we're about to return to the storm.

I am standing next to Olivia, and, as Beth goes on about Melanie and Cliff and the rest, Olivia and I exchange a look. I think her look says, *I know this isn't easy for you.* But I hold onto her turquoise eyes, grateful that someone understands, grateful that someone cares about Beth, and me, and as the elevator slows for the lobby she says quietly, "Don't worry. We'll be here."

"Look, the rain stopped," Beth observes, leaping toward the glass vestibule.

She's right. The four of us straggle off the elevator into a shaft of sunlight.

I peer back at Olivia, Amber, and Mary. "Thank you," I say softly, my voice sounding oddly hoarse to me.

I spin toward the door. Beth is hitting the buttons to get out, and as she rockets onto the street, squealing as if suddenly liberated, I turn back to give them all a quick hug, squeezing Olivia the tightest. Then I race out of the building after my sister.

"So where're we going, Beth?" I say when I reach the sidewalk, speeding along behind her toward the corner. "Melanie, and then who? Will I see Rodolpho? Estella? Who's this new driver you keep mentioning, Nino? What songs do you and Melanie like now?"

She says nothing until she reaches the corner. Then she wheels around in the brilliant light. "The year's *over,*" she says.

I stop dead, breathless, and look at her. I should have remembered, and Jesse's odd look should have reminded me. I'd been desperate at times to reach the end of the year, but I'm not desperate anymore, and I'm surprised and a little dismayed that she is sticking so exactly to the deadline.

"You don't want me to ride anymore?"

She shrugs. "I don't *kno-oh*."

We face off, and as we stand there, eyes locked together, her expression goes through a lifetime of phases: defiance thawing to longing, longing toughening to indifference, indifference ripening to affection. I can feel emotions washing across my own face, too: sadness and muddlement and testiness and caring. I can feel us breathing together.

"There's Melanie!" she says. She points up the hill, once again giddy.

The bus sails across the intersection toward us, Melanie waving from inside.

"You coming?" Beth asks, waving back.

I consider what to say, as the desire to share more time with her bumps up against my need to return to my own life.

"So?" she says.

I pause, and finally exhale, "You can go without me."

A look flits across her face — disappointment? — but before I can figure it out, the bus squeaks up to the curb and she has swiveled around to greet it.

Melanie is smiling down at us, reaching toward the lever for the door. My throat feels heavy, and I touch Beth's shoulder. "I hope that's okay," I say.

She turns back, and whatever expression had crimped her face a moment ago is gone. Now she is shaking her head from side to side.

"What?" I say.

"You're *wee-ard*," she says.

I can't help it; I laugh. "Well, sis," I say, "so are you."

The door opens. She steps toward it, and glances back to me. "Wee-ard," she repeats, and then, also laughing, she adds, "but you're cool, too. *Some*times."

Then she reaches for the railing and hauls herself in.

I stand on that corner for a long time. Too full to move, too empty to think, watching the bus pull slowly down the street until it is swallowed by the distance.

But when I finally climb into my car, it seems to know just where to go.

In the afternoon light, I drive across the city once more, making the turns the buses have taught me so well. Up this hill here, down the fork there.

Then I park across the street and look up to his third floor. That's the room where his pool table is located. The light is on. It must be his day off — and he's home.

I cross over to his house and ring the bell. He opens the door and, when he sees me there, he smiles.

"My buddy!" Rick says. "But I thought your sister —"

"Well, we were done. I could have gotten on the bus with her, but I decided not to." I pause. "Are you free?"

"For you, any time," he says.

We stand there in the surprising sunlight and shift our weight on his front step, neither of us knowing quite what to do. Then he says, "Hey, let's go for a drive." "How fitting," I tease. He grabs his coat and we get into his car.

"Where to?" I ask when he turns on the ignition.

"Everywhere," he says.

We drive and drive, and talk and talk. In the car with him, with the wind rushing by the windows, I forget about being a Somebody, or a perfect sister. I am just a woman in a car with a man, and we are making each other laugh.

Late that afternoon, as the sun is setting over the valley, he takes me up to the top of the wooded mountain. For a year I have seen this mountain from Beth's buses, and thought I was near the peak many times. But I was wrong; I'd never quite gotten to the top. I see that now, as Rick pulls up to a secret lookout spot he knows. We step out into the dusky violet light and face the wide valley below, a slice of moon hovering above us.

"Look at this," he says, holding out his arms toward the city. "Isn't it an amazing view?"

A hundred streets, a thousand streets, crisscross one another in the dying light. But there is just enough sun left for me to make out a silvery bus, moving like a fish, winding between the curbs. Maybe a bus where my sister sits. Or a bus with someone who is somehow, in ways he doesn't even know, like her. Then I look to the north and I see another bus. And to the east, there's another, and another, and another. Each one its own private history class, or luncheonette, or quilting bee, or schoolroom, or comedy theater — yet each one linked, one person at a time, to all the others. Because I can see, as Rick points it out, how they glide along, stopping for riders — riders who might have been on that run last year and are now over here, and riders from over here who might be transferring to a bus over there — and how the journeys seem separate, yet are constantly and inextricably joined together. I step back and take in all the buses coasting and turning and stopping and going — the enormous web of the world.

"Isn't it something?" he asks.

"It's beautiful," I reply.

He puts his arm around me, pointing out the sights. The air is growing cold and darkness is coming fast. We huddle close to each other to keep warm.

A Year and
a Half Later

The Miracle Maker

At three o'clock on this May afternoon, as sunlight spangles my bedroom, I stand in my slip before the mirror, in a daze of disbelief. It's not the fragrance of roses in the room that has cast a dreamy spell on me. It is that I suddenly realize that this moment is real.

Blinking myself back to alertness, flicking a look at the clock, I reach for the hanger, hooked over the wooden frame of the mirror. As I lift it up, a card that I'd stuck in the corner of the glass flutters to the floor. I crouch down to retrieve it, a Day-Glo burst of stars and exclamation marks against an orange background. I remember how pleased I was when I received it and open it now for one more look.

> to, Rachel,
> Hi. I aM. SO happy. For You.
> Cool Beth and Cool Jesse too
> (also signed by)
> Bert — best wishes
> Len
> Good luck! — Jack
> Melanie — Best wishes to you
> Congrats — wish you the best — Happy Timmy
> God bless — Estella
> Good for you — Bailey
> Years of happiness, your friend, Henry
> Marco
> Wow to ya — Karl
> May many happy and prosperous adventures be with you,
> Love, Jacob

I gaze at these signatures, executed in their handwriting with her purple pen, and think of the year and a half that has passed since my last ride with Beth and of how so much has changed. Happy

Timmy's third child was born. Jacob's health ebbed and flowed, but he held on. Often, when I came to town on Sundays or weeknights to visit Beth, sometimes meeting at the bus terminal parking lot so that, just as the buses docked in the garage for the evening, she could introduce me to her newest fellow traveler, Jacob would invite us for dinner or a car ride to take in the Christmas lights. I wondered if I might see Rodolpho, who settled down with his sweetheart, then left bus driving behind to enter the police academy. I never did, though I often ran into Estella in the dispatcher's office, or Bailey in the drivers' room, or saw Henry's wide-armed wave hailing me from a passing bus. Jack did not find his long-lost love, nor did he shift from his independent ways. Bert, inching toward retirement, cut back on his driving. Cliff, to Beth's dismay, quit to become a car mechanic. She mourned for weeks, especially after she sent him a heartfelt letter wishing him well and he never responded. "Thaz life," she told me, first with a sigh, then a shrug. Rick moved on, too, becoming a driver for another bus company that made long runs to distant cities. Melanie continued to drive.

But those were only the headlines. The more important stories lay deep inside Beth, sometimes too deep to find their way into letters: new affections, new end-of-the-line confessions, sudden downshifts in tolerance for her companionship. Throughout it all, I listened if she chose to share and offered comfort when she wanted it. Jesse steadfastly did the same. When, near the end of these many months, she had to return to the hospital, this time for a hysterectomy to eliminate the uterine fibroid problem, she sought my comfort, though once again I was only one of the people she relied on. Olivia, whose recent promotion beyond case manager had not prompted Beth to curtail her morning weather calls, phoned often, as did Wendy, who replaced Olivia. Vera, now healthy again, stopped by the hospital. Drivers old and new sent cards. Jesse sat at Beth's side while she slept, talking to me about how to take it as it comes in life. And Dad invited her to recover at his house after the surgery, and cared for her day and night while her scar healed.

But the biggest change has been my own, and on this brilliant spring morning sixteen months after I climbed the mountain with Rick, I know that it would never have happened had I not spent my year with Beth. It was she whose very presence caused the ice around my heart to thaw and who nudged me tenaciously to find the courage to go out with a man again. Rick's kind ways and fondness for me stirred me further; in the special friendship that ensued, I had let myself care. Beth's wish to have a driver as a brother-in-law has not come to pass, but through our Scrabble games in Rick's living room and our walks on rainy golf courses I came to want a different life for myself — and, for the first time, believed I was capable of having one.

This is what I am thinking, as I rise, set the card on the bed, and step into my wedding gown. I am forty-one, and, today, by incredible coincidence, Beth and I became twins again. As I stand in the bedroom, adjusting the shoulder straps of my cream-colored dress, I glance outside, down to the yard of the house where I now live with Sam: a house to which I moved last week as a fiancée and to which I will return tonight as a bride. He is waiting for me in that sunlit yard, ablaze with indigo and cranberry-colored flowers, and I know, were he to look up and glimpse me in the window, he would smile in his loving way and mouth the words we have been saying to each other for the past ten months since I called him — this time not hanging up — and we began a surprising and wondrous courtship: "It's a miracle."

I step back from the window, and then I hear, blocks away, a city bus passing in the distance. I am no longer scared, I think. I do not feel cold. I lower the veil over my face, over the same hair and eyes and — at last I can admit — love of life that I share with Beth. Then I reach forward and open the door.

Acknowledgments

The material in this book was derived from my observations and memories and from interviews with people in Beth's life. I am deeply grateful to the bus drivers and to the many others at the bus company who provided me with information. I also could not have gone forward with this project without the warmth and insight I received from Beth's service providers, both those who appear in these pages and their colleagues behind the scenes. Special thanks go as well to the members of my family, whose recollections helped me broaden and sharpen mine, and who have courageously allowed me to tell our story.

In addition, I am indebted to the friends, coworkers, people affiliated with the field of mental retardation, and readers whose literary insights, patient encouragement, comic relief, and late-night brainstorming kept me on this sometimes bumpy path: Susan Balée, Amy Burns, Angela Capio, Connie Falcone, Bethany Gorney, Patricia Hamill, Marshall Hill, Sharon Klepfer, Fran Metzman, Diana Myers, Kristine Nilsson, Sherina Poorman, Kathy Ramsland, Betty Randolph, Lari Robling, Alice Schell, the many participants on SibNet, Michael Smull, Joy Stocke, John Timpane, and David Tucker. I am particularly honored to have encountered Anne Dubuisson, a lucky happenstance orchestrated by Justin Cronin; had it not been for her compassionate tutelage, I would not have embarked on this journey, nor could I have lifted myself as deftly out of the occasional rut. I appreciate too the historians, linguists, and writers who provided background on the region, including Troy Boyer, George M. Meiser IX, Dr. Eugene Stine, Nancy A. Stine, the Pennsylvania German Cultural Heritage Center, and the Pennsylvania German Society. And an uppercase Thanks to Jayne Yaffe Kemp, my superb manuscript editor, for her meticulous eye and cheerful demeanor.

I will always marvel at the remarkable fortune that delivered me into the hands of two of the most indefatigable, perceptive, and generous spirits I know, Elaine Pfefferblit, my editor, and Anne Edelstein, my agent. One might dream of such devotion and diligence, as well as astuteness and optimism, but to find all these qualities in one's closest associates at the same time is one of life's rare gifts.

And the Number One thanks on this Top Ten list goes to the Purple Sheriff, who opened her life to me.

I feel blessed to know all of you.